UTSA DT LIBRARY RENEWALS 458-2440

D0154142

WITHDRAWN
UTSA LIBRARIES

# The Limits to Travel

For Monica

# The Limits to Travel

## How Far Will You Go?

*David Metz*

publishing for a sustainable future

London • Sterling, VA

First published by Earthscan in the UK and USA in 2008

Copyright © David Metz, 2008

**All rights reserved**

ISBN-13:          978-1-84407-493-8
Typeset by Safehouse Creative
Printed and bound in the UK by TJ International Ltd, Padstow, Cornwall
Cover design by Hugh Adams AB3 designs

For a full list of publications please contact:

**Earthscan**
Dunstan House,
14a St Cross Street
London, NW1 0JH, UK
Tel: +44 (0)20 7841 1930
Fax: +44 (0)20 7242 1474
Email: earthinfo@earthscan.co.uk
Web: **www.earthscan.co.uk**

22883 Quicksilver Drive, Sterling, VA 20166-2012, USA

Earthscan publishes in association with the International Institute for Environment
and Development

A catalogue record for this book is available from the British Library

Library of Congress Cataloging-in-Publication Data

Metz, David.
    The limits to travel : how far will you go? / David Metz.
        p. cm.
    Includes bibliographical references and index.
    ISBN 978-1-84407-493-8 (hbk. : alk. paper)
    1. Transportation–Social aspects. 2. Migration, Internal–Social
aspects. I. Title.
    HE151.M474 2008
    303.48'32–dc22

The paper used for this book is FSC-certified.
FSC (the Forest Stewardship Council) is an
international network to promote responsible
management of the world's forests.

FSC
**Mixed Sources**
Product group from well-managed
forests and other controlled sources
Cert no. SGS-COC-2482
www.fsc.org
© 1996 Forest Stewardship Council

Library
University of Texas
at San Antonio

# Contents

# List of Figures

# Acknowledgements

This book was written while I was a visiting professor at the Centre for Transport Studies, which forms part of the Department of Civil and Environmental Engineering at University College London. I am grateful for hospitality from Nick Tyler, Ben Heydecker, Peter Jones and Lin Tze Tan. Some of the research and analysis on which the book is based was carried out while I held a visiting professorship at the Centre for Ageing and Public Health at the London School of Hygiene and Tropical Medicine. I appreciate the hospitality of Astrid Fletcher, Pat Doyle, David Leon and Andy Haines. The Department for Transport funded some initial analysis through its 'New Horizons' research programme, for which I am grateful.

It seems to be the modern custom to acknowledge considerable numbers of colleagues and friends who have read parts of the manuscript in draft and provided helpful comments, or who have contributed in other ways. For this particular book, such grateful acknowledgments are due to Monica Threlfall, Ben Metz, Nick Tyler and Martin Lowson for kindly reading passages of the manuscript. This book's genesis is perhaps somewhat old-fashioned, in that I spent some years reading, observing, analysing and thinking about the subject matter, without much discussion with others. This happened largely because my line of thought took me away from the intellectual territory of the main body of transport studies and transport economics. Nevertheless, I did not disengage entirely in that I submitted papers to the peer-reviewed academic journals as well as to the professional journals. I did this to test my thinking on experts and I benefited from the comments of many anonymous reviewers (some of whom were more helpful than others, as is always the case), which I am very pleased to acknowledge. I also need to express my appreciation to the editors of these journals for their willingness to consider my submissions. Particular thanks are due to David Banister, editor of *Transport Reviews*, who wrote an encouraging editorial to accompany the first article of mine that addressed the way that time limits mobility. This encouraged me to pursue what has turned out to be the central theme of this book.

*David Metz*
*February 2008*

# Foreword

---

This is a book about travel and transport, about human mobility and its consequences. One reason for writing it is that it doesn't seem to have been done before. Of course, there are hordes of travel books – adventurous journeys to distant places that explore both the terrain traversed and the emotions of the intrepid author. There are lots of books about transport – histories of the railways for instance – or how to pass your driving test, or fly a plane or start up a budget airline. What hasn't been done is to tackle *why* we travel in relation to *how* we travel. The 'why' is the motivation, subject of the emerging scientific discipline of human mobility. The 'how' refers to the transport system in all its variety that enables – sometimes frustrates – our need to be elsewhere. And what constrains us, apart from time and money, is the impact that all this travel has on both the travellers and the environment. Traffic congestion impedes our mobility, and carbon dioxide emitted by transport is the fastest growing greenhouse gas that is warming the planet. Carbon and congestion, to put it succinctly, are the big issues for this book.

The second reason for writing this book is that thinking about transport, as an area of public policy, is incoherent. We want more mobility but less impact, and we doubt that this is possible. The choices are unpalatable and decisions are ducked, storing up problems for the future. Other related policy areas function better. On climate change, I would say that the British government has a good understanding of the issues and is taking a leading role internationally, although it doesn't escape criticism for being less than fully effectual in putting policy into practice. Energy policy, where I cut my teeth in the public service, is well understood, although there are difficult dilemmas to resolve, particularly concerning the role of nuclear power. In contrast, the civil servants and ministers involved in transport policy don't have an intellectual grip on the issues. They acknowledge that 'we can't build our way out of congestion', but continue to fund a large road construction programme. They imagine that road pricing would be a way of limiting congestion but lack the resolve to press ahead. And they recognize that forecasts of rapidly growing air travel pose a problem for policy on climate change but can't provide a persuasive rationale for their willingness to allow more runways to be built. It just doesn't add up.

In this book, I'm going to explain what has gone wrong with our thinking about travel and transport, and how to put it right. The underlying problem is that the transport economists have made a big mistake. The civil servants have been insufficiently astute to spot the error, while ministers have come and gone, doing what they were advised and making little impact.

The challenge to conventional transport economics that I shall mount is based on my own researches. Nearly all of this has been published in the peer-reviewed and professional journals, to which those with special interest can refer for details and for the full scientific literature cited. Not being an economist by training, my concern has been to see the big picture and not be sidetracked by details or methodology. So my treatment is slightly old-fashioned, being descriptive and discursive, not mathematical. The advantage is that the arguments can be understood by the non-specialist reader.

In this book I focus on personal travel, and its impact, by road, rail and plane, as well as the slow modes of walking and cycling. Lack of data constrains me to say very little about freight transport, which of course contributes to congestion and climate change, and competes for space on the transport infrastructure. Nor do I say a lot about costs, in part because these can change significantly in the long run, and I'm concerned about the long run. And in any event, we will be richer in the long run so that desirable developments become more affordable. In the short run building a tunnel seems very costly, but in the long run a built tunnel is rarely regretted.

Studies of public attitudes in Britain indicate that there is general pessimism about transport, including roads and their management, local transport, rail and congestion. People believe the transport system has got worse and is expected to get worse in the future. I will argue that in reality we are better off than we feel, and that indeed there is room for improvement if we understand more clearly the quantity and quality of the mobility we can reasonably expect.

The topics covered in this book, particularly carbon and congestion, are global, not parochial. All the rich countries are grappling with them, as increasingly are the fast growing middle-income countries. I deal with some of the relevant developments in countries other than Britain. Nevertheless, my main focus is on Britain, for a number of reasons. It is the patch that I and at least the first readers of this book know best. There is substantial engagement and analysis by the policy, academic and practitioner communities. Extensive statistics are compiled and published, to their credit, by the Department for Transport, the Office of National Statistics and other official bodies. All this provides grist for my mill. But the challenges and remedies should have application beyond these shores.

This book does not preach values or tell people what they personally should do to save the planet or anything else. Rather, my aim is to advance understanding and inform decision makers – both ourselves as individuals making personal decisions about travel, and politicians and their advisers taking decisions in a democratic society.

Human history has, among many other things, been a story of increasing mobility. This has generally been seen as beneficial. Has this form of 'progress' reached a limit, on a crowded, warming planet? Or may we aspire to yet farther horizons? I hope you'll have a sense of possible answers to these questions by the end of this book.

# List of Acronyms and Abbreviations

| | |
|---|---|
| BRT | bus rapid transit |
| CO2e | carbon dioxide equivalent |
| CTRL | Channel Tunnel Rail Link |
| GDP | gross domestic product |
| GPS | global positioning system |
| EU ETS | European Union Emissions Trading Scheme |
| g/km | grams per kilometre |
| IPCC | Intergovernmental Panel on Climate Change |
| ITC | information and telecommunications technologies |
| mbpd | million barrels per day |
| mt | million tonnes |
| Mtoe | million tonnes oil equivalent |
| PPG13 | Planning Policy Guidance Note 13 |
| ppm | parts per million |
| SACTRA | Standing Advisory Committee on Trunk Road Assessment |
| UCL | University College London |
| ULTra | urban light transport |
| WHO | World Health Organization |

# 1

# Faster and Farther

---

Travel – love it or hate it, love it *and* hate it. It's undeniably a vital part of modern life. How, where and when we travel is a constant preoccupation for most of us, whether the daily journey to work, the regular visits to shops and entertainments, weekends away, longer trips to distant destinations. Mobility is central to how we think of ourselves and how we organize our lives. Fundamentally, we are mobile beings. It feels as though the more we travel, the more we are involved with life. Stop-at-home types are out of the picture. Twist an ankle and you're temporarily trapped in a different lifestyle.

With steady economic growth, we can all hope to become richer – and most of us do. As we get richer, we travel more. The car is the prime mover, there's no doubt about it. Road traffic in Britain has increased by 80 per cent over the past 25 years. More than a quarter of households now have access to two or more cars, and there are more such households than those without any car at all. There are well over 30 million vehicles on Britain's roads. Nearly two-thirds of all journeys are by car, with bus use, cycling and walking in decline. Aviation is also undergoing huge expansion. Nearly 200 million passengers will use British airports this year, up four-fold since 1980.[1]

So we are becoming ever more mobile. But are we better off as a result? Do the frustrations and damage outweigh the benefits of more access to desirable destinations? Certainly there are frustrations. Speeds on both long-distance roads and on city streets are falling as car ownership grows. More than half those asked in surveys say that traffic congestion in towns and cities is a serious issue for them. We like new sections of roads when we happen upon them in the course of a trip – how nice to cruise on the smooth tarmac of the new bypass – but we don't want to concrete over the countryside and we would rather not live too near a busy route that disturbs our tranquillity. Thirty per cent of people say they are adversely affected by noise from traffic. The main source of noise that bothers people is road traffic, followed by noise from neighbours and then from aircraft. Although we like to fly because of where it gets us, we do not delight in having a new runway in our own backyard, or living near to the flight path of a major airport. We're not keen on the congestion at major terminals, or the sardine seating on the aircraft.[2]

We are frustrated by inefficiency – late and cancelled trains, unpredictable buses, being bumped off overbooked flights, the tedium of airport check-in, security, hanging about, bad signing on city roads, road works that take for ever, jams from sheer weight of traffic, lack of information ... the list goes on. We feel it shouldn't have to be like that.

Then there's the damage. We are anxious about the effect of vehicle emissions, particularly the 'particulates', the super-fine carbon particles that waft from tailpipes and may be responsible for a significant proportion of all lung cancer cases as well as other kinds of ill health. We are pretty convinced that our last cold was caught from someone on the overcrowded train. And looming ever larger is the contribution of transport to climate change. Much of the inhabited world would be underwater were the ice caps to melt. For the world as a whole, transport is the largest single source of carbon dioxide emissions, still on an upward trend. Carbon dioxide is the main 'greenhouse gas', increasing concentrations of which in the atmosphere are resulting in global warming. For Britain, 95 per cent of carbon dioxide emissions from the transport sector come from road vehicles. What happens to the world if the Chinese and Indians aspire to the same car-based mobility that we have achieved?

Travel, we both love it and hate it. We love the people and places to which it gets us, we enjoy the journey when all goes according to plan, but we hate the frustrations and are worried about the collateral damage. Our ideas are contradictory and fragmented. They need to be coherent and consistent if we are to make sense of human mobility and put right the many failings and inadequacies of the transport system. Making sense and putting right are the aims of this book, both for individuals and for all of us collectively. We need better to understand the fundamental nature of human mobility.

## Evolutionary origins

People living in Britain and other developed countries have become amazingly mobile over the past century. But the roots of modern mobility lie way back in our evolutionary past. There is pretty good evidence that mobility is a fundamental attribute of human nature. Let's go back to the beginning for a quick tour.

Genetic, fossil and archaeological evidence argues that anatomically modern humans originated in Africa. Then a complex series of migrations over the past 100,000 years populated all corners of the earth. Although the evidence for detailed routes is limited, the undoubted fact is that man has penetrated and resided in all territories of the world other than the frozen wastes of the Antarctic. Modern humans had arrived in Australia by 40,000 years ago and could only have arrived there by boat. Sea levels were generally below present levels up to about 10,000 years ago, with the result that Australia, Tasmania and New Guinea formed a single continent separated from south-east Asia by a stretch of open sea 100km wide or less. North America was connected to Siberia by a land bridge and the British Isles were joined to continental Europe. So colonization of most of the world could be done on foot or with simple boats. Before recorded history, man was hunter, gatherer and herder. Human settlement based on farming arose only 10,000 years ago, which is quite recent in the context of human evolution. This pervasive prehistoric mobility distinguishes man from other terrestrial animals (although birds and fish may be even more mobile than us).[3]

Endurance running is another characteristic that distinguishes man from other animals. Humans are good long-distance runners on account of particular adaptations including long tendons, big buttocks, a balanced head, short toes, a narrow pelvis and a stable foot arch. This ability may have evolved to give humans a competitive advantage over less resilient animals in the quest for scavenged meat. Surprisingly, humans can outrun deer and antelope. Although these species are faster in the sprint, the expert hunters from hunter-gatherer societies still remaining today can chase an animal relentlessly over half a day and pursue it to the point of collapse in the noonday heat. Man is equipped with sweat glands, which these animals lack. And humans are able to formulate strategies for a successful pursuit. Humans who could devise and realize such long-distance goals in the African savannah would succeed in an evolutionary context.[4]

The modern marathon runner is the heir of these early hunters. The 'runner's high' experienced by many long-distance runners is reported to be a state of euphoria induced by prolonged exercise. It may be a consequence of the release within the brain of endorphins, pain-relieving proteins. In the course of evolution, such a mechanism could give a selective advantage in a world in which dinner had to be caught before it could be cooked. Jogging should not be seen as a masochistic exercise but rather as a memory of our evolutionary past.

All in all, the available evidence supports the idea that man has evolved to travel long distances by both walking and running. As man developed technologies, these could be exploited to travel farther and faster. Thus the origins of much of the history and geography of mankind that we learnt in school, not least the willingness of people to migrate from where they were born to other cities or strange new countries in search of a better life. This has had implications for our own evolution. Steve Jones, professor of genetics at University College London (UCL), has pointed out that if one's ancestors came from the same village they may well have been related, but this is much less likely if they were born hundreds of miles apart. In 19th-century Oxfordshire, the average distance between birthplaces of marriage partners was less than ten miles. Now it is more than 50, and in the US it is several hundred. A consequence of this increasing mobility is that the world's populations are beginning to merge genetically. Steve Jones suggests that the most important event in recent human evolution has been the invention of the bicycle.[5]

Another kind of argument that mobility is an innate human attribute is inspired by observing the play of very young children. There's lots of evidence that girls prefer to play with dolls and boys with cars, trucks and other vehicles. This has been extensively documented from as early as 18 months of age. Such preferences for stereotyped play activities are regarded as one of the earliest, most pervasive and developmentally consistent manifestations of gender roles in children. The question is whether these preferences are innate, or whether they are learnt, prompted by adult expectations or by the behaviour of older children. Do such preferences follow inculcation of gender stereotypes or precede it?[6]

What is fascinating is that similar differences in toy preferences are found in infant monkeys when these are offered the same variety of toys as the infant children. This is taken to suggest that such sexually differentiated preferences are innate and arose early in human evolution, driven by selection pressures based on differentiated behavioural roles for males and females. In other words, the most successful hunters would be those who had a propensity to be mobile, which would show up in play when young. It is therefore perhaps not wholly surprising to find that model railway enthusiasts are invariably male, and that car aficionados are mostly men. Feminists might be tempted to blame our problems with the transport system on the men who very largely design and operate it – although we might debate whether it would be very different had women been in charge.[7]

More generally, we might suppose that the mobility of children, which we some-times experience to the point of distraction, reflects our evolutionary origins. I'll argue in a later chapter that some residue of this can be found in the daily travel of adults.

Related to mobility is territoriality. Human territoriality can be viewed as a strat-egy to control resources and people by controlling area. The desire to expand the territory under control in order to gain resources and opportunities is constrained by the time and energy required, as well as by the risks from exposure to predators and enemies. It is suggestive that the mean area of the territory of long-established Greek villages is about 20 square kilometres. This corresponds to a radius of about two and a half kilometres, or an hour's walk to get from the centre to the periphery and back again. No cities built before about 1800 were larger than this. Only as succes-sive transport innovations were introduced – horse-drawn trams, electric trams, buses, trains, underground trains, cars – did the effective radius of urban settlements increase, in proportion to the speed of transport.[8]

## Travel time

The amount of territory with which we can cope depends on how fast we can move – because the amount of time in the day available for travel has to be limited. Remarkably, the hour a day of travel deduced from the size of ancient villages and towns continues to apply today.

The best evidence for this lies in the data generated by the British *National Travel Survey*. This is a regular survey of individual travel behaviour carried out by the stat-isticians at the Department for Transport. The technique is to ask a random sample of the population to compile diaries that record details all of their travel over the course of a single week. Currently, around 20,000 people do this each year, a sizeable sample. The first such travel survey was carried out in 1972, so we have over 30 years of data available. One kind of data collected is the amount of time people spend on the move. All personal trips within Britain are covered, including walks of more than 50 yards. However, international travel is not counted. The trend in average travel time over the past 30 years is shown in Figure 1.1. What is striking is that the trend line is almost flat, with only a slight increase over the period. We are on the move for about 380 hours a year – close to an hour a day – on average.[9]

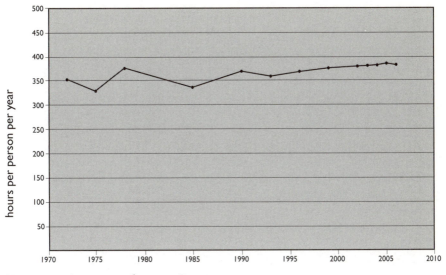

**Figure 1.1** *Average travel time in Britain*

Of course, any average conceals variation between different people. When you look at particular groups of the population, you find some variation in travel time. Older people travel less, on average about three-quarters of an hour a day for those aged 65 and over. So do children. Women spend rather less time travelling than men. And it varies by region, with average travel time in London appreciably greater than elsewhere. Londoners in their 20s are particularly mobile – getting on for an hour and a half a day, on average. Moreover, within groups such as these there'll be variation. For instance, some people with disabilities may rarely get out, while some commuters choose to travel heroic distances.[10]

Here I want to stress how surprising it is to find travel time, averaged across the whole population, holding so steady over a period of more than 30 years, as shown in Figure 1.1. It is particularly remarkable when you remember that, over this period, average incomes have doubled (after allowing for inflation), car ownership has more than doubled, from 11 to 27 million vehicles in Britain, and the average distance travelled has increased by 60 per cent.

Figure 1.2 shows how the distance travelled has increased over the period of the *National Travel Survey*. In 1972 people travelled about 4500 miles a year on average. In recent years this has settled at around 7100 miles. This figure also shows that the average number of trips made a year has held steady at about 1000 per person over the period.

So both travel time and the number of trips have remained broadly constant, on average, over the past 35 years. There can be few, if any, measures of human behaviour that show such relative stability in a context involving so much change.

This stability is not just a quirk that shows up in British data. It seems to be a pretty general phenomenon, with an average of an hour or so a day of travel time

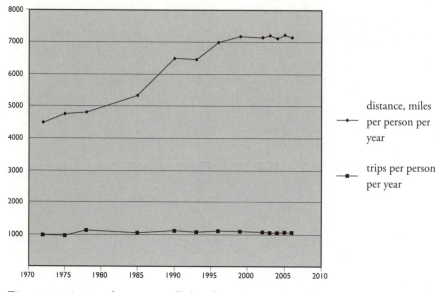

**Figure 1.2** *Average distance travelled and average number of journeys*

seen in nearly all countries where data has been gathered. If there is any trend over time, it is upwards rather than downward, with perhaps the most marked upward trend reported from the US, increasing annually at the rate of about two minutes per person per day over the period 1983 to 2001, albeit on the basis of only quite limited data. This example of American exceptionalism may reflect an increase in longer commutes associated with the phenomenon of urban and exurban sprawl (discussed in Chapter 6).[11]

If travel time is constant for countries, speed of travel certainly is not. So in rural India, people walk to carry out their daily tasks in a necessarily limited area, taking around an hour on average, whereas in countries with high levels of car ownership, the amount of time taken is similar, but of course people can travel much greater distances at the higher speeds possible.

The algebra is elementary. Distance equals speed multiplied by time. So if travel time is constant, distance increases in direct proportion to speed. If you travel faster, you can go farther in the time you can spare. This is simple but illuminating. The origins of the average travel time of an hour a day very probably date from the earliest human settlements. Over the course of recorded history, mankind has devised technologies that allow ever faster travel – domesticating the horse, the cart on wheels, the horse-drawn carriage, bicycle, train, bus, car, aeroplane. Rising incomes have made these technologies increasingly affordable. This has led both to the huge increase in mobility seen in developed countries and to the increasingly untenable environmental impact. I'll explore this fully in later chapters.

# Simplicity or complexity

A key perspective that I'm going to develop in this book is that this more-or-less one hour a day of travel time, on average, is a universal phenomenon that can help us both understand human mobility and act effectively to tackle the many challenges we face in the transport sector. However, many experts will dismiss this claim as too simplistic by far.

The world is a complex place, the experts rightly say, where cause and effect are generally hard to distinguish. Think of the complexities of our modern economy, for instance. But occasionally, I would argue, you can see something simple that allows a straightforward interpretation. Such simplicity is well worth looking out for. But whether you're so inclined is a matter of taste and pedigree. You can divide people into two types: simplifiers and complicators (whoever first said that was obviously a simplifier).

Physicists tend to take the view that the basic features of the universe have got to be simple. As Albert Einstein said: 'Everything should be made as simple as possible, but not simpler.' This of course begs the question of how far to go in stripping out complexity. Biologists, in contrast, see the world of plants and animals – the results of piecemeal evolution – as essentially complicated.

By instinct, I'm a simplifier. I've practised a variety of scientific disciplines in a varied career that has included laboratory research, civil service administration, research management and, currently, independent analysis. I've always been on the lookout for simple concepts that help us understand the world or some bit of it. When social scientists speak of a 'rich data set', I inwardly shudder, knowing that this is a euphemism for uninterpretable complexity.

As a junior scientist with a master's degree in biochemistry, aiming to start out on a career in research, I was naturally excited by the discovery of the structure of DNA, the famous double helix. It seemed to offer the promise of a simple approach to understanding the complexities of biology. So I was thrilled to be offered bench space for PhD research in the laboratory of Maurice Wilkins, who had shared with Watson and Crick the 1962 Nobel Prize for their discovery of the structure of DNA. But it turned out that while the DNA configuration was fundamentally simple, it was surrounded by complexity. Go up a level, and you find the intricacies of the chromosome. Go down a level, and you're into the complications of the chemistry of the constituent chemical building blocks of DNA. Look at how the genetic material made up of DNA replicates when the cell divides, and you're faced with multifarious enzymatic mechanisms. The beguiling 'embedded simplicity' of the double helix only emerges when you view the extraordinary complexity of the living cell at precisely the right scale from exactly the right angle. Still, such a viewpoint is well worth seeking because it helps us understand an incredibly intricate system.

Decades later, as chief scientist at the Department of Transport, as it was known at that time (more recently renamed as 'Department for Transport'), I had a strong feeling that human mobility was not being viewed either at the right scale or from the right angle. It was apparent to us that we could not continue to construct roads to match the growth of car ownership and use. While I was thinking about possible future strategies, my attention was caught by the department's statistics that showed that travel time had been holding constant at about 380 hours per person per year for the past 30 years. I thought this was remarkable and important. My colleagues did not. They seemed to think, if indeed they thought about it at all, that it was one of those statistical quirks that had no particular significance. It was only when I had left the department and had the time to reflect that I began to appreciate how this invariance of travel time could provide a crucial insight that would allow us to make sense of the history and future of human mobility.

I was not the first to identify the significance of the constant amount of travel time. Over the years, a number of analysts had drawn attention to this phenomenon. The most significant of these was Yacov Zahavi, who was born in what is now Israel in 1926, graduated as an engineer from the Technion in Haifa in 1951, and served as a graduate intern at the UK Road Research Laboratory in 1951/52. After studying and working in a number of countries he settled in Washington, where he carried out consultancy assignments for the US Department of Transportation and the World Bank. He died in 1983. Zahavi interpreted the constancy of travel time as signifying the existence of a 'travel time budget', a stable daily amount of time that people make available for travel. He also introduced the concept of a 'travel money budget', the proportion of household income spent on travel, which also seemed to be constant.[12]

Figure 1.3 shows average expenditure in Britain on travel and transport as a proportion of total household expenditure. You can see that this has held pretty steady at about 16 per cent over the past 20 years. Looking at household expenditure surveys from countries at different stages of development suggests the following pattern. Households without a car devote, on average, 3–5 per cent of their income to travel. As incomes grow, cars become affordable, and travel expenditure rises

**Figure 1.3** *Average travel expenditure as a proportion of household expenditure*

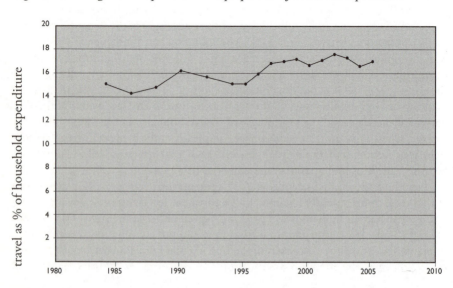

with increasing car ownership, stabilizing in the range 10–15 per cent of household income once ownership reaches about one per household. As households continue to get richer, the number of cars per household continues to rise, but the proportion of expenditure devoted to travel does not. What seems to be happening is that people make sacrifices from other areas of expenditure to get their first car because of the benefits this brings. British expenditure on travel at 16 per cent of household expenditure is at the top end of the international range, reflecting price levels for transport services – relatively high fuel tax and public transport fares.[13]

Yacov Zahavi's key papers were published in the late 1970s, when his ideas met with general scepticism. His work, though never entirely forgotten, was subsequently relegated to a footnote in the standard texts of transport studies. Had Zahavi not died prematurely, it is quite likely that the phenomena he identified would have achieved greater prominence in thinking about travel and transport, not least because the continuing accumulation of data supports his original insight. The problem was that constant travel time and constant travel expenditure didn't fit the prevailing paradigm of the transport economists and analysts, as I'll explain in Chapter 3. However, as the data in Figures 1.1 and 1.3 show, these parameters have continued to hold constant over the subsequent quarter-century, so Zahavi was clearly onto something significant.

## Why is travel time constant?

Once mankind had ceased to be ever on the move as hunter-gatherer, it seems likely that about an hour a day of travel was what was optimal for agricultural and urban peoples. Why should this be? Well, obviously there has to be an upper limit to the amount of time people can take for travel, simply because there are other things we need to do – eat, sleep, work, domestic tasks, leisure activities and so on. Interestingly, when the patterns of time use are compared for different countries, there are considerable similarities. On average, people spend about eight hours a day sleeping, four hours on homemaking and childcare, eight to nine hours on the aggregate of work and leisure, and about an hour on travel. 'We mostly sleep, work and watch TV' was the headline for the most recent British *Time Use Survey*. The main differences between countries lie in the balance between time for work and for leisure.[14] [15]

So competition for time, within the constraints of the 24 hours of the day, is what must set an upper limit to the amount of time we can allocate for travel. And it is worth making the obvious point that the 24-hour daily time limit applies to everyone, rich and poor alike, and for ever – unlike money incomes, which are unequally distributed and tend to grow over time. This is why, on reflection, the historic constancy of travel time is perhaps less surprising than it seemed at first sight.

But why just one hour a day, why not less? The main reason is that travel gets us to desirable destinations, the places we want to be, whether for a better job, a nicer home, a more stimulating leisure opportunity, or to meet friends, family and colleagues. As we become richer, we are able to spend a growing amount of money on movement, particularly on car-based mobility and air travel. When we acquire cars, we travel more. Acquisition of the second or third car by the household allows more travel. The impact of higher incomes and increasing car ownership can be seen when we look at a cross-section of society, from poor to rich. If you divide households into five bands by income, you find that individuals with the lowest incomes make on average 880 trips per year, covering 4100 miles on average, whereas those with the highest incomes make 1160 trips and travel 11,600 miles (British data for 2006). Similarly for car ownership: individuals in households that do not possess a car on average make 775 trips, spend 318 hours a year on the move and cover 3000 miles, while those in households with two or more cars make 1140 trips, take 417 hours in total and cover 9400 miles.[16]

The apparently obvious interpretation of these differences is that as people get richer and get to own a car they make more trips and take more time travelling. But that can't be right, because average travel time and number of trips a year has remained pretty constant for many years, as we have seen, over which time household incomes and car ownership have both grown very substantially. The explanation of this apparent paradox is that the direction of causality goes the other way. It's not that when people acquire a car they then make extra journeys. Rather, those people who need or choose to travel more are more likely to buy a car. What the data strongly suggest, in my view, is a positive relationship between socio-economic status and travel behaviour that applies irrespective of the overall level of household income or car ownership. Higher socio-economic status carries with it a greater propensity to travel.[17]

Think of it this way. At any point in time, people who are better off (and therefore more likely to own a car) tend to lead more active lives and so spend more time travelling and make more trips – business trips, leisure activities – while those with lower incomes are more likely to stay in one location when at work and generally get about less. To oversimplify just a little, wage earners tend to travel to work, do their job, travel home and spend the evening in front of the television. Salary earners also travel to work, but are more likely to travel while at work to meet clients and colleagues, and after work may stop off at the gym on the way home or pursue other leisure activities. Nevertheless, despite different lifestyles, as car ownership has steadily increased over the years, we are all travelling greater distances, rich and poor alike.

One reason why the significance of constant travel time has found little acceptance among transport specialists is that it seemed not to fit comfortably with data showing considerable variation in daily, monthly and yearly travel patterns for individuals. Phil Goodwin is one investigator who with his team has drawn attention to this aspect of travel behaviour. Phil and I were students at the same time at UCL. While I followed a somewhat random career course, entering the field of transport studies at quite a late stage, Phil made a very substantial contribution to research and policy in this same area, the importance of which he recognized from the outset. He is an outstandingly clear and stylish speaker who invariably attracts large audiences of transport researchers and practitioners. Phil's sense of occasion can be gauged from the opening words of his inaugural lecture as professor of transport policy at UCL on 23 October 1997, an event which filled the college's largest lecture hall: 'At this minute, 30 years ago today, Reuben Smeed, first professor of transport studies in

UCL, started his inaugural lecture, "Traffic Studies and Urban Congestion", which I attended, in the back row, as one of his first group of research students.' (Reuben Smeed, as well as being a pioneer of the subject matter of this book, is also famous for chairing a government panel on road pricing whose 1964 report supported the principle of congestion charging.)[18]

Phil Goodwin has drawn attention to the phenomenon of churn in the transport system. The individuals in the same traffic queue at the same time on two successive mornings are not, in most part, the same individuals. Every year anything up to a third of people change jobs and up to one in seven move house. People leave home, get married, have babies, their children change school, some get divorced, they retire, someone dies. All this changes travel patterns. Moreover, significant numbers of households reduce car ownership each year, but may still remain car dependent for trips, especially older people.[19]

So how might we reconcile the long-run constant nature of travel time and trip frequency, averaged across the population, with the day-to-day volatility of the travel patterns of individuals? One line of thought derives from the study of complex systems that may display behaviours that can be described as 'emergent', that is, the properties of the system as seen at a higher level may not be deducible from the behaviour of the individual components. For example, the termites in a mound can individually be described in terms of physiology, biochemistry and biological development, but their social behaviour and building is a property that emerges from the collection of termites and needs to be analysed at a higher level.

Emergence involves the arising of novel and coherent structures, patterns and properties during the process of self-organization in complex systems. Human travel using the transport system of modern societies is evidently a complex system where a wide range of individual behaviours aggregate. Average travel time and trip rate are emergent parameters that hold constant over long durations and which are properties of the whole system. This reflects the constraints of the 24-hour day, which limits travel and hence choice of opportunities at destinations, as well as the intrinsic human need for mobility that is a motivating factor in our day-to-day travel. Moreover, the relative constancy of travel time and trip rate is consistent with a system in which the structure of the population and the pattern of land use change only slowly. As one person retires and ceases making the journey to work, another enters the labour market. As one couple leaves a city-centre apartment for a house in the suburbs to accommodate a young family, another couple comes together in the vacated apartment.

People go through a cycle of mobility over the life course, from the immobility of infancy, through the peak activity in mid-life, often returning to limited mobility in late life. All these individual changes result in a churning of travel patterns that nevertheless leaves average travel time and trip rate unchanged. What does alter over time is the distance people travel, because of the benefits we get by travelling.

## The benefits of travel

This extra distance travelled arises because we find that we can improve our quality of life though mobility, despite the time spent in congested traffic – time made increasingly acceptable in more comfortable cars equipped with in-car entertainment and navigation aids, and with our mobile phones close to hand. We can seek employment within a wide area without the domestic upheaval of moving house, and can reconcile employment opportunities for ourselves and our partner through car-based mobility. We are no longer limited to working for the small number of employers in the immediate locality of home or on a convenient public transport route. Increasingly, employees are quite mobile and can pick and choose for whom they work. We get in our cars, if not on our bikes, to seek out employers who best value our services, wherever located within acceptable travelling time.[20]

Beyond work, car-based mobility means that our younger children are not limited to the nearest primary school. In fact, over 40 per cent of 5–10 year olds are taken to school by car. The parent-chauffeured car extends the opportunities for organized leisure activities out of school. But the scope for roaming around on bikes or foot has shrunk as traffic has increased, which many would argue is a bad bargain for children, although aspirational parents would probably not agree. In seeking leisure opportunities for ourselves and our families, we fill attractive resorts and rural sites to their car-parking capacity over an increasingly long season – which lengthens as the number of time-rich retired people continues to grow.

Car-based mobility is particularly attractive to women, increasing the choice of jobs and childcare facilities, which rarely turn out to be close to each other, so making use of public transport difficult. Women often find a car to be preferable, giving them the feeling that they can go where they want to go, simply and flexibly coping with multiple demands on their time. Women are more likely to be employed if they have access to a car.[21]

Most of us have chosen lives in which increasing our personal mobility – very largely by car – improves our self-perceived quality of life, despite the negative aspects of road traffic. Those of us who voluntarily forgo car use are a fairly small minority, comprising students, older people, idealists and others who choose to live in convenient and attractive urban areas, preferably with substantial pedestrian zones – places such as Cambridge, York, Zurich, Copenhagen, Amsterdam, Vienna. But even in these cities, working families with children tend to move out to the suburbs where the car can still be used for the school run, the supermarket, the commute to the business park workplace, and the weekend leisure trips.

It is going to be hard to contain, let alone reverse, this deep and strong trend towards ever increasing mobility largely based on the car. All experience shows that, as individual incomes increase in developing countries, the same car-based mobility is sought, reflecting the attractions of door-to-door convenience, and the status and autonomy associated with the private motor vehicle. Policy measures intended to constrain car use are difficult to sell to electorates, even with the carrot of improved public transport. Fiscal measures – such as higher rates of fuel duty, charging for road use or taxing business parking space – are undermined both by adverse comparisons with neighbouring countries and the increasing ability to pay these costs as incomes grow.

The big increase in personal mobility over recent decades is the result of travelling at higher speeds. Average daily distances travelled have increased substantially, reflecting the longer journeys that can be made comfortably on fast roads, by high-speed train or using the expanding aviation system, all within acceptable personal travel time budgets. Attempts to fix the problems of the transport system generally result in higher speeds, although that is not the explicit intention. For instance, you have a pinch point on a heavily used road where traffic grinds to stop–start at peak travel times. What do you do? Obviously (you might suppose), you widen the road, streamline the junction, build an underpass or the like. Brilliant, congestion disappears – or does it? Actually, it appears again somewhere on the network pretty soon after. Why? Because the road widening permits faster speeds, which allows longer journeys within the fixed amount of time we allow ourselves for travel, and longer journeys mean more traffic, which adds to congestion. And so we're back to where we started, grinding our way through congested traffic, while travelling a bit farther, and causing a bit more damage to the environment.

Conventional transport policy is badly flawed and fails to solve the big problems of congestion and environmental damage. In part this is because of reluctance by those in charge to grasp nettles. For example, one contributing factor to the growth of car use is that the cost of motoring has remained steady for many years, even falling slightly, while incomes have risen, so making the car more affordable, while at the same time fares on public transport have been steadily rising – up by 40 per cent in real terms since 1980. If you wanted to tilt the balance towards less polluting and less congesting public transport, you'd subsidize fares rather more and raise the tax on fuel to pay for it. But this is seen as too difficult.[22]

A more serious indictment, beyond lack of political courage, is that those in charge – ministers, civil servants, economists, planners and the like – don't understand their business and the needs of the people they are there to serve, as I'll be arguing. It is decidedly odd that economics ministries, such as Her Majesty's Treasury, have a better understanding of the complexities of the whole economy than transport ministries have of their limited patch.

Fresh thinking is needed. One aspect effectively ignored in official thinking and conventional transport economics is that the benefit we get from reaching our destinations is not the only motivation for travel. We also like to travel for the pleasures of the journey – for fun, one might say. Pleasure may not seem that important when driving to work through congested traffic on a wet Monday morning. But it would be a mistake to neglect the psychological boost from getting out and about, and interacting with people and places in the world beyond the home. Chuck Berry captured this well: 'Riding along in my automobile, my baby beside me at the wheel … cruising and playing the radio, with no particular place to go.' The pleasure of being on the move is decisive for lots of leisure trips, whether the bike ride on the quiet country road, the lazy riverboat, or travelling from Chicago to LA, getting our kicks on Route 66. And such good feelings are an important consideration when people choose what kind of car to buy – and not just the petrol heads.

It is the combination of places to reach plus the pleasure of mobility, a reflection of our evolutionary past, which keeps us on the move for an hour a day. We take the benefits from improvements in the transport system in the form of greater distances travelled, rather than shorter journey times. Personal investment in more and better cars, and public investment in roads, trains and airports, all these allow us to go faster. So, in the more or less fixed amount of time we make available for travel, we travel farther. This gets us to more desirable destinations, which is good, but at the price of more environmental damage, which is bad news. What we could do about this is the subject matter of subsequent chapters.

In all this the car is central. There's no denying that for most people it provides mobility, autonomy and pleasure. Growing car ownership and mileage seem an inescapable feature of our society. Road congestion is a pressing problem. Roads fill up and there is pressure to build more. But the transport sector has a big footprint, and we are increasingly anxious about the environmental damage arising from our cars.

In this book I'm going to attempt to make sense of human mobility. I will propose how we could organize our transport system in a way that better meets our needs. To do this we need a clearer understanding of mobility as an important aspect of human behaviour. Mobility is something we tend to take for granted. As a scientific topic, it has barely got going. I will pull together what is known from a range of disciplines to chart the way forward.

One proposition to be addressed in this book is that we would have to bring to a halt the ever increasing growth in mobility that has characterized human history if we are not to damage the human environment unacceptably. Would this be feasible? What would be the consequences? Would it require a change in human nature? Or could we develop new non-polluting technologies and so maintain the mobility to which we are so wedded? To find out, read on.

# Detriments and Damage

---

Every increasing access to the places we wish to reach would be a good thing were it not for the detrimental consequences, both for people and the environment. This chapter will spell out the damage from the growth of travel, and assess prospects for offsetting improvements in technology. There are three broad matters of concern. First, damage to life and limb caused mainly by cars, through both accidents and lack of exercise. Second, the local environmental impacts of roads, aviation and other transport infrastructures – air pollution, noise, intrusion into quiet areas, separation of communities, and concreting over the countryside. And third, anxieties about climate change and the part that the oil-consuming transport sector plays in this.[1]

## Crashes are not accidents

It is perhaps surprising that we are allowed to drive cars in close proximity at quite high speeds, qualified only by a driving test taken when we were beginners, mostly many years before. Were the automobile to be invented today, it's quite likely that it would be judged too dangerous for amateur drivers, and would, like buses, trains and planes, be reserved for well-qualified chauffeurs who would be obliged to submit for retesting at regular intervals. But society has grown used to the motor car over the hundred years of its existence, and has both accepted quite a considerable degree of human damage and expended considerable efforts to improve road safety.

It is, of course, the car that is the culprit of the transport system. In Britain, more than 3000 people are killed on our roads each year, almost all associated with road-traffic accidents. This compares with normally very small numbers for other kinds of transport, although train or plane crashes, or passenger ship wrecks, certainly hit the headlines, in part because these are rare events. But we also get anxious when lots of people are killed and injured in one place, and when we feel the accident wouldn't have happened had those in charge been doing their jobs properly. It's perhaps because we are to a degree forgiving of ourselves as amateur drivers that we accept quite a substantial level of road traffic accidents.

In Britain in 2006, 3172 people were killed on the roads (none on the railways). Rather over half were in cars. The remainder comprised mainly pedestrians (675 individuals), motorcyclists (599) and cyclists (146). Many more people were seriously injured. Nevertheless, these numbers are on a declining trend, particularly the figure for those seriously injured, down by a third since the late 1990s. The government has set itself a target reduction of the numbers killed and seriously injured of 40 per cent by 2010, and looks likely to achieve this through a variety of measures including publicity and enforcement of drink-driving laws, changes to learner driver training, and improved arrangements for pedestrians and cyclists.[2]

While road casualties are undoubtedly an important detriment of a transport system that so strongly features personal motorized mobility, this is less a source of public concern than the absolute level of death and injury might imply. Not only does the popularity of the motor car weigh in the balance, but a well conceived, widely endorsed programme of action at national and local level ensures that the trends are downwards. Moreover, within Europe, Britain's record for the rate of road deaths is bettered only by Sweden and the Netherlands.[3]

Globally, however, 1.2 million people die each year as the result of road-traffic accidents – accounting for 2 per cent of deaths worldwide – and 50 million are injured or disabled. The vast majority of this carnage occurs on the increasingly crowded streets, roads and highways of the developing world. The Commission for Global Road Safety forecasts that global road deaths could double by 2020 unless action is taken.[4] Given the favourable experience of the developed economies, there is plenty of scope for measures to reduce deaths and injuries in the developing countries. This will happen naturally to a degree, given that as incomes grow so does the value that society places on a human life and hence the cost of the effort that we are willing to expend to prevent loss of life. Nevertheless, as Margaret Chan, director general of the World Health Organization puts it: 'Road traffic crashes are not "accidents". We need to challenge the notion that they are unavoidable and make room for a pro-active, preventive approach.'[5]

Transport can detract from good health not only through accidents but also by depriving us of healthy exercise. Physical activity is one of the most basic human functions. Yet the combination of too little activity and too much nutritional intake is leading to the increasing prevalence of obesity in the developed countries. Expert opinion advocates at least half an hour of moderate-intensity physical activity on most days of the week. There is evidence that this enhances many aspects of health, including heart disease, diabetes, cancer, the musculoskeletal system as well as psychological well-being.[6] Walking or cycling, rather than taking the car or the bus for short trips, can be a convenient way of improving your health without the bother of going to the gym. One maxim that I particularly like is: 'Eat less, walk more.'[7] Another, applicable to the decision whether to walk up the stairs or take the lift: 'Take every opportunity to exercise.'

# Local impacts

Busy roads damage the local environment and cause harm to individuals and communities in the vicinity. At the same time, the very activity on the roads is a consequence of people being mobile, going about their business and gaining access to desired destinations. So there are trade-offs to be made, with winners who gain mobility at little environmental cost, and losers living close to busy roads who are harder hit by noise and poor air quality, and who may not gain if they lack access to a car. Local and national politics grapple with the issues of equity between different parts of the community and between the social classes. 'Not in my backyard' is a cliché but reflects an understandable and widespread sentiment.

The main local issues in respect of the road system are noise and local air quality. In the countryside, there are particular concerns about the impact of new roads on the quality of the landscape (including trunk road lighting on the night sky), on rural tranquillity and on biodiversity. A related anxiety is the experience that new roads attract additional traffic, over and above the trend growth, which exacerbates the damage. In urban areas, there is the problem of severance of one part of the community from another by a busy road, and the impact on townscape. Protecting the heritage of historic and archaeological resources is important to many people. And, this time from the viewpoint of the road user, there is the ambience of the journey – the contrast between the pleasant open road crossing rolling countryside and the narrow-lane road tunnel.

For aviation, noise for those under flight paths near airports can be a severe affliction, as can local air pollution from aircraft and the density of road traffic. Damage to the countryside, impact on wildlife and tranquillity, are big local issues when the expansion of airports is proposed.

Poor air quality in the vicinity of roads and airports is of particular concern because of possible impacts on health. The main pollutants are nitrogen dioxide, carbon monoxide, ozone and microscopic particles. The consequences for health include: reduced life expectancy through long-term exposure; early deaths or emergency admissions to hospital, particularly for those already in poor health, caused by episodes of high pollution; and periods of breathing discomfort for many. Exposure to ultra-fine particles can cause respiratory and cardiovascular disease. Estimates for 2002 suggested that more than 600 deaths in the UK and a similar number of hospital admissions were brought forward by exposure to particles, although it was not possible to know by how much (and transport was responsible for less than a quarter of the total particulates).[8]

The Los Angeles smog motivated the first US standard for the control of automotive emissions, while European emission-control regulations, such as requiring three-way catalytic converters, were driven primarily by the need to reduce acid rain. The European Union (EU) has set stringent emissions standards for cars and light vans from 2001 (the Euro III standards), as well as tighter fuel quality specifications for petrol and diesel.[9]

Developments in engine and fuel technologies in recent years, including the catalytic converter for car exhausts, have reduced emissions from vehicles substantially, so we may expect the health impacts to lessen. Life expectancy – how long on average we might expect to live – has been rising quite rapidly in recent decades. Between 1984/86 and 2004/06 life expectancy at age 65 in the UK increased by 3.6 years for men and 2.6 years for women.[10] A wide range of environmental, medical and lifestyle improvements have contributed to this impressive trend, including the reduction of transport sector pollution. On the other hand, the gains from further pollution reduction in developed countries seem unlikely to contribute much to further improvement in life expectancy across the whole population – the law of diminishing returns – although some argue that there remains a case for specific action in the centres of large metropolises with dense traffic. And in developing countries there is enormous scope for cleaning up vehicle emissions, with big health benefits.

A low-emission zone covering the whole of London was introduced in February 2008 with the aim of improving air quality by accelerating the retirement of older diesel lorries and encouraging adoption of the newer cleaner vehicles that meet current standards. The health impact assessment for this proposal concluded, somewhat equivocally, that 'there would be important but relatively modest reductions in the health impacts associated with air pollution', and specifically that for the period 2005–15 the zone would lead to '5,200 years of life lost gained [sic], 43 respiratory hospital admissions avoided, and 43 cardiovascular hospital admissions avoided'.[11] This health gain is indeed very modest and would hardly be measurable, given that half a million Londoners would be expected to die over this decade. It will, nevertheless, be good to get the remaining dark-smoke-emitting vehicles off the roads of London, not least for the benefit of those, like myself, who are regular cyclists around town.

There are two useful ways of thinking about local environmental impacts. First, how to weigh these detriments in the balance, against the claimed benefits of expanding the transport system. Second, how to mitigate these detriments – with the London low-emission zone as one example of what can be contemplated.

The standard approach to balancing benefits and detriments of any new public sector scheme, whether a physical construction or some new process, is known as 'cost–benefit analysis'. The essential idea is that monetary values are associated with all the costs, including cash expenditure and detrimental consequences, as well as with the benefits. If the benefits are seen to outweigh the costs, the project may be worth pursuing.[12]

For transport schemes, whether roads, railways or airports, the main benefit is conventionally supposed to be the time saved by travellers as a result of the improvement. For instance, it is argued that widening a congested road will reduce congestion and save the time of motorists. Such time savings can be valued ('time is money') and on average amounts to about 80 per cent of the total monetized benefits of new road capacity. We'll return to this idea of 'travel time saving' in Chapter 3.

The other 20 per cent of the monetized benefits derive from fewer accidents, a consequence of new roads being better designed for safety than the roads they replaced. It is possible to make plausible estimates of the average value of a life lost in an accident, and also of major and minor injuries, as a basis for computing the value of the benefits of fewer accidents. On the other side of the equation, we have the cash costs of construction of the new road, together with the value of the detriments arising from local traffic – extra noise, pollutants and so on. Although cost–benefit analysis has been employed to appraise transport schemes for the past 40 years, until fairly recently it had not been possible to put a monetary value on the environmental and non-accident health damage. This meant that the economic component of the investment appraisal excluded important costs (i.e. the value of damage to the environment and health). So if decision makers focused on the hard numbers, the damage to the environment tended to be downplayed, while if they wanted to give full weight to these detriments, they found themselves comparing apples and oranges. This difficulty has prompted considerable efforts to value environmental and health consequences of transport schemes. Currently there is an established approach to valuing the impact of increasing noise levels. For other detriments, for which a monetary impact cannot as yet be calculated, the practice is to state the impact in terms of, for instance, the number of properties affected by worse air quality and the number by improved air quality.[13]

As well as not being able to capture the value of much of the significant environmental damage of new road schemes, another problem with cost–benefit analysis is that it cannot handle questions of equity – the way that some people consider themselves as losers from a particular project, while others experience clear net gains. All this means that the public is not much persuaded by the argument of the proposers that there would be an overall net benefit from some new transport infrastructure project, or even a benefit-to-cost ratio that is positive and higher than other projects competing for funding. Cost–benefit analysis is appreciated by economists and by civil servants who want a respectable rationale to justify capital programmes. I'll argue in Chapter 3 that cost–benefit analysis in the transport sector has been a distraction and has lead to bad decision making based on misconceived principles. However, one virtue of cost–benefit analysis, as with any approach that requires numerical values to be attributed to the key features of a project, is that it prompts much more rigorous thinking about the future streams of activity and value – which improves the chances of good outcomes.

# Mitigation

I turn next to how the local environmental impacts of transport activity might be mitigated. Consider noise generated by road vehicles. Transport noise affects well-being; it may cause nervous stress; and there is evidence that night-time traffic noise increases cardiovascular disease and fatalities. Of all the sources of noise, transport noise is the most pervasive. We are concerned with noise from both engines and from the tyre on the tarmac or concrete road surface.[14]

EU legislation, binding on all member states, has laid down limits on noise from passenger and goods vehicles, and motorbikes, and these have been steadily reduced over the past four decades. The noise from individual cars has been reduced by 85 per cent since 1970 and from trucks by 90 per cent, a very considerable achievement. This illustrates what can be achieved through regulation that drives development in an area of technology which is ripe for progress. In economic terms, noise is a negative externality, meaning that it is a cost to people who have no direct control over its presence. There is no market for noise and so taxation is difficult as an incentive, unlike the position with carbon (see below). The impact of this noise-reduction legislation is apparent as modern cars purr quietly along our urban streets and the newest buses creep up on unsuspecting cyclists who in the past could hear them coming yards away.

But in the countryside vehicles at higher speeds generate tyre noise that detracts from rural tranquillity. At above about 40mph tyre noise dominates over other noise sources. There are trade-offs between noise reduction, tyre and tarmac durability, and skidding safety in the wet. Tyre rolling resistance accounts for about 30 per cent of the fuel used by cars, but it turns out that there is no relationship between noise and rolling resistance, which means we could have low-noise tyres that are economical to run on. EU legislation is putting pressure on manufacturers to market such tyres. Some surfacing materials are designed to reduce noise but these can be less hard-wearing than conventional materials. As well as developing quieter tyres and road surfaces, noise barriers alongside busy trunk roads can alleviate the impact on nearby houses. These take the form of earth barriers or timber fences up to 3.5m high.[15]

This example of noise from road traffic shows that is possible to make progress through a combination of continuing public pressure to reduce noise levels, government regulation (at European level for vehicles that are marketed internationally), technological development, and expenditure on noise-alleviating measures by public authorities. My impression is that the problem of traffic noise has been mostly solved for most parts of most urban areas of the more civilized cities. But there are still busy roads with unwelcome levels of traffic noise, as well as some places where noisy motorbikes continue to be tolerated despite breaching regulations. Well-used trunk roads with fast traffic still detract from our desire for rural tranquillity. So there is some way to go before we could say that the problem of road traffic noise has been cracked.

Beyond roads, aircraft noise remains a problem. Although today's aircraft are far quieter than those operating in previous decades, the reduction in noise from individual aircraft has, in many locations, been offset by the increased number of aircraft landing and taking off. There are prospects for significantly quieter planes being introduced, with perceived noise being reduced to half of current average levels by 2020. There is also some scope for alleviating measures including provision of acoustic insulation for existing buildings near airports, action by pilots and air traffic controllers to minimize noise from overflights, limiting use of airports at night, and withdrawal of older noisier aircraft. Nevertheless, given the scale of expansion of air traffic generally envisaged (discussed in Chapter 6), aviation noise is likely to become a bigger problem.

For both roads and aircraft, technological progress in tackling noise pollution is occurring and can be driven forward by policy and regulation in response to public concern. But working against this is the growth of traffic, an aspect to which we will return in subsequent sections of this book.

Apart from noise and air pollution, there are other undesirable local environmental consequences of transport – intrusion into quiet areas, separation of communities, and concreting over the countryside. For these there are similar stories to tell involving trade-offs between costs and benefits, technology and traffic growth, mitigating measures and public expenditure, and with winners and losers.

# Transport and climate change

Beyond the local effects of transport systems there are the regional and global consequences. In the 1970s we recognized how acid rain could damage forests and fisheries beyond the national boundaries of the originating fossil fuel combustion plant. In the developed parts of the world these regional problems were tackled by international agreements to clean up emissions from power stations and other large sources. Now we have to tackle the global consequences of the emissions of the so-called greenhouse gases.

The story of greenhouse gases and climate change, and what we need to do, is becoming increasingly well known. So I'll provide only a succinct résumé.

The earth is illuminated by the sun and it radiates energy back into space. Gases in the atmosphere reflect some of this radiated energy back to the earth, which makes the surface of our planet warmer than it would be otherwise. The atmosphere acts like the glass of a greenhouse – hence the term 'greenhouse gases'. The most important 'anthropogenic' (meaning generated by human activity) greenhouse gas is carbon dioxide which is the main product when carbon-containing fossil fuels are combusted in air. Carbon dioxide is produced on a grand scale when coal, oil or natural gas is burned in power stations to generate electricity, when we heat our homes and offices with gas, and not least when we drive our cars and fly in aircraft. Carbon dioxide is not the only greenhouse gas, however. Other significant contributors to global warming are methane and nitrous oxide from agricultural sources, and water vapour from aircraft engines at high altitudes.

Man-made additions to the greenhouse gas content of our atmosphere have become significant since the industrial revolution got well underway in the 19th century. Before the industrial revolution, the carbon dioxide concentration was about 280 parts per million (ppm). It is currently 380ppm and rising at the rate of nearly 2ppm a year. The effect of this rise in carbon dioxide concentration has been to increase the average temperature of the earth's surface by about 0.2°C per decade.[16]

The scientific possibility that human activities might cause significant warming of the earth's atmosphere has been recognized since the 19th century. That this might be important practically was first signalled by James Hansen and his colleagues in a 1981 paper in which they predicted that anthropogenic warming should begin to be detectable over and above natural climate variability by the end of the 20th century. At the time of publication, I was a civil servant in the then Department of Energy. I recall Bill Burroughs, a colleague, and ex-scientist like myself, mentioning this paper over lunch. Bill had been a researcher in atmospheric physics and has since published a number of popular science books on the weather and climate. We could see that this prognostication of climate change might be the beginning of something important, although when it might begin to impact on policy thinking was hard to guess.[17]

Since Hansen's seminal paper, an enormous amount of scientific effort has been brought to bear to understand the phenomenon of man-made atmospheric warming and its practical implications. The outputs of extensive programmes of research and analysis have been brought together since 1988 by the Intergovernmental Panel on Climate Change (IPCC), conducted under UN auspices. The IPCC, which has drawn on the work of more than 2500 scientists from around the world, has so far issued four substantial sets of assessment reports, the most recent in 2007. As the research and analysis has progressed, confidence in the validity of the conclusions has grown. The key findings have been agreed by more than 100 governments. The consensus view among these scientific experts best placed to judge is that, although there remain significant areas of uncertainty, warming of the climate is unequivocal, with most of this very likely due to the observed increase in anthropogenic greenhouse gas concentrations.[18]

There are a few researchers who have taken a sceptical view and, because of the high public interest in the topic, get more media coverage than their numbers and arguments might otherwise warrant. Contrarian views are quite normal, and indeed honourable, in science, where progress is made through theoretical speculations being put to the test by the gathering of empirical evidence. The evidence is never complete and is always open to interpretation, hence the possibility of scientists taking different views. Nevertheless, I find impressive the convergence of expert opinion on the causes and consequences of the build-up of greenhouse gases. While more research and analysis is certainly needed, I do not believe that a reasonable case could now be made for any course of practical action that failed substantially to acknowledge the current forecasts of global warming. The consequences of climate change are global, long-term, uncertain, but potentially large and irreversible. So doing nothing would be very risky. Even the Bush administration and the main US industry groups now accept the need to tackle carbon emissions.[19]

There is a wide consensus that it would be desirable to limit the global temperature rise to no more than 2°C if we are to avoid dangerous consequences such as large changes to agriculture, to water supplies and to the sea level. That aim implies that the atmospheric concentration of carbon dioxide be limited to the bottom end of the range 450–550ppm. To achieve this would require a major reduction in the emission of greenhouse gases, particularly by the developed countries whose past combustion of fossil fuels has been the main source of present concentrations above the pre-industrial level. Twenty-five countries are responsible for 80 per cent of global anthropogenic carbon emissions. The Kyoto Protocol of 1997 accordingly places the initial responsibility on the developed countries to reduce their greenhouse gas emissions. Sufficient countries – over 160 – have signed the Kyoto Protocol to activate it, and it came into force in 2005. However, the US resisted, arguing that the protocol places no obligations on the major developing economies, particularly China, which has now overtaken the US as the biggest single emitter of carbon dioxide, albeit based on a population over four times the size. The Kyoto Protocol covers the period to 2012. At the international conference held in Bali in December 2007, it was agreed that government officials from 187 countries would meet regularly to agree by 2009 what to do after 2012.

The UK has a commitment under the Kyoto Protocol to reduce emissions of greenhouse gases by 12.5 per cent of 1990 levels by 2008–12. The government says it expects to achieve a reduction of about twice this amount by 2010 and has adopted a demanding longer term target by submitting to parliament a Climate Change Bill, as the basis of a legal framework that will underpin the UK's contribution to tackling climate change and show leadership internationally. The legislation will put in place a statutory goal of a 60 per cent reduction in carbon dioxide emissions by 2050 (against a 1990 baseline) through domestic and international action, with reduction in the range 26–32 per cent required by 2020. This will involve a new system of carbon budgets set at least 15 years ahead. In a speech on 19 November 2007, Prime Minister Gordon Brown recognized that the evidence now suggests that developed countries may have to reduce their emissions by up to 80 per cent and that Britain would need to consider whether our own target should be tightened up to 80 per cent.[20] There are various ways in which carbon dioxide emissions might be reduced. In general, the requirement is to attach a financial penalty to carbon emissions. One approach would be to tax each tonne of carbon dioxide emitted, so creating an incentive to emit less. However, new taxes tend to be unpopular, and it would be hard to judge at what level it should be set to deliver the scale of carbon dioxide reductions required of a signatory country to the Kyoto Protocol. So the generally preferred approach is what is known as 'cap and trade'. Governments, individually or collectively, set the overall ceiling on emissions for a particular period – the 'cap', which reduces progressively from period to period. The cap is divided into permits which allow the holder to emit one tonne. These permits are either issued to the main emitting companies by the government, or they could be auctioned. Any company that does not need all its allocated permits can sell the surplus to a company that needs more. An 'emissions trading scheme' facilitates such transactions and allows a market price to be established.

The attraction of the cap-and-trade approach is that it focuses clearly on the objective of reducing emissions. It is economically efficient because it creates incentives for emission reductions in the form of spare permits which can be sold, and avoids imposing unpopular taxes as well as having to secure international agreement to imposing such taxes. Politically, cap-and-trade is gaining cross-party momentum, being supported by both leftish environmentalists and rightish pro-market and business people.

There are, though, a few prominent figures on the political right who resist the call for action on climate change. Vaclav Klaus, President of the Czech Republic, writing in the *Financial Times* on 14 June 2007, sees the biggest threat to freedom, democracy, the market economy and prosperity as ambitious environmentalism which wants to impose a sort of central global planning. Another opponent is Nigel Lawson, now Lord Lawson, a former Chancellor of the Exchequer. His first cabinet-level post was Secretary of State at the Department of Energy, where he brought to bear a tough-minded approach, endorsing markets and privatization and not believing in 'energy policy'. This stance persists a quarter of a century later, for instance in evidence given to a parliamentary committee in May 2007 when he argued that people are extremely adaptable and it was therefore implausible to suggest that we would have huge difficulty in adapting to a 3°C temperature rise over 100 years.[21]

The main disadvantage of cap-and-trade is fluctuation in the price of permits, which makes investment decisions more difficult. The economics of new electricity generation is largely about carbon prices. For instance, if the price of carbon is high, nuclear and renewable sources could be good investments, if low they may provide poor returns. The problem for investors is to assess what the carbon price is likely to be over the lifetime of the investment. This price is seen as in part dependent on government policy, given that governments create the trading arrangements for emissions permits. Some experts argue for a mechanism to increase the certainty about the price of carbon over at least 10–20 years. What is not yet clear is the extent to which the development of a futures market will provide such assurance.[22]

The first successful emissions trading scheme was developed for sulphur dioxide – the main cause of acid rain – in the US and has been in operation since 1995. The European Union Emissions Trading Scheme (ETS) for carbon dioxide was launched in 2005. At present it covers emissions from 11,500 installations across Europe for five 'dirty' industries – electricity, oil, metals, building materials and paper. About half of UK carbon dioxide emissions are included. There are plans to extend it to transport (see below). The EU ETS is linked to the 'clean development mechanism' set up under the Kyoto Protocol. This provides that emissions reductions in developing countries can be certified by the UN and can then be sold to businesses in the EU needing permits. Gaining cash for emission reductions generates additional incentives for investment in developing countries.[23]

Incorporating a charge for carbon emissions would add to the cost of goods and services that depend on fossil fuel combustion. The consequences for the world economy of measures to limit global warming have been considered thoroughly in the report prepared by Sir Nicholas Stern for the British government. He estimates that the costs of inaction far exceed the costs of mitigating action – which would be worth around 1 per cent of global gross domestic product (GDP). A sensible stabilization range is 450–550ppm 'carbon dioxide equivalent' (CO2e, which expresses the total effect of all greenhouse gases in terms of the equivalent carbon dioxide concentration; the current level of greenhouse gases is 430ppm CO2e). Anything higher than 550ppm, in Stern's view, is a very dangerous place to be but the most severe damage could be avoided at affordable cost. Anything lower than 450ppm is simply too expensive to be realistically attained under current technologies and would not justify the damage avoided.[24]

Because the stock of greenhouse gases is growing, the costs of meeting these targets increase for every year that action is delayed. So there is the need for strong urgent international action. Based on income, historic responsibility and per capita emissions, Stern argues that the rich countries should take responsibility for emissions reductions of 60–80 per cent from 1990 levels by 2050. What is needed is to create a common global price signal for the cost of carbon, with the EU ETS – the largest carbon market – becoming the nucleus of future global carbon markets.

Tackling global warming requires a substantial reduction in greenhouse gas emissions on the part of the developed countries. This will require big changes to the fossil-fuel-using parts of the economy, of which the transport sector is but one. What's special about transport is that its carbon emissions are growing, while those of other sectors are shrinking or static. In 2004 transport (other than international aviation) was responsible for 27 per cent of total UK carbon dioxide emissions (21 per cent of all greenhouse gas emissions), which represented a 10 per cent increase on 1990. Road transport emissions grew by 8 per cent from 1990 to 2000 even though average fuel efficiency of new cars has improved by 10 per cent since 1997.[25]

But even though it is a growth sector for greenhouse gas emissions, this does not mean that transport must be singled out for special measures. The logic of cap-and-trade is that the *source* of emissions doesn't matter. What matters is the *effect*, in respect of which a tonne of carbon dioxide from a power station chimney is no different from a tonne from a road full of cars. (A special case in this context is the effect of aircraft emissions at high altitude, a topic for Chapter 6.) So if transport greenhouse gases were to be included in the ETS, then the price of carbon would find its market level and the cost of emissions would become incorporated into the cost of doing business in transport, electricity generation and all the other sectors of the economy.

At present the EU ETS applies to a limited category of large carbon dioxide emitters, albeit which amount to about half of all carbon dioxide emissions. There are proposals to include aviation. The Department for Transport has published a discussion paper on options for including road transport in the ETS. It is envisaged that, in the short to medium term, the effect of including road transport in emissions trading is likely to be that the transport sector buys permits from other sectors and uses carbon credits from investment projects in developing countries. This is because the cost of carbon dioxide abatement in road transport is expected to be higher than in other sectors, which means it would be more cost-effective to reduce carbon emissions in other sectors than to try to achieve the same levels of emissions abatement in transport. So carbon dioxide emissions from transport could continue to grow. However, in the long term, the carbon price is likely to be higher and sufficient to support the use of renewable energy in road transport and support investment in fuel efficiency technology.[26]

It will take some time for road transport to be incorporated into the EU ETS, and longer before all the significant sources of greenhouse gas emissions could be incorporated into this and other regional or national trading schemes, and for these schemes to be linked to achieve global trading at a global carbon price – the ultimate destination for any tradable material in a global economy. In the meantime, it is sensible to pursue reinforcing policies including increasing road fuel duty, agreeing limits for carbon dioxide emissions from new cars, and setting a target for the minimum use of biofuels in road transport (all discussed further in Chapter 8).

Suppose global arrangements for greenhouse gas trading are achieved, operating within an overall cap that reduces over the years such that climate change is kept within acceptable limits. What would be the implications for transport?

At this stage it is hard to say. Much depends on what happens with fossil fuel consumption beyond transport. The more that it is possible to avoid fossil fuel use for electricity generation, the more scope there is for transport based on oil, within the UK's overall greenhouse gases cap. Some 75 per cent of Britain's electricity is generated from fossil fuels at present, very largely from coal and natural gas. In contrast, in France nearly 80 per cent of electricity is generated from nuclear power, while Denmark hopes to generate 50 per cent from wind power by 2025. Similar opportunities arise with housing, where it is possible to reduce carbon emissions very substantially through better insulation and other measures, and indeed the British government intends that all new homes should be 'zero carbon' within a decade. However, new construction each year is equivalent to only 1–2 per cent of the existing stock, so the important question is what will be done to reduce energy loss from existing buildings, where energy savings of nearly 50 per cent should be possible cost-effectively or nearly so.[27]

So if we are able to make substantial progress in reducing carbon emissions from electricity generation, from industry and from housing and other buildings, then we'll have more headroom for transport and the price of carbon should not be too high. Such a scenario would be consistent with Stern's estimate that the cost of avoiding dangerous climate change would be of the order of 1 per cent of GDP per annum. Additional costs of this magnitude, as they feed through the economy, might not result in much reduction in the amount of travel that people undertake.

Conversely, if reducing carbon emissions proves to be tough and slow, then the price of carbon would follow a rising pathway, which would make all kinds of fossil-fuel consumption substantially more expensive – including transport – which in turn would reduce demand. Of course, a high carbon price will incentivize all kinds of technological innovations that reduce carbon outputs, as will be considered in Chapter 8.

As a pretty trivial illustration of the priority that we might give to travel, consider patio heaters. Most heat from these is wasted. Over a year of use, each generates as much carbon dioxide as one and a half cars. Suppose, following the ban on indoor smoking, every pub purchased two patio heaters. The impact might be equivalent to adding 200,000 new cars.[28] So, will the rising price of carbon eventually drive out the patio heaters, while we keep running our cars? Or will we warm our patios using renewable or nuclear electricity? Or will we dream up a better solution to the problems of outdoors recreation? My guess is that we'll want to keep running our cars, one way or another, so we'll make carbon economies elsewhere.

# 3

# The Economics of Travel Reconsidered

Traffic problems are nothing new. Ancient Rome, a city of more than a million inhabitants without a planned street system, had traffic problems probably not very different from that of modern cities. There was legislation, the *Lex Julia Municipalis*, which limited the daytime use of heavy wagons in order to relieve traffic congestion. Goods traffic had to move by night.[1]

King Charles II issued an edict in 1660 to ban stationary carriages, wagons and horses from the streets of Westminster and the City of London because they were creating a public nuisance. They were required to wait for their passengers off the main thoroughfares to allow the traffic to flow more freely. Nineteenth-century cities were incredibly crowded places where most people walked to work or lived above or behind their businesses. Streets were characterized by horses – the excrement, noise of steel shoes on granite, and the smell of horse-drawn wagons, buses, carriages and cabs, with traffic at times dense beyond movement. Stables to house the horses could be three or four storeys high. Later came quieter, cleaner steam-powered vehicles and then electric and diesel, which allowed people to live farther from their work, and commuting began. But the city centre remained congested. Even in modern central London, where a scheme for charging of vehicles on the move has been introduced, congestion remains a problem.[2]

Historically, traffic congestion has been a defining characteristic of urban living. It reflects the density of the population and the need of the people for mobility. Hamish McCrae, a commentator on economic affairs, agues that we should welcome congestion as an inevitable part of increasing prosperity and as a great social leveller, for sitting in a jam we are all equal. Or not exactly equal, because the time of people working long hours or earning high salaries is worth more. So congestion in practice is an extremely progressive tax which bears most heavily on the rich.[3]

# Building roads

In our era, congestion has spread beyond city centres to the suburbs, main inter-urban routes, and attractive tourist destinations. This reflects our desire for ever increasing mobility for ourselves and our families, to gain access to an ever expanding range of choices. We look to government for solutions, but satisfactory solutions are hard to identify.

The standard response to any growth in demand is to increase the supply. This is the response of the market. It works well for cars, but not for roads which are publicly provided. In the past, the perceived role of government, both central and local, was to predict the growth in demand for travel and to provide the infrastructure to satisfy that demand. Most roads have been paid for out of taxation, so the transport ministries had to bid for funds from the national treasuries, which were rarely sufficient to meet the desires of road users for journeys unconstrained by congestion in the face of steady growth in car ownership and longer trips.

One solution to the problem of limited public funds has been for private sector operators to be granted franchises to build inter-urban toll roads. The tolls pay for the operating and maintenance costs of the road as well as servicing the cost of capital and providing a return to the investors. This approach has been used in countries such as France and Italy, although in other places self-financing toll roads have been operated by public authorities.

Tolled roads need space for toll booths, and toll plazas may need to be quite large to cope with the flow of traffic. In part for this reason, tolled roads are unusual in Britain, where the population density is high, space for roads is at a premium and where many exits are needed to link motorways to the local road system. Accordingly, the vast majority of British roads are free of charge to road users and therefore must be financed out of taxation.

# Travel time savings

What then is needed is some basis for justifying expenditure on new and improved roads, so that the Department for Transport can first make a convincing case to the Treasury for a construction programme, and then decide just which projects up and down the country should be funded. One approach would be a purely political process in which arguments are invoked, patronage sought and arms twisted to fund particular schemes. In the US this is 'pork barrel' politics – the benefits go to the constituents of particular politicians in return for campaign contributions or votes. Japan has run a road building programme on the same basis. In Britain we have generally managed to avoid this approach to decision making on transport schemes or other public works, although the Humber road bridge, opened in 1981, was constructed largely as a political gesture (to help win a by-election) and has been financially unsustainable with the tolls charged.

The system that has been developed to justify public investment is known as 'cost–benefit analysis'. The idea is that the sum of all the anticipated benefits of a particular project is compared with the total of all the anticipated costs. If the benefits are greater than the costs, the project is potentially worthwhile. Where there are more possible projects than funds to finance them, then best value may be obtained by preferring those projects with the highest ratio of benefits to costs.

Cost–benefit analysis allows for the flow of benefits and costs over time by bringing these to a single point in time for comparison (using a 'discount rate' – somewhat analogous to an interest rate – to reflect the fact that £1 next year is less valuable to us than £1 today). Cost–benefit analysis also requires that all benefits and costs can be expressed in monetary terms, which in practice can be problematic (as discussed in Chapter 2, in relation to environmental detriments).

For public sector transport investment in Britain, cost–benefit analysis has been a central part of the decision-making process for over 40 years, since pioneering work to estimate the benefits of the M1 motorway and the Victoria Line underground rail service in London. For these studies, the benefit was assumed to be the time saved by travellers by using the new road or rail line, compared with making the same journey by the previously available route. In economic terms, the point of travel has been seen as permitting people to get to destinations that allow more value to be gained than by staying at home. So travelling to work allows income to be earned, and travelling to the shops allows goods to be purchased. If, for simplicity, we assume that the origins and destinations of our journeys are not altered by making available a better transport link between them, then the benefit of the investment could be the total travel time saved by those making these journeys (since the benefits associated with the destinations would be unchanged).

Time is money. If travel takes place in working time, then less productive work is done. And travel in non-working time means that we are deprived of activities that we would otherwise wish to do. So if we are able to reduce travel time for the trips we need to make, that represents a gain in value. Techniques have been developed for estimating how much value we attribute to travel time savings for different kinds of journey. For instance, time saved on journeys during working time is considered to be worth some five-fold more than time saved on non-work trips. These values of time saved are multiplied by the number of people benefiting from the time saving to estimate the benefit from some new transport infrastructure improvement.[4]

There is, however, a bit of a problem with cost–benefit analysis in which the predominant benefit is time saved by travellers. As I pointed out in Chapter 1, average travel time has remained pretty constant in Britain since data were first collected in the early 1970s, with similar findings for other countries. If anything, travel time tends to creep up slowly, never down. This prompts the question: what has happened to all the travel time savings claimed to justify public expenditure on roads in Britain of around £100 billion over the past 20 years? One possible answer would be that average travel time would have been higher than it has been, had it not been for the time savings associated with this investment. However, the pattern of investment in road infrastructure in Britain over the past 20 years has shown marked swings in expenditure, as fashions for road building have come and gone. Spending on roads has varied between £3.5 and £6.4 billion a year (at constant 2004/05 prices). The amount of new road capacity coming on stream would show a similar swing. But the steady trend of travel time seen in Figure1.1 of Chapter 1 shows no hint of any such variation in new capacity. There is no support for the idea that average travel time would have been higher in the absence of new road construction.[5]

An alternative interpretation of Figure 1.1 is that people take the benefit of investment in the transport system – private investment in vehicles as well as public investment in infrastructure – in the form of additional access to desirable destinations, made possible by higher speeds, in the time available for travel. From this viewpoint, travel time savings would be at best transient phenomena.

We might ask whether researchers have in fact been able to measure the travel time savings expected to be associated with infrastructure investment, such as a new or widened road that has been built with the intention of generating such savings. When I searched the research literature – specialist books, journals and databases – I was very surprised to draw a blank. The concept of travel time saving is absolutely crucial for standard cost–benefit analysis of transport projects. So it is remarkable that there appear to be no empirical studies of travel time savings in the literature. In this context 'travel time saving' makes available time to be spent on other activities by reducing the time spent travelling. There are certainly studies that demonstrate time saving for vehicles as a result of widening a particular road in a road network (such as the evaluations of new roads, five years after opening, commissioned by the UK Highways Agency). And of course the railway timetable demonstrates the speedier journeys made possible by faster trains on modernized track.

Such particular journey time savings would result in overall travel time saving per person per year if the origins and destinations of all journeys remained unchanged – which in general cannot be assumed. To detect travel time savings that might arise from particular investments, it would be necessary to employ travel diary techniques, as used for instance in the *National Travel Survey* (discussed in Chapter 1). A five-minute saving through reduced congestion on a regular two-way commuter journey would amount to a reduction of around 10 per cent of the average overall annual travel time. This should be detectable in a suitably designed survey using travel diaries. However, the effort would not be trivial. Perhaps the supposed reality of travel time saving is so deeply embedded in the thinking of transport economists and analysts that no one considered this worth substantiating through empirical investigation.

So, there is no evidence for travel time savings in consequence of investment in transport infrastructure. This lack of direct evidence does not mean, however, that travel time savings do not exist, since the absence of evidence is not evidence of absence, in this and many other instances. But given the long-term constant nature of average travel time, any travel time saving would necessarily be a transient phenomenon. Think of it this way. The prospect of travel time savings as a short-run benefit motivates us to take a new and better route or transport mode, when that possibility arises. Subsequently this time saving is used for further travel, as the benefits of additional access are recognized. For instance, a new bit of road on your daily journey to work by car might save you five minutes both going and coming. You might leave home five minutes later and return five minutes earlier. But at the weekend, you might use the new road to get to some better leisure or shopping opportunity, which you wouldn't have bothered with before on account of the traffic. In the longer run, when you contemplate moving house or changing job, this new road allows you more choices, within the amount of time you are willing to use for travel. And if you're happy to stick to the usual destinations, then there's more space on the new route for others to make longer trips – which is one reason why average travel time remains unchanged despite extensive road improvements over the years.

We see that, for individuals, the long-run benefit of investment is the additional access to desirable destinations. Because the average annual journey frequency has held remarkably constant over time, at 1000 trips per person per year in Britain (discussed in Chapter 1), this additional access involves longer journeys to the same kinds of destinations, not extra trips to new destinations.

Conventional transport economists generally reckon that the value of travel time saving represents some 80 per cent of the economic benefit of major road schemes. But if travel time savings have significant value only in the short run, as I argue, then it follows that the economic benefit of long-lived investment has been wrongly specified. The bulk of the economic benefit of road schemes and other transport infrastructure investment is associated with making possible additional access to preferred destinations. This is consistent with the concept that travel is what economists call a 'derived demand'. The idea is that travel is not something that is desirable in its own right. Rather our demand for travel depends on the value of the activities at the destinations we reach, which has to be sufficient to outweigh the time and money costs of the journeys. (I'll return below to this idea that travel is essentially a derived demand; for the moment we can live with it.)

The emphasis on travel time saving as a measure of the economic benefit of an improvement to the transport infrastructure arose in a context in which trip origins and destinations were assumed unchanged – this goes back to pioneering cost–benefit analyses in the 1960s. This assumption meant that the values of activities at trip destinations could be disregarded since these would be the same in the 'do minimum' and 'do something' cases. (These are the conventional expressions used to describe the consequences of making an investment, for instance widening a busy road – 'do something' – and not making the investment but perhaps adopting some low-cost improvements – 'do minimum'.) Subsequently, it has been recognized that the demand for travel may vary in response to the availability of new infrastructure, so that in consequence people may choose new destinations, for instance preferring a more distant supermarket to the nearest one. But what has generally been overlooked is the consequent need to estimate the economic benefit associated with the new destinations. In the limiting case – the long-run situation discussed above where all initial time savings are used for extra travel – the entire economic benefit arises from activities at the new destinations and none from time savings.

## Induced traffic

My argument is that the benefits of new transport infrastructure are taken by travellers in the form of greater access, not time saving. This is not merely a nice theoretical distinction. It has practical implications. Indeed, I believe that an important reason for the failure of much transport policy lies in this mistaken perception about where lie the benefits from new construction. The transport economists have led us badly astray.

One obvious consequence of these benefits being taken in the form of additional access, made possible by higher speeds, is that there will be extra travel. In fact, this additional travel is already well recognized as the phenomenon known as 'induced traffic', the traffic which arises from increasing the capacity of the system.

For a long time most transport economists and road builders resisted the idea that simply building new road capacity would result in more traffic, even though those who protested against road construction stressed the detrimental effects of the extra vehicles. When the M25 orbital motorway around London speedily filled with traffic within months of opening, most of us could agree that the new road was 'creating' traffic. It took a major review by the government-appointed but independent Standing Advisory Committee on Trunk Road Assessment (SACTRA), which reported in 1994, before professional opinion would generally accept that induced traffic is real. It is supposed that the main responses of travellers to new road capacity include changing route, retiming journeys, choosing a new destination for the same journey purpose, increasing journey frequency, making entirely new journeys, as well as changed land-use patterns. All these responses can result in extra traffic. Induced traffic is regarded as the additional vehicle kilometres, comparing the 'do something' and 'do minimum' cases.[6]

However, while the phenomenon of induced traffic is now accepted in principle, is seems as though it has regularly been forgotten and has had to be rediscovered since it was first identified in 1925 when a new section of the Great West Road was opened. Indeed, induced traffic was not mentioned in the four-volume 2006 report by Sir Rod Eddington, former chief executive of British Airways, which was jointly commissioned by the Chancellor of the Exchequer and the Secretary of State for Transport to examine the long-term links between transport and the UK's economic productivity. Eddington describes existing economic appraisal, which includes time saving for freight and business travel, as forming part of the bedrock of transport project appraisal. To make funding decisions involving choices between different projects he recommends that decision makers should 'listen to the numbers' so that decisions reflect the relative returns offered by competing schemes. Eddington's analysis draws on a Department for Transport database of 170 actual and proposed investments in the transport system. However, 90 per cent of road schemes considered by the Department over the past ten years have neglected the possible consequences of induced traffic. So Eddington's approach is defective in two important respects. Not only is travel time saving *not* the benefit that travellers receive from investment in infrastructure. But also induced traffic is very largely disregarded, which tends to inflate the returns to investment by overstating the time savings benefits from reduced congestion. The underlying problem is that induced traffic doesn't fit into conventional transport economic theory and so is overlooked, even in such an important study as Eddington's.[7]

There is also debate over the amount of induced traffic. There is a tendency by those proposing new road construction to underestimate the magnitude of induced traffic. In part this is due to lack of a good theory that would suggest the scale of induced traffic. But it is surely also a matter of what is known as 'appraisal optimism' – a bias that presents a proposal in the best light. Appraisal optimism is a risk for all protagonists of capital projects, but a particular hazard for those in the public sector where a cost overrun cannot bankrupt the organization. The main manifestation of appraisal optimism is the underestimation of project cost and timescale. If uncon-scious, this might be considered as reflecting the natural enthusiasm of the project leader to get agreement to a proposal in which he or she has invested substantial time and effort. If the underestimation is conscious, and intended to increase the likelihood of getting the project into the budget, it can be condemned as 'strategic misrepresentation'.[8]

A further manifestation of optimism bias for road schemes is to underestimate the likely scale of induced traffic, both because the more such traffic, the less the reduction in congestion and hence the less the travel time saving (which is the main conventional economic benefit). Underestimation also lessens opposition to the project from those living nearby who may be affected by the extra traffic. The under-estimation of induced traffic can be substantial. Consider the case of the famous Newbury bypass.

The Newbury bypass in south-east England was the site of the largest demonstra-tion against road building of the 1990s. The bypass is a nine-mile section of dual two-lane carriageway located to the west of Newbury. It was designed to divert heavy traffic away from the town, where through traffic together with local traffic was giving rise to significant congestion for long periods of the day. The bypass formed part of a series of improvements to the A34 trunk road from the Midlands and Oxford to the south coast, in particular the port of Southampton.[9]

There was public consultation about the road in 1982 and public inquiries in 1988 and 1992. The Highways Agency, the arm of the Department for Transport responsible for the trunk road network, reviewed scheme in 1995, including assessing the potential for induced traffic. The 'worst case' assumed 10 per cent extra traffic on the bypass. Environmental concerns identified as part of the proposal included intru-sion into the North Wessex Downs Area of Outstanding Natural Beauty, together with noise and visual impacts.

From July 1995 protesters began to occupy the land that was scheduled for clear-ance in an effort to stop the felling of trees. Many lived in tree houses, while others occupied home-made tents on the ground, made from hazel branches covered with tarpaulin and known as 'benders'. Another method used by protesters to stop the clearance work was the digging of underground tunnels. A network of tunnels ten feet down was dug at Snelsmore Common in the belief that heavy machinery would not drive over them in case they collapsed, burying the protesters inside. From the beginning of January to the end of March 1996 the clearance of approximately 360 acres of land to make way for the building of the road led to exceptionally large anti-road protests. Around 7000 people demonstrated on the site of the bypass route and over 800 arrests were made. Nevertheless, the road was built and the Newbury bypass opened to traffic on 17 November 1998. But quite possibly this will have been the last substantial new road to be built across open greenfield land in Britain.

The Highways Agency commissioned a 'five years after' evaluation, covering the period 1998–2003, which was published in July 2006.[10] The main analysis focused on traffic counts, before and after the bypass was opened. The bypass has been well used. As expected, traffic on the old route through Newbury town centre fell signifi-cantly, reducing by 28 per cent in the year following opening, but subsequently growing slowly. Heavy goods vehicles, which comprise 20 per cent of traffic flow on the bypass, have been reduced on the old route by over 80 per cent.

What is striking is that across the 'narrow corridor', comprising the old route plus the bypass, traffic volumes increased by around 50 per cent between 1997 and 2003, compared with regional growth rates of around 14 per cent in same period. The majority of this increase occurred in 1999, the first year after opening. This step change, which had not been predicted, certainly seems to support the arguments – made by those who oppose the building of new roads or the widening of existing roads – that additional road capacity gives rise to extra traffic, over and above the long-term trend in traffic growth. Hence building new roads is no solution to the problem of congestion – the new road simply fills up with traffic. Observed traffic flows on the Newbury bypass have been as much as 100 per cent greater than predicted in the traffic model employed by the Highways Agency when making the case for construction, where, as I mentioned, the 'worst case' sensitivity test indicated that there could be 10 per cent extra induced traffic. More than a suspicion here of appraisal optimism, I feel. Some might suggest a case of strategic misrepresentation.

So induced traffic can be much greater than the road builders usually allow. This has implications for detriments, as discussed in Chapter 2, which are related to traffic volume. One of these is deaths and injuries. Generally, proposals for major road schemes to be funded with public money take credit for the reduced accident rates expected when modern roads replace those of an earlier era. About 20 per cent of the economic benefits are conventionally considered on average to derive from accident reduction. However, what is not properly recognized is that a greater volume of induced traffic would give rise to greater numbers of accidents, and this would offset the expected accident savings. For a portfolio of British trunk road schemes, I have estimated that the economic value of the extra accidents arising from induced traffic is of the same order of magnitude as the value of the savings claimed for the improvements, with considerable variation from scheme to scheme. A retrospective evaluation of the effects on road safety of nine new urban arterial roads in Sweden showed that average induced traffic amounted to 16 per cent while the reduction in average accident frequency was 18 per cent, yielding very little net change in the expected number of accidents. The improved safety performance of the new roads was offset by the extra traffic that was subject to accidents.[11]

As well as increased accidents, vehicle emissions would be higher on account of induced traffic than would otherwise be estimated, since emissions are proportional to distance travelled. So new road construction will result in increased carbon emissions as people travel to more distant destinations. There would also be land-use implications of the extra travel, as I'll discuss in Chapter 6. All these aspects affect the benefits to be expected from proposed new road capacity. It is therefore important to base the appraisal of such schemes on the authentic behaviour of travellers, who in fact take the benefits in the long run via additional travel, not time savings.

Induced traffic across a road network is predictable in magnitude, given the conservation of average travel time – a theoretical advance, I'd claim. The extra traffic is proportional to the increase in average speed that results from the increase in capacity. Standard estimates of induced traffic made by transport economists and analysts tend to be a good deal smaller than my theory predicts, in part because until now there has been no established theoretical basis for making such estimates.

We can say more about the nature of induced traffic. As noted above, the average trip rate holds constant in the long run at about 1000 journeys per person per year. This implies that induced traffic in aggregate does not arise from increased journey frequency, or making entirely new, additional journeys. Rather, induced traffic is generally the consequence of the choice of more distant destinations for the same journey purposes.

## The real benefits of travel

If we are to think sensibly about the economics of transport, we need to be clear about the economic benefits of travel. The purpose of personal travel, first and foremost, is to reach destinations at which individuals may acquire benefits – whether from employment, leisure, shopping, education, visiting people and so forth – which could not be achieved by staying at home. The farther it is feasible to travel, the more choice of destinations of any particular kind. This is why higher speeds are attractive, given that travel time is constrained. All else being equal, access and choice increase with the square of the speed (because these are proportional to the area of a circle of which the radius is the distance travelled in the available time; area = $\pi r^2$ from school geometry). However, the additional benefit from access to any particular kind of location would tend to decline as choice increases – a case of the well known economic concept of 'diminishing marginal utility'.

To understand what this means, consider a road improvement that allows you to gain access to an additional supermarket within the time that you are willing to allocate to travel for shopping. The magnitude of the benefit would depend on whether, prior to the improvement, you had access to one, two or more competing supermarkets. More supermarkets mean more choice of purchases and more price competition. The UK Competition Commission has studied access to supermarkets, finding that 75 per cent of consumers travel to supermarkets by car, with 90 per cent travelling for 20 minutes or less each way. Supermarket catchment areas are based on travel time, routinely calculated when potential new stores are being evaluated. In assessing the extent of competition among supermarket chains, the Commission took the view that the presence of at least three stores within a 15-minute catchment area would provide consumers with adequate choice, while the presence of only one or two would be likely to limit choice, a situation which would justify intervention on competition policy grounds. The Commission concluded, in effect, that the marginal benefit to consumers outweighed the costs of regulatory intervention to ensure access to a third supermarket but not a fourth.[12]

Most other kinds of destination exhibit similar characteristics of declining marginal utility – meaning that the more access you have, the smaller the benefit of a bit more such access. This applies to employment, education and leisure, although the appropriate scale of choice would depend on the nature of the activity. For instance, most people might prefer more choice of job opportunities than leisure opportunities. Choice of where you live is more complex, of course, with costs and benefits associated with location, amenity, size and quality of living space, as well as travel time and money costs for the journeys to the workplace and to family and friends.

Nevertheless, higher speeds on the journey to work permit a greater choice of places of residence, and diminishing marginal utility of benefits generally applies.[13]

In principle, the value of access to different classes of destination could be established by standard techniques used by economists (known technically as the willingness-to-pay approach, in which people are asked to state their preferences). However, it would be necessary to identify the value of access at the margin, for example to the second, third and fourth supermarkets (as opposed to the average supermarket). It would then be necessary to allow for the fact that an improved road permits increased access not just to shops, but also to employment, educational, leisure and other opportunities, each with their own willingness-to-pay-at-the-margin characteristics. Moreover, it would be desirable to take into account household income since what people are willing to pay in money terms for access must depend on what they can afford. So, while in principle it would be possible to put an economic value on the access that results from improvements to the transport system, in practice the task is not trivial. I'll discuss the implications of this later in this chapter. But first there is one particular implication of diminishing marginal utility that we need to consider.

Over the years, travel speeds have increased and individuals have gained more access, but, as I argue, the marginal benefits of this additional access have tended to decline. You might suppose that, on this account, average personal travel time would tend to fall over the years. That is, as the amount of choice increased, people would find the extra increment of choice progressively less valuable, and might therefore tend to spend less time on the move. However, no evidence of any downward trend is seen in average travel time, as depicted in Figure 1.1 of Chapter 1 or in other data for travel time. This requires explanation.

## Travel for its own sake

The perspective of conventional transport economics is that travel is essentially a 'derived demand', that is, a demand that derives entirely from the benefits found at the trip destination. It is not supposed that there is any demand for travel 'for its own sake'. However, the general finding of constant average daily travel times has prompted suggestions from researchers that there may indeed be benefits from travel over and above those associated with the destination of the journey, and this could be a reason why travel time is conserved. Suggestions made include the idea that there is an 'intrinsic utility' based on satisfaction obtained by moving; hence the total utility of travel is this intrinsic utility – limited by boredom, monotony and fatigue – plus the derived utility associated with the destination. The kinds of factors that contribute to intrinsic utility would be psychological needs and motivations including enjoyment of movement, of speed, curiosity or information seeking, variety seeking, need for escape, independence, desire for freedom, satisfaction from skilfully handling a vehicle, and display of travel or vehicle as status symbol. Another way of putting this is to say that travel may be desired for its own sake, 'undirected travel' so to speak, in which the destination is ancillary to the travel, rather than the converse. In the context of an ageing population, I myself have suggested that there are 'destination-independent' benefits of travel – including the psychological benefits of movement, exercise benefits and involvement in the local community – the loss of which lessen the quality of life in old age. There is some evidence to suggest that an individual's liking for travel has a strong positive impact on their desire to increase the amount of travel. Survey data point to positive preferences for travel among a good proportion of respondents, as well as evidence that people often engage in 'excess travel', that is, travelling farther than the minimum distance to reach a desired destination, taking the scenic route, for instance.[14]

Much recreational travel is evidently attractive on account of the means and style of travel, for instance sailing, horse riding, hiking, as well as motor touring in favourable circumstances – the open road amid pleasant scenery. This intrinsic utility of mobility is likely to be experienced, to some degree, with more utilitarian kinds of journey. The enormous range of new car models available is also suggestive – in Britain currently there are over 300 distinct model ranges and nearly 9000 distinct variants.[15] While some of the choices made from this vast array would be prompted by practical matters such as passenger numbers and luggage space, quite a lot must reflect desires linked to the pleasures associated with ownership and driving.

As well as the benefits of travel associated with mobility, another class of destination-independent benefits comprises those arising from the fruitful use of time while on the move. You can make productive use of the time involved in travelling, particularly by rail, for instance for using a mobile phone and notebook computer, reading, listening to music, thinking, self-improvement and so forth. Such productive uses extend to waiting time, for example in the airport lounge, and are hence incidental to travel. This contrasts with the intrinsic benefits associated with mobility which obviously do not arise while waiting for a connection. Suppose you have the choice of commuting to work by train or by motorbike, and that it takes about the same amount of time whichever mode is taken. On the train you can make full productive use of your time (assuming you can get a seat). On the bike you experience the pleasures of mobility as you cut through car congestion. Both these experiences have value, and both are neglected in conventional transport economics.[16] A further benefit of taking time to commute to work is the psychological space it creates. If you ask employees what their ideal commuting time would be, they often say about 20 minutes, because this gives people a buffer between the stresses of home life and the workplace.

The evidence for the existence of an intrinsic utility to travel is very suggestive, in my view, if not yet conclusively demonstrated and well understood. The reason is that the topic has attracted few researchers. Nevertheless, the possibility that such intrinsic utility may be significant is one that we need to take into account in our thinking. There is nothing in economic principles that would argue against there being a benefit from travel for its own sake, in addition to the benefit of reaching the desired destination.

One implication of there being an intrinsic utility to travel is that it suggests a reason why people do not take advantage of improvements to the transport system to reduce the total amount of time they spend on the move – because this would reduce the benefits from travelling for its own sake. If people take advantage of infrastructure improvements to travel farther (as they do), this is because the utility associated with the destination plus the intrinsic utility of the trip must be at least equal to the value of the travel time saving that might otherwise been made.

Consider a recreational walk you might take, starting and finishing at home. If you've judged the distance well, the intrinsic utility derived from the exercise, getting out and about, and so on, would equal the value of the time expended (which is travel time that might have been saved by not making this trip). If now such a recreational walk is combined with a visit to a shop, the utility associated with this destination would need to be added to the intrinsic utility on one side of the equation. Generally, the benefits of travel comprise both such destination-dependent and destination-independent components, although the relative magnitudes will vary from case to case. Observing the traffic flows into any city in the weekday morning peak, you would not expect many drivers to be there for the fun of it. Observing at the same location the traffic flowing out of the city on a Sunday morning, you would expect that quite a few people may be travelling for fun, flexibly, to opportunistic destinations.

## Costs and benefits

Let's get back to cost–benefit analysis, which has been important in justifying public investment in transport infrastructure. Travel time savings have been the source of the predominant part of the quantifiable economic benefit, although recently so-called 'agglomeration' benefits and other benefits to business have also been recognized as benefits not captured by estimates of time savings.[17]

There are, however, a number of problems with cost–benefit analysis as presently employed to appraise transport projects. First, as I have argued, it is in principle wrong to justify investment in long-lived infrastructure mainly on supposed short-run travel time savings. The value of access at the margin should be used in place of the value of average time savings – although the task of creating an economic methodology based on the value of access could be considerable. In any event, the value of travel time saving, as currently estimated, overstates the value of access at the margin because of the contribution to the value of the trip of the intrinsic utility, as explained above.

Second, as is well recognized, not all benefits and costs are capable of monetary valuation. Although there have been some recent additions to those that can be valued – noise, local air quality, greenhouse gases, journey ambience, and physical fitness for walkers and cyclists – there remain many others for which this has not proved possible, despite years of effort (as discussed in Chapter 2). In consequence, decision making involves considerable judgement, with the relative weighting to be attached to the monetarized and non-monetarized benefits unclear. Either you focus on those aspects to which money values can be attributed – and then find yourself accused of neglecting other important consequences merely because these cannot be so valued – or you aim to take all consequences into account, but then find yourself trying to add apples to oranges. Perhaps for this reason, cost–benefit analysis does not resonate with the public at large or those who take a close interest in new transport schemes. Estimates that show benefits comfortably exceeding costs do not command credence from objectors at public inquiries.

While cost–benefit analysis is used quite widely for transport infrastructure appraisal in Europe elsewhere, it is by no means used universally to justify other kinds of public sector capital expenditure. In Britain, the Treasury guidance advocates the use of cost–benefit analysis across the range of public investment. Nevertheless, for major areas of such expenditure, including the large capital programmes in health and education, cost–benefit analysis is not in fact employed. While the monetary costs are naturally quantified, the benefits are not. It is not practicable to assess the value of the benefits of replacing an old hospital building by a new one, or of new school buildings. It is difficult to identify the causal relationship between the modern building and improved health or educational outcomes, as well as to value such outcomes. Rather than attempting cost–benefit analysis, what is done is to assess cost-effectiveness in achieving policy objectives. The focus is on achieving best value for money in reaching the desired policy objective.

Cost-effectiveness analysis can take place at different levels. For a hospital building programme, for instance, there will be decisions about which hospitals up and down the country should be rebuilt, taking into account such factors as the state of the existing premises and the local demand for in-patient care. And then for each particular hospital, there will be options having different costs, with the number of beds an important consideration.

Given the difficulties in the way of employing cost–benefit analysis to appraise transport projects, there would, in my view, be attractions in applying instead cost-effectiveness analysis to the various means of achieving agreed policy objectives. This would tie economic analysis more closely to policy. It would mean that proponents of new roads would need to focus more clearly on what it is they are seeking to do by way of improving the transport system. Rather than relying on theoretical economic benefits, they would need to spell out the choices available and the costs involved for each options. I'll take up this theme again in Chapter 5.

## Modelling

Before concluding this chapter on the techniques used by transport economists and analysts, I want briefly to touch on another area where things have gone wrong – transport models.

Analysts build models to simulate a part of the real world and thus help forecast the future. Economists in the Treasury have a model of the British economy that allows forecasts of the consequences of changes in policy. The meteorologists build models of the atmosphere to forecast the consequences of global warming. The Department for Transport has constructed a *National Transport Model* as a means to compare the consequences of alternative national transport policies, against a range of background scenarios that take into account the major factors affecting future patterns of travel. All these models are of course constructed in software and run on powerful computers.

The question of whether travel time is saved or conserved is relevant to the practice of transport modelling. In general, conventional transport models (of which the *National Transport Model* is one) make the assumption that travellers minimize the 'generalized costs' of the journey. By 'generalized costs' is meant the combination of money costs and time costs, summed using monetary values of travel time. Minimization of generalized costs would be consistent with the idea that travellers take advantage of improved infrastructure to save travel time. However, it is not obviously consistent with the evidence that in the long run travel time is conserved.

Another inconsistency arises from the finding that the proportion of household income spent on transport and travel holds constant over time, once the level of car ownership has reached around one per household, as discussed in Chapter 1. You'll recall that in Britain this expenditure has fluctuated around 16 per cent for the past 25 years. This too does not fit well with the idea that travellers are motivated to minimize travel costs, at least in the long run.

The case for thinking in terms of minimization of generalized costs may be defensible when modelling short-term effects such as transport mode choice in response to cost changes – for instance, the proportion of travellers likely to switch from train to other forms of transport if rail fares were to be raised. But for longer term modelling of transport supply and demand, or of transport and land use, it seems more appropriate to assume that travellers aim to maximize access, subject to time and money constraints. Or better still, that travellers value additional access at the margin and perceive intrinsic utility in travel, while subject to competing demands on their time as well as to a money constraint. As Professor Phil Goodwin has observed: 'We would probably make more accurate forecasts if we start from the assumption that the average total travel time is constant and then seek special reasons why it might not be in particular cases, than … by completely ignoring such a powerful well-established but as yet not fully understood phenomenon.'[18] (One purpose of this book is to help understand this phenomenon.)

Transport models, as with all other models involving people and populations, are essentially models of human behaviour. If the basic features of behaviour are wrongly specified, then the model cannot be expected to make reliable projections. In my view, this is the problem with the *National Travel Model* and other similar conventional transport models. Generally, there is a lack of critical evaluation of such models, asking how good they are in predicting future travel behaviour. In the case of the Newbury bypass that I mentioned earlier, there was a huge discrepancy between the traffic levels predicted by the model and the outcome, even one year after the road opened. Analysis of other new roads has also shown traffic to be higher than forecast.[19]

The world of the transport modellers is very technical and somewhat introverted. There is little critical engagement with others beyond their community and reluctance to be self-critical in public lest this undermine the belief of clients in the validity of the outputs of models. But when modellers gather together in private, or when models are subject to audit, serious doubts can emerge. One transport and land-use model used by the Department for Transport generates results that are counterintuitive – for instance, building more housing in the Thames Gateway region to the east of London is not predicted to increase traffic on the M25 London orbital road, for reasons that are not apparent.[20]

There is another kind of transport model based on a technique known as 'micro simulation'. In this the movement of thousands of individual vehicles operating in a road network may be simulated on a computer, rather like computer simulation games but focusing on traffic. The behaviour of vehicles is governed by parameters which specify aspects of driver behaviour such as the acceptable gap between vehicles and the propensity to change lanes. The resulting behaviour of individual vehicles can be aggregated to display the characteristic features of congested traffic flow. Driver behaviour, as observed in particular locations, can be used to calibrate such a model, for instance the minimum distance between vehicles that a driver will accept before changing lanes. Such models can recognize the behaviour of individuals at a more basic level than that of route choice, transport mode choice and the other stand-ard behavioural variables of conventional macro-level models. The analogous basic behaviour in conventional models is the minimization of generalized cost, which seems never to have been considered as a candidate for variation to secure the better fit of the model to the observed data. So while micro-simulation models of traffic have the potential to be valid and useful, conventional models are suspect because, fundamentally, they make erroneous assumptions about human behaviour. Unless transport models are based on authentic behaviour, they cannot be relied on to make valid forecasts.

## Behavioural economics

Transport economists and model builders have been professionally deficient in that they have made assumptions about underlying human travel behaviour which they have not validated through empirical research. In particular, the assumption that the main benefit of investment is 'travel time saving' has been the centrepiece of transport economic analysis for approaching half a century. The idea is simple and attractive. We have better things to do than travel, so if travel time could be reduced through improving the infrastructure, then there would be a quantifiable economic benefit to set against the cost of the investment. The lack of empirical evidence for travel time saving is therefore surprising. Travel time saving has the quality of a myth – a traditional story accepted as a factual. Travel time saving is what economists term a 'stylized fact', a pretend fact so to speak, as opposed to a real, empirical fact.

This traditional focus on travel time savings in economic appraisal, and on the minimization of generalized costs in transport modelling, may be contrasted with the approach of the important subdiscipline of 'behavioural economics'. This considers the possibility that people in the real world do not behave as the idealized utility-maximizing participants of standard economic frameworks. Behavioural economics is concerned to identify the ways in which behaviour differs from that of stand-ard economic models, as well as to show how such behaviour matters in economic contexts.[21]

While much work in mainstream behavioural economics has focused on finance and saving, one interesting study concerns the behaviour of New York City taxi driv-ers who pay a fixed fee to rent their cabs for a 12-hour shift and then keep all their fares. Their work hours are flexible – they can quit early and often do – and income fluctuates because of the weather, day-of-week effects and so forth. Many drivers say they set a daily income target to cover the rental fee, fuel and desired take-home pay, and then quit when they reach that target. Drivers who set a daily target will drive longer hours on low-income days and quit early on high-income days. This behaviour is the opposite of an income-maximizing strategy over the longer term (a week, say) where you would put in more hours when business is brisk but quit early when there are few customers. Because many drivers think one day at a time, it's harder than it might be to find a cab in New York City on a rainy day – not only is demand for cabs higher, but the supply is less as drivers meet their income targets and go home.[22]

The conservation of average daily travel time suggests that a similar targeting process may be at work here. People are comfortable with a certain amount of daily travel. Many people would say that their ideal commuting time would be about 20 minutes because this provides a buffer between home life and work life. So they arrange their lives to include a daily 'travel fix'. The amount of daily travel time is subject to an upper bound determined by competition between the various uses of time within the 24-hour day, and a lower bound reflecting the benefits to the individual arising from mobility unlinked to the particular destination.

Conventional transport economics supposes that people seek to save travel time, whereas what they actually want is additional access. Conventional transport economics disregards the attraction of mobility for its own sake. As a consequence, conventional transport economics cannot explain induced traffic, the extra traffic that appears when a road is widened – which I attribute to the additional access made possible by higher speeds combined with the desire to maintain a certain amount of daily travel time. The failure of transport economists to base their analyses on the authentic behaviour of travellers has serious implications for investment appraisal, modelling and transport policy. Standard cost–benefit analysis is not a reliable guide to the value of infrastructure investment and should be abandoned. Conventional transport models are not based on validated behaviour of travellers and cannot be relied on to predict the consequences of policy or operational interventions. Transport policy makers need to recognize that interventions that have the effect of increasing speed will promote traffic growth. I'll pursue these practical implications of a methodology that is 'not fit for purpose' (to use a current term of disapprobation) in Chapter 5 and will there suggest how a coherent approach to thinking about travel and transport can be based on an understanding of authentic human behaviour.

One important message to take from this chapter concerns the choices that are made possible by increasing mobility. Such choices increase rapidly with increasing speed of travel – roughly with the square of the speed. On the other hand, the value of each additional possible destination that we might choose is less than the previously available possibility – diminishing marginal utility, as it is described by economists. What this means is that our need for choice is not open ended. It can be met by a finite transport system. Indeed, for most of us living in developed economies, it may well be that the mobility we already have is very largely sufficient to meet our day-to-day needs.

# 4

# Global Travellers and Global Oil

Throughout history, poor people have been trapped in their villages by bad roads. Better transport helps increase prosperity through both trade and access to better jobs. People migrate to the growing towns which provide employment opportunities. This happened in Britain in the 19th century, and is happening in India and China now. In the growing towns people need transport to get around – public transport, bicycles, motorized two-wheelers and cars.

When people get rich enough, they are willing to devote a significant slice of their income to buying and running a car. As average income grows, so does car ownership. Figure 4.1 shows how car ownership per 1000 inhabitants in four European countries has increased over the past 35 years. Mass car ownership took off earlier in the more developed Italy and Britain, rather later in Ireland and Poland, but regardless of the starting point, the rate of growth is similar and saturation seems likely to occur at similar levels. In low-income countries, households without a personal car devote only 3–5 per cent of expenditure to travelling. With increased ownership of cars, household expenditure on travel rises until it stabilizes in the range 10–15 per cent when car ownership rates exceed 200 cars per 1000 inhabitants.[1]

This increase in car ownership with rising income has happened in all societies with market economies because of the fundamental attractions of personal mobility. Once people can afford the basic necessities, they are willing to spend a growing proportion of their household incomes on car ownership, at least up to the point at which there is about one car per household. We must expect the Chinese, the Indians and the peoples of other developing countries to want the same personal mobility. This is exactly what is happening, with big implications for global oil demand.

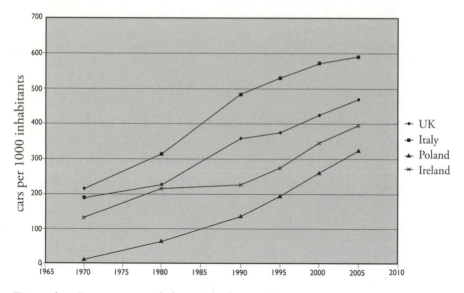

**Figure 4.1** *Cars per 1000 inhabitants for four European countries*

*Source*: European Commission (2006), Directorate-General Energy and Transport, 'Energy and Transport in Figures, statistical pocket book 2006' Table 3.6.1 Road: Motorization

## China and India

China and India are the world's largest developing countries. Together, they had more than 2.4 billion inhabitants in 2005, accounting for 37 per cent of the world's population. While per-capita incomes are still quite low, they have risen considerably in recent decades. Between 1980 and 2005, average real per-capita income (adjusted for inflation) more than doubled in India and more than quadrupled in China. One result of higher incomes has been a rapid increase in motor vehicles in both countries. Since 1990, the total number of motor vehicles has roughly tripled in India and has increased ten-fold in China. Current per-capita energy use in China and India is far lower than in Europe and North America. Nevertheless, total energy use in these two countries is high due to their large populations and is rising rapidly as the economies grow. If these countries continue on the path toward rapid motorization, their increasing contributions to greenhouse gases levels and energy use will have a major impact on the rest of the world.[2]

Both China and India are still primarily rural but are urbanizing rapidly, with especially rapid growth of the largest cities. Indian cities are increasingly being surrounded by unplanned, haphazard suburban sprawl, while Chinese cities remain fairly compact and well planned, even as they grow outward to accommodate increasing populations.

For many years urban transport in China was dominated by bicycles, with extensive cycle paths, lanes, signals and parking provided in most cities. However, this picture is changing. From 1980 to 2002, highways doubled in length, freight traffic quadrupled and passenger traffic grew ten-fold on highways. From 1990 to 2002, motor vehicle production grew six-fold, private vehicle ownership twelve-fold, and passenger car production thirty-fold. From 1990 to 2000, energy consumption grew by 80 per cent for transport in general and 160 per cent for highway transport in particular, so the highway share of energy use for transport grew from half to two-thirds. Petroleum is by far the dominant fuel for transport in China, accounting for nearly 90 per cent of total transport energy consumption in 1998.[3]

Nevertheless, the level of car ownership in China is still relatively low compared with the European countries of Figure 4.1. Although the number of privately owned vehicles increased from 2.5 million in 1995 to 6.25 million in 2000 and to 14.8 million in 2004,[4] the population of China is about 1.3 billion, which means that car ownership is only about 15 per 1000 inhabitants, or about 3 per cent of the British level. However, it is found that when the GDP per capita reaches $1000, families start to buy cars in large numbers. GDP per capita has reached that level in large Chinese cities like Beijing, Shanghai, Guangzhou and Shenzhen, where much of the growth in vehicle population has been seen.[5]

One special feature of China is the development of smaller, simpler, indigenous vehicles of a kind that are virtually unknown outside that country. Over 3 million Chinese Rural Vehicles were produced in 2002, three times the number of conventional passenger cars, with a total in use of about 22 million. The rural vehicle industry is unusual in that it evolved largely outside the control of government regulation and policy, using local technology and resources. These vehicles are mostly three-wheelers that employ inefficient single-cylinder diesel engines originally designed for stationary agricultural machinery. They now consume one fourth of the diesel fuel used in China and play an important role in rural development. However, the future of this class of vehicles is unclear in the light of increasing government regulation of emissions and safety, despite the possibility of this being the basis of a low-cost vehicle to foster rural development.[6]

Large numbers of low-cost motorized vehicles are a feature of the towns and cities of developing countries. The most easily affordable motorized mode in India is two-wheeled motor vehicles – scooters, motorcycles and mopeds. These can manoeuvre their way through congestion, offer reliable door-to-door service, require little parking space (indeed, can be parked securely inside the home), and can carry passengers as well as luggage. They provide mobility equal to that of cars at a fraction of the cost. While the poor majority rely on bicycles for personal mobility, the middle classes, for whom cars are out of reach, use overcrowded, slow buses only when unavoidable, and purchase scooters as soon as affordable. One television channel poll defined a middle-class person as one who owns either a two-wheeler or a four-wheeler or a colour TV or a telephone. On this definition, the middle class represents 20 per cent of population. In India, two-wheelers have been the most rapidly growing vehicle type, doubling every 5 years, and represent around 70 per cent of motor vehicles nationally. On the negative side, they contribute significantly to the adverse impacts of the transport sector, accounting for nearly half the total gasoline consumption in India, and high shares of urban air emissions and road fatalities.[7]

Since the late 1980s, urban incomes in India have increased substantially due to economic liberalization, and the two-wheeler vehicle and buyer profiles have changed significantly. Because of large numbers of young professionals with substantial disposable incomes, as well as college students with well-to-do parents, there has been a growth in the demand for individual mobility, as opposed to a scooter onto which the whole family could squeeze. Motorcycles, with their more rugged appearance and higher road speeds, have become the two-wheeler vehicle of choice. The upshot is that motorcycle sales have increased dramatically since the 1990s and continue to grow. The share of motorcycles of total motorized two-wheeler vehicle sales, only 21 per cent in 1994, and 43 per cent in 2000, now stands at around 77 per cent.

The rapid growth in motor vehicle and other energy-intensive activities has caused air quality to deteriorate rapidly in Indian cities. In Delhi, for example, suspended particulate matter levels, which are strongly linked with respiratory and cardio-vascular illnesses and deaths, exceeded World Health Organization (WHO) guideline limits almost daily during the 1990s, with peak levels as high as 6–10 times the limit at many sites. The introduction of and steady growth in less polluting four-stroke motorcycles starting in the mid-1980s happily coincided with the more stringent emission standards.

Economic development in India will undoubtedly result in an increase in mobility, travel and use of the transport system As always, being able to afford to go faster allows people to reach more destinations in the time for travel they have available. This in turn offers a greater choice of destinations and wider opportunities generally. An average Indian travelled 3470km in 2000, over 90 per cent by road. One recent study projects this to increase to nearly 10,000km by 2020, involving a proportionate decline in the use of public transport from almost 80 per cent to 50 per cent, with a corresponding increase in the use of motorized two-wheelers and cars. This absolute growth and changed pattern of personal travel will have major implications for energy demand and carbon dioxide emissions, the latter projected to grow by four- to five-fold over two decades.[8]

As well as increasing personal mobility, growing populations will add to transport energy use and carbon emissions. In recent years India's population has grown at almost twice the rate of China's, due to the latter's strict family planning policies that generally limit a couple to only one child. The current population of India is 1100 million, and of China 1300 million. In both countries, population growth has been concentrated in cities, largely due to in-migration from economically depressed rural areas. Official statistics, which may underestimate, record the Chinese urban population rising from 178 million in 1978 to 524 million in 2003, and in India from 160 million in 1981 to 285 million in 2001.

For the world as a whole, the current population of 6.6 billion is projected to rise to over 9 billion by 2050. While one billion of the present population, mostly in Africa, have poor prospects for economic development, the middle 4 billion are experiencing rapid and accelerating growth in per capita income. They too will want the benefits of mobility.[9]

# Travel in cities

The rapid growth of urban populations in both Chinese and Indian cities has dramatically increased demand for land and travel in urban areas, thus putting enormous pressure on transport and other kinds of public infrastructure. The sheer increase in the urban population would be sufficient to generate serious transport problems, but this is compounded by the growth of personal motorized transport. As these cities have grown in population, they have also spread outward to the suburbs at lower densities than previously. Many low- and middle-income households in China have been moving to peripheral suburban areas because of the lack of affordable housing in the central cities. Employment has also decentralized, with factories relocating to the suburbs and the development of new industrial and technology parks on the fringe of urban areas. Similar developments are found in India, in part a result of planning policies to limit city-centre densities and to encourage suburban growth, as well as the fostering of large technology parks on the urban fringe. The decentralization of the cities has increased the length of trips for many urban residents, leading to more overall travel demand and thus more traffic on the roadways and public transport systems. Moreover, increased trip distances make walking and cycling less feasible than before, thus encouraging a shift from non-motorized to motorized modes.[10]

Personal motorized mobility in the large cities of Asia is encouraged by the unattractive buses – often overcrowded, slow and unreliable – and limited provision of rail-based public transport. Bangkok, the metropolis of Thailand, has in recent decades seen a dramatic expansion of the middle classes, who have moved out to homes in low-density suburbs while continuing to work in the central business district. The middle classes are highly dependent on private motor vehicle travel for commuting, for which they show a strong preference partly on account of a perception of reduced exposure to pollution. This preference attracts support from the public authorities despite high levels of congestion. This middle-class bias of Thailand's urban transportation policy is both detracting from the quality of the public transport service for lower income groups and reducing mobility for everyone.[11]

It is possible, however, to attract the middle classes to use public transport by a combination of high quality rail-based travel and only very limited opportunities for car parking at work destinations in central business districts. Hong Kong has a diverse multimodal public transport system which carries around 11 million passengers a day. In contrast, it has only about 27,000 on-street and publicly operated parking spaces available for some 400,000 private cars, this for a population of 7 million.[12]

The central districts of many European and some North American cities are also sufficiently well served by public transport to meet the needs of the well paid. One example is in London's Docklands, the fast developing area to the east of the traditional financial district, where you find Canary Wharf. This 100-acre site of high-rise offices includes London's tallest building, into which the first tenants moved in 1991. Currently 80,000 people work there, predominantly in the financial services sector, plus supporting business services. The connecting roads are not of especial quality and there are only 3000 parking spaces. Three-quarters of those who work there commute by public transport, mostly by good underground rail and surface light rail services, which is remarkable given that these people are probably on average the highest paid in Britain.[13]

So there are feasible forms of urban development other than suburban sprawl and car-based commuting. What is needed is an attractive, dynamic central business district together with high quality rail-based public transport. However, while this can make a big impact on the use of the car to get to work in these locations, it does not lessen the attractions of car ownership where there is space to park at home and opportunities for shopping and leisure trips in the suburbs.

So we must expect growth in demand for oil to fuel the increasing car populations of China, India, Thailand and other fast developing countries. What impact will this have on global oil supplies?

## Oil demand

China has doubled its oil consumption over the past ten years and already is the world's third largest oil consumer after the US and Japan. A major cause of the increase in Chinese oil consumption is the rapid growth of the transport sector in general and motor vehicles in particular. Because domestic oil production capacity is limited, China currently imports about a third of its total oil consumption (70 out of a total of 210 million tons in 2000). One study suggests that road vehicle oil consumption could rise to 360 million tonnes (mt) by 2030, compared to about 100mt at present, although with the adoption of vehicle fuel economy measures this could be reduced by up to 85mt. Another study puts China's transport energy demand in 2020 in the range from 191 to 363 million tonnes oil equivalent (Mtoe), with a mid-case estimate of around 264Mtoe. Fuel use, and hence carbon emissions, in China's transport sector seem certain to rise sharply under any reasonable assumptions.[14]

Similarly, for India, the expected rapid increase in mobility and switch to personal motorized modes will have huge implications for energy demand and carbon dioxide emissions from passenger transportation. One study projects emissions to increase from 20 to over 90 million tonnes carbon equivalent over the period 2000 to 2020, although with improved energy efficiency this might be kept down to about 75 million tonnes.[15]

The prospect of rapidly growing private vehicle ownership and usage in developing countries is a major concern for the future levels of global greenhouse gas emissions. If these nations follow the same path of automobile dependence as developed nations, the resulting emissions from millions of new vehicles look set to overwhelm the reductions that could be achieved through improved fuel and propulsion technologies (which I will discuss in Chapter 8). Currently there are about one billion motorized vehicles worldwide. One business-as-usual scenario investigated by the International Energy Agency projects 2.6 billion vehicles by 2050, with the main growth being in what are at present the less developed countries.[16]

One approach to estimating the global consequences for oil demand and carbon emissions of the projected growth in vehicle numbers and in personal mobility generally is to apply the idea, explained in Chapter 1, that people spend, on average, a constant fraction of their time and expenditure on travel. Applying these constraints allows projections to be made of carbon emissions from global personal travel. However, the outcomes depend on what is assumed about the limits to human mobility, particularly the extent to which carbon emissions from the transport sector will need to be constrained on account of global warming – a question to which I'll return.[17]

Over the past 40 years, energy use in transport for the core EU countries has grown in line with the growth in the economy and the growth in travel, whereas overall energy use has grown much more slowly. The main change has been the huge growth in travel distance by car – nearly five-fold.[18] There is every sign of a similar growth in personal motorized transport underway in China, India and the other developing countries. The question is whether there are constraints that will prevent this very substantial growth in car-based mobility. There are two main kinds of constraint. In Chapter 2 I took an initial look at the constraints that may be imposed by climate change, a topic to which I'll return in later chapters. I now consider the availability of oil.

## Oil supplies

The growth of the transport sector is critical for future demand for oil. In the developed countries, oil is now primarily consumed for transport. More than 70 per cent of oil consumption in the US powers transport and is responsible for roughly one-third of its greenhouse gas emissions, or about 8 per cent of the global total. Although its emissions are growing very quickly, transport is perhaps the most difficult sector to regulate because of the sheer size of the vehicle fleet, its fairly slow turnover, and the complex web of institutional interactions and personal attitudes relating to vehicles and land use, local politics and the marketing power of the auto and oil industries.[19]

At present, about 35 per cent of China's oil consumption is for transportation, a proportion set to increase as car ownership grows. Average per capita petroleum consumption in China is still a modest two barrels a year, compared to 12.5 barrels a year in Europe and 26 barrels a year in the US, where more than half of the cars sold in recent years were gas-guzzling sport-utility vehicles.[20] Over the past 40 years, world oil production and consumption has increased by nearly three-fold, from about 33 million barrels per day (mbpd) in 1966 to about 82mbpd in 2006. Over the same period, China's oil consumption has increased by about 25 times, to 7.5mbpd, and India's by nine times, to about 2.5mbpd. Although oil is a fossil fuel, reserves of which have ultimately to be limited, published data for world 'proven reserves' have doubled over the past 25 years to about 1200 thousand million barrels, reflecting continued exploration and development.[21]

There is, however, a major debate under way about the prospects for future oil supplies. This centres on the idea of 'peak oil' – that world oil production is at or approaching peak output, after which an inexorable decline will set in, with widespread implications for the global economy.

It is undoubtedly the case that for any mineral that is mined or extracted, output from a given geological source builds up following initial discovery as the most accessible, lowest cost material is recovered, and reaches a peak as the costs of recovery rise. There is then a phase of decline as geological conditions become less favourable and costs therefore increase. Oil and gas production from the British sector of the North Sea, which got going in the 1970s, reached a peak in 1999 and looks set to be in long-term decline at a rate of 5–10 per cent a year.[22]

The best known example of a prediction about peak oil output is that made in 1956 by geologist M. King Hubbert. He forecast that US oil production would peak in the early 1970s. At the time, almost everyone rejected this analysis. However, in 1970 crude production in the lower 48 states (not including Alaska) started to fall and the US became dependent on imports. Around 1995 several analysts began applying Hubbert's method to world oil production. Most estimated that the peak would occur between 2004 and 2008, after which it would fall, never to rise again.[23]

Naturally, the peak oil story is rather more complicated than that. Although Hubbert correctly predicted the date of maximum production, he underestimated the volume of oil subsequently discovered in the US, as improved extraction techniques were developed. In 2005, US production in the lower 48 states was 66 per cent higher than Hubbert predicted. Where state oil companies are responsible for production, as is the case for many key oil resources (although not for the US), the rates of development and subsequent decline may be extended. Nevertheless, the peak for world oil discovery was in 1965: the biggest Middle East oil fields were discovered over 50 years ago, a few more big discoveries were made in 1970s (Alaska and the North Sea), but none since; and the last year in which we discovered more oil than we consumed was a quarter of a century ago.[24]

There is debate about how much oil remains to be exploited. Pessimists, often geologists who have worked in the oil industry, tend to believe that one trillion barrels of oil or less remain, which would imply that peak output would be reached in the present decade. Optimists, who tend to be economists, think that two or more trillion barrels remain to be exploited in oil reserves and reasonably expected future discoveries, suggesting peak production in the 2030s, followed by an undulating plateau for a decade or more before declining slowly. This would allow time to bring in alternatives to oil.

Optimists point to amounts of oil that can be recovered from operating fields through the use of new technologies. Globally, only about 35 per cent of the oil present in established fields is actually produced. The most easily recovered oil is extracted through traditional drilling. Then secondary extraction is employed, using techniques such as injecting water or carbon dioxide to drive more oil out of the rocks. Lastly, many fields undergo tertiary extraction, usually by injecting steam to lower the viscosity of the oil. What limits extraction is the cost, so if oil prices rise then abandoned fields can be reopened. Moreover, new offshore technology allows access to deep water reserves. One of the biggest oil fields found in the Gulf of Mexico, the Thunder Horse field, is in deep water, its reservoir lying some three miles beneath mud, rock and salt, topped by a mile of ocean.[25]

Another source of optimism lies in the scope for exploiting unconventional sources of oil that becomes possible when prices are relatively high. The source that has attracted most attention is the extensive oil sands of Alberta, Canada, which might yield 1.7 trillion barrels of oil. These thick bitumen sands need energy-intensive treatment to get them to flow, and new refineries must be built. Two tons of sand and clay must be mined in the open pit to yield a barrel of oil. Alternatively, steam injection can be used to free deeper deposits at lower cost, but this needs quantities of fresh water which become contaminated. Two thirds of the energy recovered is used in the extraction process, which generates six times more carbon dioxide than conventional oil production. The rise in oil prices in recent years has set off what has been called North America's biggest resources boom since the Klondike gold rush more than a century ago. In 2006 the oil sands contributed nearly half of Canada's oil output. Huge investments are planned, based on expectations of long-term value if oil prices remain above $50 a barrel. But there are major risks arising from the possible yo-yo of oil prices, environmental concerns, and strains on local services in the remote north of Alberta. And it will be all but impossible for Canada to meet its carbon dioxide reduction goals under the Kyoto Protocol to which it is a signatory.[26]

The debate about the timing and profile of peak oil is influenced by the professional mindsets of geologists and economists, although the protagonists do not fall neatly into two camps by profession. Geologists tend to focus on the distinguishing physical properties of a resource – a fixed stock depleted by consumption. Economists tend to see an economic commodity whose available quantity is determined by the profitability of extraction when competing with other sources. From this perspective, reserves are available that producers replenish from the resource base through exploration and development to offset consumption. The aim is to keep the size of reserves fairly constant over time since small reserves could lead to risk of supply shortages and loss of market share, while large reserves would imply excess expenditure on development. Hence the reserve-to-production ratio for global conventional oil has stayed fairly constant over the past century at between 20 and 40 years.[27]

Economists, as well as geologists of a similar bent, emphasize the importance of the oil price in incentivizing technological advances that enhance recovery from reservoirs and the search for new geological sources. High oil prices also mean that it can become economic to make oil from coal, of which there are very extensive supplies (perhaps 400 years on current trends). The topic of alternative sources of oil for transport is one I'll return to in Chapter 8, along with other technological solutions to dilemmas of transport policy.

The remaining question for this chapter is 'how much oil can we afford to burn?'

A key analysis is found in Sir Nicholas Stern's review of the economics of climate change, prepared for the British government and published in December 2006.[28] He concludes that about 2.7 trillion barrels of oil equivalent of gas, oil and coal have been used up. Another 40 trillion remain in the ground of which 7 trillion can be considered as economically recoverable. This is comfortably enough to meet fossil fuel demand to 2050 on a 'business as usual' scenario, in the absence of constraints to counter global warming. So increasing scarcity of fossil fuels alone will not stop the growth of carbon emissions over time since the stocks of hydrocarbons that are profitable to extract under current policies are more than enough to take atmospheric carbon dioxide concentrations to well beyond 750ppm, with very dangerous consequences for climate-change impacts.

Nevertheless, constraints on oil supplies that manifest themselves in the form of a peak or plateau in world output in the coming decade or two seem likely to be important in influencing the climate change outcome. The possibility of 'peak oil' will encourage expectations of sustained high oil prices. This in turn would create an incentive to invest in transport technologies as well as other energy technologies that use oil more efficiently or which don't use oil at all – which will be a helpful response to counter global warming.

But while the prospect of peak oil is helpful for actions to avert climate change, a world in which oil supplies are tighter is worrying from the perspective of security of energy supplies. The transport sector, so dependent on oil and with such a tight supply chain, is particularly vulnerable to interruption in a steady flow of fuel. The possibility of industrial or political action at some point in the system prompts us to top up our tanks a bit earlier than we otherwise would. Queues appear at the petrol pumps, which attract others to join before the local supply runs dry. And before long we have a crisis on our hands, with people not getting to work and goods not getting to shops and businesses. The government is expected to fix the problem, but its ability to do so is limited, particularly if the origin of the problem is overseas, in the politically sensitive Middle East for example. Holding stocks of crude oil and refined products is one way of buying time. The developed countries that are members of the International Energy Agency have agreed to hold oil stocks equivalent of at least 90 days of net imports of the previous year. In the event of an oil supply disruption of 7 per cent or more they would release these oil stocks, restrain demand, switch to other fuels, increase domestic production and, if necessary, share available oil. These arrangements should be helpful as far as they go but have yet to be fully tested in the face of a major supply disruption. All in all, the dependence of transport in the developed world on oil supplies from the major producers in the Middle East, Russia, Nigeria and Venezuela must be a source of continuing anxiety.[29]

A further worrying aspect of peak oil output and long-run high oil prices is the affordability of energy for people on low incomes – 'fuel poverty', as the problem is often described. This is most serious for domestic heating, rather less so for transport. For buses, fuel costs represent about 10 per cent of operating costs, which means that even a big fuel price increase would have only limited impact on fares. For aviation, fuel amounts to a quarter of total operating costs, so is more vulnerable to oil price increases. For the motorist, tax accounted for two-thirds of the pump price of petrol in Britain in mid-2007, which means the proportionate effect of a steep increase in oil price is uncomfortable rather than absolutely unaffordable. One response open to the proverbial hard-pressed motorist is to trade down to a car with smaller engine, thus saving money and emitting less carbon to the atmosphere. That would be a prudent decision for motorists in a warming world, faced with the prospect of oil output peaking very probably within their lifetime, possibly even within the lifetime of their car.

# Policy Failure

Sometimes travel arrangements work well and the transport system delivers what is promised. But all too often that is the exception, not the norm. If we are to do better, we need to understand why we are subject to delays and disappointments.

The main reason for disappointment is that our collective demand for travel outstrips the capacity of the transport system to meet our needs. A shortage of capacity leads to congestion and overcrowding. In the past, the natural response of operators and policy makers was to provide more capacity wherever possible, although this was not always feasible in city centres. Travel demand grew in parallel with the economy as a whole, so predicting the future need for transport infrastructure and aiming to provide it was for a long time a respectable policy approach. However, 'predict and provide' led to accusations that the Department of Transport was in thrall to the road builders and their supporters – the road freight operators and the motoring organizations – and so neglected the impact of new roads on the environment. In the 1990s, attitudes began to shift as environmental concerns moved up the policy agenda. It became quite usual for ministers to state that 'we can't build our way out of congestion'. The question then is what could be achieved by a substantial road building programme. In Britain this involves investment in road infrastructure currently running at the rate of some £5 billion a year, with costs escalating quite rapidly. There are some extremely expensive projects – for instance widening the M6 motorway has been reported as likely to cost £1000 per inch, the most expensive piece of tarmac ever laid.[1]

## The consequences of road construction

The ostensible purpose of this large programming of road construction is to reduce congestion and improve journey time reliability in the face of growing traffic. But is this really possible? I am sceptical. The root of the problem lies in the human desire for movement, which limits the impact of the instruments available to those responsible for transport operations and policy.

We have seen in Chapter 1 that average travel time in Britain and elsewhere has held relatively constant at around an hour a day. The key insight that flows from this is that, in aggregate, *the benefits from policy and operational measures that increase average speeds are taken wholly in the form of extra travel on longer journeys.* The benefits are not taken in the form of reduced travel time, averaged across society as a whole, as explained in Chapter 3. Nor are they taken in the form of more frequent trips, since the average annual number has remained steady at about 1000 a year. Of course, some individuals may save travel time if they choose to make the same journeys, between the same origins and destinations, following transport system improvements which allow higher speeds. But others then take advantage of the road space thus vacated to reach more distant destinations while increasing their travel time, given the overall unchanging amount of travel time on average.[2]

It is therefore crucial to make a distinction between those transport policy and operational measures that have the effect of increasing average speeds, and those which do not. Investments and operational measures that have the effect of increasing average speeds would result in longer journeys, which in turn would have implications for carbon dioxide and polluting emissions, congestion, accidents and noise. While such measures would provide some additional benefits to travellers in the form of a wider choice of destinations, the disbenefits would also be increased.

We can consider the typical measures proposed in the transport plans of national authorities, including those of the British Department for Transport and its Highways Agency which is responsible for the motorway and trunk road network. Most measures that *have the effect* of increasing average travel speeds are not primarily *intended* to increase speeds. The test is whether the outcome involves higher speeds. For instance, much new road construction is aimed at 'debottlenecking' congested sections of the trunk road network. The aim is to cut time wasted in traffic congestion. A bottleneck arises at a location where the capacity of a road is suddenly reduced. Permanent bottlenecks require very careful study to determine whether or not they should be eliminated. Many bottlenecks perform a metering function, by reducing the flow at one point to a level that can be sustained in downstream sections of roadway. Removal of the bottleneck in one location may simply result in transferring the bottleneck to another point farther downstream. In many cases, the newly formed downstream bottleneck may result in worse traffic conditions than maintaining the original bottleneck. Thus, bottlenecks may often play a useful and important function in regulating flows and controlling the level of congestion that occurs on a road network.[3]

Suppose, nevertheless, the bottleneck is widened and initially the traffic does indeed flow faster. Subsequently, however, the traffic builds up quite rapidly. In part this arises from existing trips being rerouted to take advantage of the improved road. Over a longer period, further traffic growth is the result of decisions by individuals about the trips they make between home, work, shops, schools and so on which have to be managed within the amount of travel time they find manageable and acceptable. Time savings through improvements to a regularly used route allow a wider choice of destinations, as we have seen. So overall congestion is not lessened by widening the bottleneck since the benefit of the extra road space is offset by the extra space needed between vehicles, which rises with increasing speed. A new congested equilibrium is established, involving longer journeys with the same average travel time per person. The net result is some increase in access and choice for individuals, no change in congestion overall, and some increase in carbon emissions, pollutants and noise. And because there is no change in congestion, the logic dictates a continuing programme of debottlenecking road improvements. Road building need never stop, which suits the professional and commercial interests of the civil servants and construction companies concerned.

A second important class of road construction is bypasses. These are constructed for environmental reasons, to relieve a town or village of the adverse impact of through traffic (assuming that this is greater than the adverse impact of the new road on the countryside through which the bypass runs). In practice, however, bypasses are faster roads than the routes they replace and offer time savings which are a main factor in conventional economic justification. Bypasses therefore have the effect of increasing distance travelled within the overall travel time constraint. It has long been recognized that a series of bypasses on a route between two towns amounts in effect to a new fast route, the effect of which is to increase traffic flows. On the one hand, this is good for access. On the other, it's bad for environmental impacts. For congestion, it's neutral.

Recall the case of the Newbury bypass that I discussed in Chapter 3.[4] For the old route through the town and the bypass taken together, traffic volumes increased by around 50 per cent between 1997 and 2003, compared with natural growth rates in the region of around 14 per cent in same period. The majority of this increase occurred in 1999, the first year after the new bypass opened, a step change which had not been predicted by the advocates of the road at the public inquiry. Indeed, observed traffic flows on the bypass have been as much as 100 per cent greater than predicted in the traffic model employed when planning the road. For instance, for 2003 traffic counts of 33,000 vehicles in a 12-hour period were observed, compared with 16,000 and 19,000 predicted in the low- and high-case forecasts respectively. Prior to construction, the 'worst case' sensitivity test indicated that there could be 10 per cent extra induced traffic on the bypass. This is a striking example of the tendency of those who propose new road construction to underestimate the scale of induced traffic.

Where did all this traffic come from? That's not entirely clear because the data collected was limited to traffic counts. If the consultants who carried out the study had asked travellers about trip origins and destinations, we'd have a much better idea. The consultants' best guess is that traffic has been attracted away from other strategic routes serving southern England. In addition some traffic may have been diverted from smaller local roads that were subject to rat-running, and there may be traffic from changes in land use, as well some entirely new trips. I'm a bit sceptical about diversion from other strategic routes since the fairly modest impact of a nine-mile bypass hardly seems likely to cause area-wide rerouting of the kind that would be expected from a more substantial length of new trunk road. I suspect that the main traffic growth has arisen because the bypass has permitted people to make rather longer trips at higher speeds than was possible previously when they had to go through the centre of Newbury. So they have more choices of destination accessible within the time they have for travel, and they've exercised those choices.

# Road pricing

Perhaps the biggest idea in current transport policy is that people should be charged to use road space, rather than it being free at the point of use. We are used to paying for road space on which to park. In central London and elsewhere we are becoming used to paying for the road space on which we drive. Road pricing is nevertheless controversial, as is the somewhat more sophisticated concept of 'congestion charging' where what we pay is dependent on the amount of congestion to which our journeys contribute.

The enthusiasm for road pricing among economists, transport planners and many policy advisers stems from the perception that we are faced with a seemingly inexorable growth trend in car ownership and use, a reasonable belief that 'we cannot build our way out of congestion' through road construction, and increasing anxiety about the contribution of transport to climate change. Road pricing is seen as a means both to dampen the growth in travel demand and carbon emissions, and to tackle traffic congestion. Transport economists advocate pricing as a rational means to allocate scarce road space to those who place highest value on mobility and can best afford vehicle use, particularly at times of peak demand.

Road pricing, also termed road user charging, originated as a means for raising money to help finance new road construction. Tolled roads are common in many countries. More recently, road pricing, also in this context termed congestion charging, has been introduced with the prime purpose of reducing congestion. Congestion charging was introduced successfully in central London in February 2003,[5] and was extended to an adjacent area to the west in February 2007. The British government has adopted a positive, albeit wavering stance towards the idea of a national system of road user charging, and the report from Sir Rod Eddington, commissioned by the Treasury and the Department for Transport and published in December 2006, endorsed this view.[6]

Road pricing in one form or another is operating in some 14 countries, although only two – Britain and the Netherlands – are contemplating schemes that are national in coverage.[7] While partial national schemes exist in some countries in the form of lorry road user charging arrangements, the large majority of existing and intended charging schemes are local in scope.

There is a close relation between the technology required to implement road pricing and the structure of the tariff, which in turn is in part a reflection of the economic incentives to behavioural change that pricing is intended to generate. The London congestion charging scheme, for instance, employs cameras to read the number plates of vehicles within the charging zone. Drivers of vehicles that have not paid the daily charge by the specified deadline are subject to a penalty charge. This straightforward technology – self-declaration plus enforcement – has worked well, although it is quite expensive to operate (see below). However, the tariff permitted by this technology is limited to a fixed daily charge for a presence in the charging zone, however brief, during the daytime operating hours, with some classes of vehicles and drivers exempt from the charge.

The London scheme does not allow charges to be varied to reflect either actual traffic conditions on particular roads within the zones, or historic experience of such conditions. To develop a more refined approach to road user charging, it would be necessary to employ a technology that allowed greater discrimination of such aspects as the section of the road network which the vehicle is traversing, the time of day, the class of vehicle, and perhaps the actual traffic conditions. There are two broad technological approaches to this more sophisticated charging, both of which require vehicles to be equipped with a device that can interact with the other part of the charging system located in the infrastructure.[8]

First, there are roadside beacons that use radio-frequency identification technology to detect the in-vehicle device (also known as the smart-card, tag, transponder or on-board unit). The system then registers the appropriate charge for that vehicle on that section of road at that time of day. The smart card may either be a prepaid card or it may operate like a credit card, the vehicle owner then being billed retrospectively for payment. Such systems are in common use on tolled motorways in Europe and elsewhere, and in Britain on the Dartford river crossing on the M25 and the M6 toll road north of Birmingham.

The second kind of technology uses global positioning system (GPS) devices in each vehicle to identify the section of the road network being traversed at the particular time. The in-vehicle device then calculates the appropriate fee, and sends a note of the amount and the journey details to the toll collection centre via mobile radio signals, allowing a bill to be dispatched to the driver. In Germany, such arrangements operate for lorries using the autobahn system, which is divided into 5000 segments for charging purposes. The charge also depends on the vehicle's emission class and size. To make it difficult for charges to be avoided there are 276 enforcement gantries over roads which use detection devices to ensure that lorries are properly equipped and are paying the charge. There are a similar number of mobile enforcement units.[9] The British Department for Transport's feasibility study of road pricing concluded that a national system which charged on the basis of time, distance and place would not be practicable using roadside beacons. Accordingly a GPS or other positioning system would be required, although this technology is not yet regarded as mature enough for use.[10]

The road pricing schemes that have been introduced so far have generally involved a published tariff of charges so that drivers can estimate in advance the costs they are likely to incur. It is possible, however, for charges to be continuously varied to ensure free flow of traffic on the tolled road, with vehicles preferring not to pay having the option of using a parallel untolled route. The one example of such 'dynamic road pricing' is the high occupancy toll lanes on the Interstate 15 in San Diego, California, which are available to solo drivers for a fee, as well as to high occupancy vehicles. The fees are adjusted continuously, depending on traffic levels, to ensure the free flow of traffic. The transit time under free flow conditions of the eight-mile section of tolled road is about six minutes, whereas the delay due to congestion on the untolled lanes can add up to 20 minutes travel time.[11]

Dynamic pricing means that the cost of using the tolled route is not known precisely in advance, although in the case of the I-15 scheme the driver is able to decide whether or not to use the tolled lanes in the light of the prevailing charge, shown on a variable message sign. In the case of the ten-mile toll route on State Route 91 in California's Orange County, tolls vary by time of day according to a published tariff. However, tolls at times of peak usage may be adjusted at six-monthly intervals according to a procedure that reflects traffic flows in the previous period and has the aim of maintaining free flow travel.[12]

We see that there are a variety of approaches to road pricing which employ different technologies and which are suited to different charging arrangements. At present, the only system operating nationwide is that for lorries in Germany. Otherwise, systems are local. One question that arises is how to manage the transition from local schemes to a national scheme. The British government has indicated cautious support for a national system of road pricing, but at the same time is reluctant to mandate a standard in-vehicle device, given the rapid pace of development of the relevant technologies. It would accordingly be desirable to conduct trials of different technologies in local schemes, to see what works best. What is envisaged is some kind of technological migration, paralleling the geographical spread of charging, starting with payment by drivers enforced by number plate monitoring, moving on to roadside beacons and then to GPS.[13] However, I suspect that such diversity of technologies would inhibit the adoption of road user charging. What is needed is the kind of European standard that facilitated the continent-wide uptake of mobile phones based on a single technology. Indeed, the EU has adopted a directive with the long-term aim of ensuring that in-vehicle units would be interoperable with all electronic charging systems within the EU.

A further concern about road pricing concerns 'diversion'. If some roads are tolled and others are not, then you would expect some traffic to divert from the former to the latter. This could have adverse consequences for safety and the environment if the untolled roads are less suited to high traffic volumes. Such a problem was experienced following the introduction of charging for lorries using the autobahn system in Germany, as well as with some parts of the motorway networks in Hungary and Japan.[14] One advantage of charging based on GPS location is that it could be applied to all roads, without the need to install beacons or gantries on each road section, and hence in principle diversion could be deterred by suitable charges on alternative roads – although this raises questions of public acceptability (see below).

The cost of installing and operating a national system of road pricing would depend on the technology chosen, as well as on the arrangements for billing and enforcement. Costs could be substantial. In the case of the London congestion charging scheme, Transport for London estimated for 2006–07 that operating expenses amounted to £90 million and income from charges and penalties £213m, giving net revenues of £123m. But these revenues do not allow for implementation costs of £162m for the original scheme and £118m for the western extension.[15]

As part of its feasibility study of national road pricing, the Department for Transport commissioned a review of the costs of implementing such a scheme. These are huge. The set-up costs were estimated to be in the range £23–62 billion at 2004 prices, the wide range largely reflecting uncertainty in the cost of the in-vehicle unit.[16] Annual running costs might be in the range £4–5bn, which compares with the gross annual income of £9bn. The conclusion of the feasibility study was that a national distance-based charging scheme does not seem to be affordable now, but could become affordable in the future as and when the costs of technology fall.

The costs cited above include payment and enforcement activities. Adequate enforcement is important if significant revenues are not to be lost and public accept-ability prejudiced through perceptions that some drivers are able to avoid payment. In London, a quarter of the revenue in 2006–07 arose from penalty charges, which indicates the importance of enforcement.

The revenue generated by a national scheme for road pricing would depend on the level of charges set. As I mentioned earlier, for certain short lengths of tolled road in the US, charges are set to achieve the free flow of traffic. There would be no case for higher charges than that if the main motivation is to tackle congestion. The London congestion charging scheme, however, has not aimed to achieve free flow conditions, in part because a zonal charge is too crude an instrument for such a purpose. In 2005, congestion in the charging zone was estimated to be 22 per cent less than in 2003, before the introduction of charging, which is smaller than the 30 per cent observed immediately after the scheme's introduction (in 2006 congestion was only 8 per cent lower than the precharging value but this disappointing finding is attributed to the exceptional amount of street works).[17]

For the Department for Transport's feasibility study mentioned above, charges were estimated on the basis of what the economists regard as necessary to achieve economic efficiency. This is termed the 'marginal social cost' – which means setting prices to reflect the external costs that a vehicle at a given time and place imposes on society.[18] With a maximum price cap of 80p per kilometre, it was estimated that congestion could be reduced by some 40 per cent, resulting in an economically opti-mal level of congestion.

There is a trade-off between charges and congestion reduction. Free traffic flow is a clear objective with evident attractions for those willing to pay the user charge, but with charges set higher than economic efficiency would justify. Charges set on the basis of marginal social cost would be lower, and on that account more acceptable, but would not result in a clearly specified outcome – just a reduction in congestion below what it would otherwise have been.

Charges for road use may be expected to increase over time. The initial charge in central London of £5 per day was increased to £8 after two years, to intensify the effect of the scheme and to generate additional revenue. More generally, there are three reasons why charges would need to increase over time. First, unless road user charges increase at least at the rate of increase in average earnings, use of the road network becomes more affordable, hence usage would increase and so would conges-tion. Second, because car ownership tends to increase as earnings increase, road user charging would need to increase at a faster rate than earnings if the effect of increased ownership on congestion is to be countered. And third, charges would need to be raised to counter the induced traffic that may be expected.

Induced traffic, as explained in Chapter 3, is the additional traffic that appears following the construction of extra road capacity, over and above the trend traf-fic growth (the Newbury bypass case, discussed above, is a good illustration of the phenomenon). It is the consequence of the additional distances at higher speeds made possible by the new capacity, given that average personal travel time holds constant. In a similar way, because road user charging reduces congestion, one expected consequence would be to permit those willing to pay for faster travel to gain access to additional desired destinations by travelling farther in the time they have available. This potential for induced traffic is a factor largely missing from analyses of the consequences of introducing road pricing. As yet, induced traffic arising from congestion charging has not been directly demonstrated, although there is evidence that a significant number of London commuters, especially from outer boroughs, appear to have switched to car use as a result of the introduction of the congestion charging scheme. Moreover, an economic evaluation suggests that induced traffic could offset a third of the estimated reduction in traffic due to congestion charging in central London.[19]

Charges for road use aimed at stabilizing congestion at some chosen level would therefore need to be increased regularly by an additional amount, over and above that needed to cope with the earnings and ownership effects, to counter the growth of induced traffic. Accordingly, road use charges would need to rise over time at a rate significantly faster than the rate of increase of average earnings. This could prove problematic as regards public acceptability, which leads us on to the politics of road pricing.

## The politics of road pricing

The story of the fuel price protests of 2000 is worth bearing in mind. The British government had increased road fuel duty at a rate significantly higher than the rate of price inflation during the period 1993–2000 with the aim of reducing the environmental impact of road transport. However, in 2000 there were strong protests against this policy by lorry drivers, who blockaded the oil refineries. This led to panic buying at the petrol pumps. The government backed down and ceased the duty increases.[20] In contrast, protests against fuel price increases in the period since 2003, due to the increase in the cost of crude oil, have been quite muted. This suggests that increases in the costs of road use driven by rises in external costs are more acceptable than increases driven by policy purposes. Road user charge increases to contain congestion may well appear more like the latter than the former. If so, then one risk arising from the introduction of a costly national scheme of road user charging is that it would not be politically possible to increase charges at a rate which prevented congestion from worsening over time.

Fairness is also important for public acceptability. Different road users will experience different costs and benefits from any particular scheme of road pricing. There will be winners and losers, and the protagonists and promoters will need to address the concerns of those who see themselves as disadvantaged, particularly vulnerable groups susceptible to social exclusion.[21]

The Department for Transport's feasibility study envisaged a national charging scheme such that a typical drive to work might be cheap for the first part, becoming more expensive as traffic builds up on the main road into town, finally hitting a higher charge for the last kilometre where demand for limited road space is highest. The charges would also vary according to time, so at the peak of the rush hour they would be higher than earlier or later periods. A driver would have a choice between paying the higher rate for a better journey at the time of their choosing, or a lower rate to travel at a different time. Or they may chose to share a car with a neighbour to reduce the cost, or to transfer to public transport, choices that free up road space for the benefit of those willing to pay the charge.

The acceptability of a scheme of road user charging would depend in part on the numbers displaced from their preferred mode and time of travel. Of the million people commuting to central London each day, only 9 per cent use a car or van, which is an important reason why charging has proved generally acceptable. Nationally, however, the proportion of trips by car for commuting or business purposes is 70 per cent, so a far wider range of people would be affected.

While people on low incomes are less likely to own a car than those who are better off, and hence are less likely to have to pay road user charges, those that do own cars already spend a greater proportion of their income on travel. In the poorest 10 per cent of wards in England, half the households do not own a car. Nevertheless, motoring accounts for a quarter of the weekly expenditure of households in the lowest fifth (by income) of households that own cars.[22] Households owning cars in the lower half of the income distribution spend £30 to £50 a week on motoring, which may be compared with the £40 a week that would be incurred for daily travel by car within the London congestion charging zone or for daily two-way use of the M6 toll road.[23] This suggests that there is unlikely to be much scope for the payment of road user charges in congested conditions by low-income motorists who are dependent on their cars for getting to work, for instance because of lack of suitable public transport or because of working unsocial hours when such transport is not available. The position of such low-income motorists would depend in part on whether other motoring costs such as fuel duty could be reduced, and whether the proceeds from road user charging could be employed effectively to boost public transport provision (as has been the case in central London).

Opinion polls and focus groups consistently find that the public does not regard road user charging as a particularly effective or popular means of tackling traffic congestion.[24] One core concern is 'fairness'. You would expect that the public acceptability of road pricing would depend, among other things, on the proportion of those affected who perceive themselves as likely to be worse off to a significant degree. This in turn depends on what is done with the net revenues from the scheme. These could be used to offset other motoring costs, or to fund transport improvements. Or they might contribute to general government expenditure or serve to reduce general taxation.

In the case of the London congestion charging, there is a requirement to use the proceeds to further transport strategy, with the main effort in practice devoted to supporting bus operations. For a national scheme, the debate is focused on whether to favour 'revenue neutrality' or not.[25] With revenue neutrality, the additional costs experienced by vehicle users on account of road pricing would be offset by reductions in taxation specific to vehicles and their use, principally vehicle excise duty and road fuel duty. Such an approach has the political and presentational advantage that motorists collectively would be seen to be no worse off, although the expense of implementing the scheme would then be borne by the government. Alternatively, if only the net proceeds (after such expenses) were used to offset taxation, then motorists would be worse off. On the other hand, a serious disadvantage of revenue neutrality is that the cost of fuel would fall, which would run counter to the desire to improve the fuel efficiency of vehicles in order to reduce carbon emissions.

Public acceptability must also influence, and be influenced by, political attitudes and leadership. Where winners are seen clearly to outnumber losers, and where there is a strong political commitment, city-centre congestion charging can prove publicly acceptable, as in London and, more recently, in Stockholm following a trial and a referendum.[26] On the other hand, initial public support may ebb away and voters may reject a proposed scheme, as in Edinburgh where matters were less deftly managed.[27] In any event, city centres suited for congestion charging are characterized by a small proportion of travellers who regularly use cars, together with a dense network of public transport. Such conditions are not generally found elsewhere. So experience in city centres is not necessarily a guide to likely public attitudes to a national scheme of charging.

Research on public attitudes indicates that the acceptability of road pricing increases when the revenues are dedicated to the improvement of transport generally. Fairness is important, particularly the impact on those with low incomes and those who do not have viable alternatives to using their car. There is also hostility that reflects concerns that road pricing would be ineffective, would amount to additional taxation, and would limit people's freedom of choice in getting around. Concerns about privacy are also significant, but less than concerns about costs.[28] An electronic petition to the Prime Minister that opposed road pricing and vehicle tracking attracted 1.8 million signatures by the time it closed in February 2007.

The difficulties I've outlined amount to a fairly formidable set of hurdles that would need to be overcome in order to implement a national scheme of road pricing. So we need to consider alternative ways of coping with congestion. The traditional comparison for transport investments is the 'do minimum' case in which the minimum reasonable action is taken. In the present context this might involve a variety of traffic management measures, some quite modest investment in road infrastructure, perhaps local road pricing schemes, but no national scheme. For such a case, conventional transport modelling would forecast increasing traffic and increasing congestion. However, congestion is self-limiting. As we have seen, both average personal travel time and trip rate have changed little over the past 35 years and are unlikely to change much in the future. It follows that the likely behavioural response to the build-up of congestion is a stabilization, or even a reduction, in average distance travelled – an aspect that is underestimated in conventional modelling. Such stabilization can be observed in practice. As we saw in Figure 1.1 in Chapter 1, the average distance travelled has been stable over the past decade at a little over 7000 miles per person per year. Another example of stability is that traffic on the heavily used M25 London orbital road did not increase (in fact decreased slightly) between 2001 and 2006, whereas for the motorway system as a whole traffic increased by some 8 per cent.[29] Naturally, such constrained travel, and the constrained access it implies, is likely to be seen by some, particularly businesses, as a regressive development. There would therefore be pressure on policy makers to take positive action to tackle congestion. I'll return in Chapter 8 to what might be done with the aid of technology.

Adoption of a national scheme of road pricing would be seen as a fairly fundamental change in the terms of use of the national road system. There seems to be a general acceptance that the costs of construction of a new road, bridge or tunnel could reasonably be funded from a toll, particularly where there exists an untolled (albeit inferior) alternative. However, there must be a major question about the acceptability of new charges affecting the generality of drivers for use of existing roads. At present, road usage in Britain is very largely free of charge, as is health provision through the National Health Service or school-level education – all services financed out of tax revenues. Arguments could be made for user charges to contribute to the costs of running all these public services, as well as to limit demand. But there are counter-arguments arising from concepts of equity and fairness which point the other way.

Transport is a relatively egalitarian domain. The first-class passenger arrives at the same instant as the budget traveller who shares the train or plane. The top-of-the-range motor car is as much impeded by congestion as its mass-market counterpart. There is some competition between modes, for instance between road and rail, allowing trade-offs between speed, comfort and cost. But otherwise the options for paying more to arrive faster are limited by the exceptional expense involved, for example, in travelling by helicopter. We choose to live in crowds, most of us in urban areas that offer many conveniences and attractions close to hand. The price we pay is more mutual proximity than we would wish when we travel, which is the origin of traffic congestion. One possible solution is road pricing, which appeals to those who believe in markets as a means to maximize efficiency, as well as to the well-off who could comfortably afford the charges. But many others would reject 'economic pricing' and economic efficiency in favour of equity, of common and equal rights to enjoy the traditionally free use of the public highway. We can even view congestion in a positive light – as a symptom of economic success and a shared experience in the common public space that all members of society are constrained to occupy when they wish to travel. In a society increasingly concerned about widening inequalities between rich and poor, it is not obvious that we should exclude low-income motorists from busy roads so that high-income motorists could travel faster.

The impediments in the way of implementing a national scheme of road pricing seem not inconsiderable. It is little wonder that British politicians are proceeding cautiously, even though the economists, civil servants and most informed commentators are supportive. The present uncomfortable situation has arisen because the economists' thinking is overly simplistic, and the civil servants concerned lack both a deep understanding of the transport system and the imagination to identify alternative courses of action. Ministers equivocate, sometimes showing some enthusiasm, sometimes backing away.

I spent over 20 years working in Whitehall departments, as civil servant and scientist. The British Civil Service has a high reputation and attracts able senior staff, the best of whom are to be found in the most prestigious departments such as the Treasury. I myself was impressed by the quality of the administrators I encountered when dealing with energy policy matters. As a new entrant, fresh out of the laboratory, wearing a new suit, I was allocated to a job concerned with civil nuclear policy. I benefited from having as my first boss Richard Wilson, an exceptionally able and kind man who later became Head of the Civil Service, as well as having as colleagues a bright group of people who had been assembled to deal with the policy issues that had come to the forefront following the first oil shock in the 1970s. When I eventually moved from the energy sector of government to the Department for Transport, I have to say that I found the collective capability somewhat disappointing.

The transport ministry has never ranked high in the Whitehall hierarchy and has rarely attracted the best and brightest talents among civil service entrants. Secretaries of state are often on their first or last cabinet jobs, or are keeping their heads down in the hope of a better posting before long. No minister in recent decades has made a significant impact or achieved fame as head of the Department for Transport. John Prescott had a shot, soon after appointment as head of a combined transport and environment department, following the Labour election victory 1997, when he stated: 'I will have failed, if in five years time there are not many more people using public transport and far fewer journeys by car. It's a tall order but I urge you to hold me to it.' However, Prescott's Ten Year Transport Plan, published in 2002, was soon effectively dead and its key target to cut road traffic congestion abandoned. Instead, traffic congestion is now forecast to increase and carbon dioxide emissions from road transport to grow. Transport white papers have been published at regular intervals, with minimal practical impact.[30]

There are two contemporary politicians who can be taken seriously for their contributions to transport policy, neither of whom has been, or is ever likely to be, Secretary of State. Steven Norris was a well respected Minister for Transport, the number two post in the department, from 1992 to 1996. He continued his involvement in transport matters when he left parliament and convened the group of transport experts that contributed to the Conservative party's 'Blueprint for a green economy' submission to the shadow cabinet in 2007. The group sensibly argued that grandiose programmes of road building are part of the problem, not the solution. After buying short-term relief from congestion at tremendous cost, they induce more traffic. The group saw a strong case for a comprehensive review of cost–benefit analysis regime and a moratorium on all plans for motorway and trunk road widening pending such a review. They proposed a hold on all plans for further airport expansion while in each case such plans are tested against the challenge of climate change.

The other politician with transport credentials is Ken Livingstone, who stood for Mayor of London on a manifesto which included the London congestion charging scheme. This he promptly and effectively implemented, using the proceeds to improve public transport. The powers of the mayor are quite restricted, responsibilities for London being shared with the boroughs and national government. Transport is the aspect where the mayor can make the biggest impact and where Ken Livingstone has made good progress.

# Freight

This book is about personal travel. But the transport system is also responsible for moving freight. There is competition between people and freight for space on roads, railways and at airports. It would be simpler to tackle the transport problems faced by business if there was a wholly separate system for freight.[31] But in practice transport infrastructure is shared, and so what can be done by way of improvement to aid business is limited by the response of personal travellers. Freight hauliers press for the widening of trunk roads to ease the congestion that results in unreliable delivery schedules. However, the space from widening is largely taken up by car drivers accessing more distant destinations, so the lorry drivers are disappointed in the outcomes.

It is beyond the scope of this book to deal fully with freight transport, and in any event there is a lack of good data relevant to the kind of analysis that needs to be carried out. Moreover, the importance of transport for business should not be overemphasized. Although the Eddington transport study focused on the role of transport in contributing to economic success, it also recognized that transport costs typically account for 4–5 per cent of total input costs for firms and that the 5 million business trips a day represent only 4 per cent of personal travel.[32]

I will deal here with just one important aspect of freight travel by road.[33] The phenomenon of constant average travel time applies to the travel behaviour of people. I want to suggest that the analogous concept for freight is that of *acceptable delivery times*. For any class of goods in any particular period, there is a more or less fixed delivery time that is acceptable to the generality of customers. This varies from 24 hours or less from order to delivery for fresh food, to months or years for capital goods. The market determines what delivery time is acceptable. Improved delivery times can be a source of competitive advantage for suppliers and a means to reduce inventory on the part of customers. Occasionally there may be a step change in requirement, as occurred with the introduction of just-in-time delivery in the motor manufacturing industry.[34]

As the UK motorway system was developed and trunk roads upgraded, the pattern of road freight logistics changed in response. Advantage has been taken of the higher speeds possible to reduce the number of warehouses, thus making savings in inventory and estate costs, while retaining acceptable delivery times. Centralized distribution warehouses, which tend to be clustered around motorway intersections, are playing an increasingly important role in the supply chains of the economy. Logistics companies can deliver to 75 per cent of the UK population from their West Midlands warehouse hubs in a half-day truck drive. The area around the M1, M62 and M18 motorways in South Yorkshire is becoming a golden triangle for distribution and logistics with 'supersheds' constructed on cheap land with good access to roads and ports. The average length of haul for road freight has increased since 1980. At 87 kilometres, it is now 31 per cent higher than at the start of the period. An increasing proportion of freight is moved by articulated vehicles, which carry goods on average about twice as far as rigid vehicles.[35]

For the supermarkets, road network improvements allowed a depot to supply a wider geographical area, permitting reduction in the number of depots, saving in stock levels, and generating economies of scale. We were helped to understand these developments by David Quarmby when he was joint managing director of Sainsburys. An economist specializing in transport, he had earlier been an economic adviser to the Ministry for Transport and subsequently became responsible for logistics at the supermarket chain. Currently he is chairman of the Independent Transport Commission, a think tank. Quarmby observed that the trend in retail distribution, especially of food, involved large multiple chains controlling their own distribution because this was more efficient, and led to better quality of service, flexibility and management control. Traditional suppliers or wholesaler-controlled supply networks have more depots in or near towns to supply all outlets in the area. In contrast, retailer-controlled networks employ fewer larger vehicles which spend less time unloading and operate out of relatively few depots located close to the trunk road network. This mode of operating the supply chain depends on a good motorway and trunk road network.[36]

Manufacturers and retailers generally see spatial concentration of production as a dominant trend, which allows both customers and manufacturers to reduce inventory levels. A consequence is increased journey lengths. For instance, Boots The Chemist, which operates some 1500 stores in Britain, has been reported as planning to close 17 regional distribution centres as it centralized operations in the form of a new £70 million automated warehouse at its headquarters in Nottingham.[37]

In the case of the ubiquitous 'white vans' that carry the technicians who sustain our service economy, a similar situation seems likely to apply. There will be an acceptable response time for call out, whether routine or emergency. For routine servicing, there will be an acceptable balance for the service organization between the time spent travelling and the time spent on customers' premises. For public emergency services, such as fire and ambulance, targets for response times are set and monitored.

In all these cases – freight and service vehicles – the number of depots needed to serve a given geographical area will depend on the average speeds attainable, all else being equal. Higher speeds would allow economies to be made in depots. Conversely, declining speeds would necessitate more depots. Because perceptions of growing traffic congestion seem to threaten the economies gained from past road improvements, it is natural that business should urge further road construction. Without this, firms feel they would have to make additional investment in depots and inventory, which seems to them to be regressive and inefficient.

Although there is a lack of empirical data, a reasonable assumption is that acceptable delivery and response times for freight and services change relatively slowly. It follows that business takes the benefits of higher speeds made possible by improved transport infrastructure in the form of economies in inventories and real estate, not through reduced travel time. In this regard, business transport and personal travel are similar. Understandably, business seeks ever more public investment in transport infrastructure in order to reduce its own costs. Whether that represents a good deal for the nation as a whole is another matter.

*6*

# Travelling Together

How much and how we travel depends on where we live. Most travel is within and between cities and towns. Where routes are well used, we are able to travel together in what is conventionally known as public transport. Collective transport might be a better term, to distinguish it from personal transport – mainly by car. The question of collective versus personal, public versus private, is important since public transport offers the possibility of lower carbon emissions, as well as less congestion.

One long-term global trend is the movement of people from the countryside to cities in search of a better life. According to the UN Population Fund, this year for the first time more than half the human population, 3.3 billion people, will be living in urban areas. However, while people are flocking to the cities, the cities themselves are becoming less dense in terms of numbers of inhabitants per square kilometre. Average urban densities have been declining for the past two centuries. As transportation continues to improve, the tendency is for cities to use up more and more land per person.[1]

## Sprawl

In the early 20th century US cities grew upwards as tenements and luxury apartments replaced low-rise dwellings. But at end of this century compact urban cities had been replaced by suburban sprawl, malls, office parks and houses on larger lots. At first people lived in suburbs and commuted to city centres, but then jobs followed the people and now metropolitan areas are characterized by decentralized homes and jobs. Sprawl, the dominant urban form in the US, is made possible by the ubiquitous automobile. The main problem, some would say, is the underclass of people left behind in the inner city.[2]

In Europe, where cities have traditionally been compact, there are signs that sprawl and suburbanization are increasing. Between 1969 and 1999 the urbanized areas in France increased by five times, while the population of these areas grew only by 50 per cent.[1] In Britain, planning policy in the form of the 'green belts' around cities has limited urban sprawl. One consequence has been the movement of people, housing and jobs into the towns and villages beyond the green belts. This has prompted calls for an 'urban renaissance' aimed at preserving both the vitality of the central core of cities and the countryside from further housing built on greenfield sites. In the US, concerns about inner city dereliction have led to the advocacy of policy measures to encourage 'smart growth' of metropolitan areas, including denser urban infill and more compact 'sustainable' communities which are less dependent on the automobile and more in tune with traditional urban patterns.[3]

The 1999 report of the Urban Task Force, chaired by the architect Richard Rogers (described by John Prescott as 'an evangelist of urban renaissance'), made a strong plea for policies to regenerate inner city areas. The response of the British government, in the Urban White Paper of November 2000, was to state that: 'We wholeheartedly support the vision set out by the Urban Task Force.' This statement should not necessarily be taken at face value, however. Will Hutton, a well placed observer, has written: 'I know at first hand the reaction of ministers and senior civil servants to the Urban Task Force's report ... apart from an honourable minority they regard it as largely misconceived.'[4]

Why might there be doubts about the case for urban regeneration? One criticism is that jobs have been neglected. The typical image of a revived urban centre shows people at leisure, chatting and promenading in the sunshine. The city centre is an attractive destination in its own right. Copenhagen, the only European city to have prevented growth in car traffic over the last 30 years, decided in 1962 to pedestrianize the main shopping street, both to control traffic and make the city more attractive. Public transport was improved, cycle paths created, parking places cut at the rate of 2–3 per cent a year. All this proved to be popular and commercially attractive, with 25 per cent more journeys on foot in the centre and a 65 per cent increase in cycling since 1962, a quarter of all journeys in the city now being by bicycle.[5] Where people work did not seem to be a matter that needed addressing.

However, people need to live where they can get access to employment. In Britain in recent decades, jobs have been lost from manufacturing while employment opportunities have opened up in the service sector, such as finance, distribution, transport, hospitality and communications. Successful towns are attractive to both companies and workers. Features sought include pleasant living and working environments, the absence of 'industrial baggage' (urban decay, poor skills, social problems, negative image), large numbers of consumers, a skilled workforce, good infrastructure (especially roads), and generally an ambiance suited to new kinds of working practices that require mobility.[6]

Employment opportunities are not moving in a single direction, however, as can be seen from the development of London as a vibrant, growing global city, drawing in workers from around the world, particularly to the thriving financial services and media sectors. To explain why some cities and regions grow faster than others, economists have invoked the concept of 'agglomeration', based on productivity benefits which include: better matching of people to jobs and access to skilled labour, as a result of dense labour markets; better connection to suppliers and markets; and information spillovers between firms. For consumers a wider range of goods and services is to hand.[7]

Transport can facilitate agglomeration. For instance, transport played a pivotal role in the development and longevity of the Lancashire cotton mill cluster in the mid 19th century. The cluster consisted of a number of textile towns, each specializing in a particular stage of the production process, with no single town offering an advantage over the tight cluster of individual specialized towns. Rail links supported the movement of intermediate goods between towns, and to and from the port, while international shipping provided imports of raw cotton and export of finished goods.

Agglomeration can be slightly elusive, however. It may be recognizable at the time, but hard to predict in advance, and not easy to forecast for the future. Already the geographical focus of hedge fund activity, the top end of the financial services market, has shifted from the City to London's West End. And the national newspapers have long since dispersed from Fleet Street – surely in its heyday a textbook example of the benefits of agglomeration.

For some employment sectors then, there are centripetal forces at work that draw people into the city centre. But the centrifugal trend still seems pretty powerful, notwithstanding the many voices of architects, planners, academics and government officials across the affluent world who believe that suburban sprawl is economically inefficient, socially inequitable, environmentally damaging and ugly. Aspects that make the suburbs and more distant locations attractive include lower commuting times to nearby good jobs, more living space and gardens, car parking, good schools and avoidance of problems associated with the inner city. In Britain, only 9 per cent of us live in the urban core. Movement out has been taking place since the 1920s at varying pace, but never reversed.[8]

However, any simple dichotomy between urban and suburban will risk misleading. Robert Bruegmann, who is sceptical of the case against sprawl, notes that US suburbs are becoming denser. Suburban lot sizes peaked in 1950s and have been declining ever since even as houses themselves have grown in size. A surprising amount of new housing at the edge of US cities is row houses (terrace, as we British would say) and garden apartments for working-class Americans. Los Angeles has become much denser over the past 50 years, and is now – surprisingly – America's most densely populated urbanized area. It is in fact considerably denser than New York or Chicago. Although LA has no high density core, it has relatively high density housing spread over an extremely large area, with no very low density extraurban sprawl because of the relatively high cost of supplying water.[9]

The English too are a suburban people. Eight out of ten live in suburbs or 'exurbs'. These are not predominantly dormitories for city-centre office and shop workers. Most of their residents live, work and play in the suburbs and visit city centres only from time to time. Suburbs comprise mixes of homes, shopping centres, business parks, universities, research labs, airports and hotels, all essential parts of the country's economy. They provide today most of the services found in cities in the past. Suburbs are expected to grow because they offer more land and bigger houses for lower prices. As households become more affluent they tend to demand more living space. Having been designed around cars and lorries, suburbs could not exist without them.[10]

The result of such developments in the US, and in Britain beyond the green belts, is that home and job location have become increasingly uncoupled. Radial travel from suburb to city centre is less common, commuting patterns more complex and journey lengths longer. Increasing mobility has allowed people to seek and take jobs over ever wider areas. As people become increasingly specialized as workers, they are increasingly unlikely to find jobs near home. People in better jobs tend to be willing to commute farther, a trend likely to increase as the workforce becomes more professionalized. Commuting patterns are becoming more complex, suburb to suburb or small town to small town. Households increasingly fix a residential base and cope with job changes by commuting from accessible suburban or non-urban locations. Job advertisements nowadays rarely offer to pay removal expenses. Dual-career professional households choose optimal domicile location to further both careers.[11]

An example of this complex pattern of travel can be seen in South and West Yorkshire where congested sections of the motorways and trunk roads are used in peak periods by very large number of commuters with largely single car occupancy. Origins and destinations of journeys are well dispersed. Some people travel very long distances and only a small proportion of car commuting trips end in town or city centres. This pattern has grown up because people prefer to live in an environment of their choice, in houses they can afford, with family and friends nearby, where their children attend schools of their choice, and where they can access a wide range of employment locations via the strategic road network. Increasingly, jobs are less secure and people are unwilling to move house to be nearer a job which they may have to change in the foreseeable future. There has been a considerable migration of population from inner urban areas towards suburbs and smaller towns where housing is of better quality and more affordable. New employment opportunities tend to be located on out-of-town sites, in business parks, and retail and leisure developments adjacent to a good trunk road network. Car prices have not increased in real terms over a long period, and have decreased in recent years.[12]

Decisions on where to live are likely to change over the life course. A study of people who live in five higher density neighbourhoods in London identified three classes of resident: 'urbanites' who positively opt for high-density living; 'suburban leavers' (both from and to the suburbs) such as 'empty nesters' whose children have left home and young families who will soon leave the city for the outskirts; and 'trapped residents', particularly long-term council tenants, older people, the poor and others with limited choice about where they live. Those who are not trapped may well opt for spells of urban, suburban and rural living according to their life stage.[13]

Faced with this range of issues, planners are becoming increasingly frustrated. The prospects for being able to plan sensibly for housing, jobs and travel are fading at the very time the agenda of sustainable development and urban regeneration requires them to do more. What I now want to discuss is the scope for transport policy to influence these location issues.

## Transport and place

Given that travel time is constant at around an hour a day on average, then building new roads or railways that permit higher speeds would result in people travelling farther. Railways, including metros and undergrounds, allowed people to move to the suburbs and surrounding towns while still being able to work in the city centre. Orbital roads around the cities, such as the M25 around London, were intended to divert through traffic around the congested centre. In practice they have provided faster travel for commuters and other local traffic, thus permitting the diversity of employment and residential locations discussed above. To the extent that commuting times are reduced by working in the suburbs rather than the centre, more time is available for other journeys, preponderantly by car.

Would it be possible to reduce the amount of travel by encouraging higher density settlements in which people live closer to their jobs and the facilities they need, as well as to public transport facilities? This is a policy aim of the British government, set out in Planning Policy Guidance Note 13 (PPG13), which is consistent with promoting sustainability and reducing carbon emissions in particular. However, there are reasons to be sceptical about the practical effect of this policy. There is no evidence as yet that by themselves measures intended to reduce the need to travel contribute to an actual lessening of traffic growth, or that the provision of choice of travel modes will actually make much impact on modal share in absence of restraint on car use. It's hard to see how development planning could have more than a very marginal impact on travel demand across large parts of the country. The need therefore is to focus on areas where major land use and development change is in prospect.[14]

Quite apart from the question of whether such higher density settlements would be attractive while lower density alternatives remain available (for the reason discussed in the previous section), I would expect two consequences that run counter to the policy intention of PPG13. First, less time spent travelling to work and other regular destinations would permit longer trips to optional destinations, given constant travel time. Second, more use of public transport instead of the car would reduce congestion and thus permit higher speeds and longer journeys for those who decide to continue to use their cars (a further example of induced traffic, as discussed in Chapter 3).

Given the attractions of car use for suburban living, planning measures alone are unlikely to reverse the popularity of the personal vehicle. More potent influences would be needed. In the sunbelt states of the US there are new suburbs in which every house sits on an acre of land. Low density makes public transport impracticable. Without cars, such places are uninhabitable.[15] For more densely populated areas, public transport (known as transit in the US) may have better prospects for stemming the trend to car use, which tends to increase as average income rises.

Cities vary widely in their characteristics. Peter Newman and Jeffrey Kenworthy have studied 84 cities around the world, 15 in detail. They find that fuel consumption for private cars is as high as 3000 litres per person per year in Atlanta, the city with the lowest population density in the world, but less than 500 litres for western European cities, while for developing country cities the range is 30–300 litres. Public transport use is the opposite: de minimis in most US cities, over 20 per cent of vehicle-kilometres in western European cities, 50 per cent in east Asia with as high as 73 per cent in Hong Kong.[16]

Newman and Kenworthy distinguish different classes of city according to population density. They find that constant average travel time defines the shape of cities. 'Walking cities' were and remain dense, mixed-use areas no more than 5km across. These were the major urban form for 8000 years, but substantial parts of cities such as Mumbai and Hong Kong retain the character of a walking city, as do most of Krakow and central areas of New York, London, Vancouver and Sydney. 'Transit cities' developed from 1850 to 1950 based on trams and trains, which meant they could spread out 20–30km from dense centres along corridors following the rail lines. Most European and wealthy Asian cities retain this form, as do the old inner cores of US, Australian and Canadian cities. Many developing cities in Asia, Africa and Latin America have the dense corridor form of a transit city but do not always have the public transport system to support them, so they become car saturated. 'Automobile cities' from the 1950s on could spread 50–80km in all directions at low density – as for many US, Canadian, Australian and New Zealand cities.

Public transport is heavily subsidized in almost all cities because of what economists term its large 'positive externalities', meaning reduced need for road space and reduced congestion, but also to ensure access by poorer people. Cities face pressure to keep fares affordable for those on low incomes, but in doing so they sacrifice bus quality and comfort. Middle-class riders react by buying scooters, motorcycles and cars as soon as they can. With the flight of the middle class, transit revenues diminish, and operators reduce quality further as they serve a poorer clientele. The quality of service suffers first, and a decrease in quantity of service often follows. With inadequate financial support and management, public transport can enter a downward spiral of decline. One result is the excessive car congestion found in Bangkok (Chapter 4).[17]

Professor Ricky Burdett, an urban expert from the London School of Economics who has studied 16 world cities on all the continents, argues that one of the three things that make a successful city is that people should be able to travel to work at relatively low cost with dignity. Public transport is ultimately about justice, in his view.[18]

## Urban travel

Attractive high-quality public transport in developed cities requires a 'carrot and stick' approach, to discourage car use and to foster public transport. London, Barcelona and Singapore are among the few major cities in the world to have been successful in this objective. Those cities that focus only on public transport investment have not been able to secure significant change to travel behaviour. The hoped-for benefits from such investment – fewer journeys by car and less congestion – have not been sustained, as the vacated road space has simply filled up with new traffic. Since 2000 London has achieved a 5 per cent shift in modal share from cars to buses, a change in travel behaviour that started before the introduction of congestion charging and which has been facilitated by policy interventions to reduce road space such as more bus lanes, more pedestrian crossings and pedestrian phases at traffic signals. The only other city which even comes close to this figure is Barcelona, which has seen public transport use up by 1.7 per cent and car use reduce by 3 per cent between 1999 and

2002 (by restricting car use and improving public transport and ticketing). On the other hand, while bus use in Dublin increased by 40 per cent between 1996 and 2003, the lack of car restraint measures has meant that car use rose during the same period by 28 per cent. Even a city such as Zurich, which has long had an excellent public transport system with one of the highest levels of use in the world, is now battling rising car use.[19]

In many European cities trams provide smooth access from suburbs and neighbouring towns straight into a partly pedestrianized city centre where the bus network is timetabled to link with the tram network. But trams can be expensive, which is why bus rapid transit (BRT) is viewed by some experts as perhaps the most important transportation initiative today. The main features of BRT systems include some combination of segregated bus lanes, techniques to hasten boarding and alighting using elevated platforms as for trains ('stations' rather than bus stops), fares collected prior to boarding, priority given to buses at intersections, and effective coordination at stations and terminals. The aim is to emulate rail transit without the high cost. Indeed, a few BRT operations have been able to move almost as many passengers in one bus lane as on one rail line and at a fraction of the cost. Rail lines in urban areas typically cost over \$100 million per mile in developing countries, whereas BRT costs less than one-tenth as much.[20]

For almost two decades, the only successful example of BRT was in Curitiba, Brazil. In the 1990s BRT systems were put in place in a number of major cities including Quito, São Paulo, Nagoya, Ottawa, Pittsburgh, Mexico City, Bogotá, Jakarta and Beijing. I have ridden the system in Quito, capital of Ecuador, where at one end of the route the buses snake through the narrow roads of the historic city centre. The speed of progress and quality of the journey is more like a train than a conventional bus. At present 33 US cities and 50 elsewhere have adopted BRT systems. There are five such schemes in Britain, where light rail schemes (trams and metros) are difficult to finance, and more should be possible on the basis that BRT can achieve 90 per cent of the patronage of light rail at 50 per cent of the cost.[21]

Where the road space is not available for long lengths of dedicated bus lanes, a variety of measures can be employed to promote bus use. London is a good example where improved bus services have been introduced in parallel with and funded by revenues from congestion charging. Bus patronage in London has increased by up to 7 per cent per annum over the last few years while traffic volumes have remained static, delivering a 4 per cent reduction in car-based modal share and up to 30 per cent reduction in congestion in central London. In contrast, in the same period, the other English metropolitan areas have collectively averaged a 4 per cent per annum decline in bus use, and seen a 7 per cent increase in traffic volumes, together with consequential increases in car-based modal share and traffic congestion. Nevertheless, in some larger urban areas like Nottingham, Brighton and Reading, as well as smaller to medium-sized towns like York, Cambridge and Telford, similar results to London have been achieved, often with modest investment.[22]

The other feature of public transport in London is of course a substantial underground rail system together with an extensive surface rail network. The public transport system as a whole is responsible for most travel within the city during the daytime when congestion charging operates. Of the million people commuting to central London each day, only 9 per cent use car or van, whereas nationally the proportion of trips by car for commuting or business purposes is 70 per cent. One consequence is considerable social inclusion. As I noted in Chapter 4, 80,000 people work at Canary Wharf, the 100-acre site of high-rise offices in London's Docklands. Three-quarters commute by public transport, which is remarkable given that these people are probably on average the highest paid in Britain and could certainly afford car-based commuting, were that feasible.[23]

## Trains

Railways were the great 19th-century transport innovation. The fate of this heritage in the early 21st century is surprisingly varied. In the US and most Latin American countries, passenger railways faded away as road and air travel developed. In Europe the typically shorter intercity journeys are well served by rail. France in particular has created a high-speed rail network on new tracks which competes effectively with air travel for internal journeys.

In Britain, the scope for such new fast rail routes is limited by existing land use and population location. Nevertheless, by the mid-1990s the long-term post-war decline came to an end and since then rail traffic has increased by 40 per cent, despite a number of problems resulting from the way the privatization of the former nationalized industry was carried out. However, rail's share of the total passenger market is only 7 per cent (expressed as passenger kilometres); cars and vans take over 80 per cent. This means that even if rail's share were to increase substantially, the impact on road use would be limited. The problem is that railways are very largely constrained to operate along historic tracks, and cannot adapt to meet the needs of the more varied and complex journey patterns outlined in previous sections.

The British government published a White Paper on the future of the railways in July 2007. The long-term ambition is to handle double today's level of traffic. The investments to achieve this include some new or substantially improved routes: the Channel Tunnel Rail Link, the West Coast Main Line with its tilting trains, the reinforced Thameslink service north to south through central London, as well as the east to west corridor Crossrail route. In addition there are plans to lengthen trains and platforms to reduce overcrowding, and to improve signalling techniques to permit a higher frequency of services on busy routes while maintaining safety.[24]

Those who support the White Paper approach argue that rail connectivity enables regeneration and resurgence of cities such as Manchester, Birmingham, Leeds, Bristol and many others, as well as London, both for interurban travel and commuting.[25] However, in thinking about the merits of this programme, which involves the government providing in excess of £15 billion of grants over a five-year period, it is important to recognize that investments that result in higher speeds will lead to people taking longer trips, given that average travel time is constant. So, the Channel Tunnel Rail Link (CTRL) knocks 20 minutes off travel time between London and Paris, and the West Coast improvements cut the London–Glasgow journey by about 45 minutes. These higher speeds should help rail compete with air travel for the full distance trips. But an important impact will be more long-distance commuting between intermediate stations, in particular longer commutes into London – in the same way that motorways designed for long-distance travel are used over short distances by car-based commuters. For instance, from Ebbsfleet on the Thames estuary, with 9000 car parking places at the station, commuting time to central London will be a mere 17 minutes along the new high-speed CTRL track.

Another example of this phenomenon is to be expected in the case of Crossrail, the east–west rail route, which requires an expensive tunnel under central London. This segment of Crossrail will reduce the travel time between the Paddington rail terminal in the west and the City by about 10 minutes. One consequence, I predict, is that the commuting range from the salubrious counties to the west of London will be extended by 10 minutes of high-speed rail and by a similar amount of time by car from villages more distant from intermediate stations. Is this extension of the catchment area for well remunerated City types – a particular instance of agglomeration benefits – worth the cost of Crossrail, I wonder?[26]

A virtue of Crossrail is that it will increase the overall capacity of London's railways by 10 per cent. In particular, capacity to Canary Wharf will increase by 50 per cent, and to the City by 20 per cent. What I think represents better value for money from rail investment are those measures that increase the capacity of routes without increasing speed – longer trains and platforms, and better signalling to permit more trains on the tracks, which unlike roads are empty most of the time, given that a seven-mile gap is currently required between trains on intercity routes in the interests of safety. There is certainly a need for more capacity on London's Underground, given population growth, but I suspect we'd get better value by improving signals in the existing tunnels to increase train frequency and reduce overcrowding.

Some rail enthusiasts were disappointed by the government's White Paper, seeing it as down playing the potential of high-speed rail.[27] I'll return to the potential for technological advance on the railways in Chapter 8. But with a journey time of a little over two hours between London and Manchester in modern trains running on upgraded track, it is not obvious we need to travel a lot faster.

One reason why there is enthusiasm for rail is that this is seen as less environmentally damaging than other modes of transport, particularly the underoccupied car and the aeroplane. Comparisons of carbon emissions for different modes of travel can be controversial since a number of assumptions must be made, particularly about the source of electricity and passenger occupancy. Underground trains perform well in respect of carbon emissions per passenger kilometre because of high occupancy, whereas for local trains emissions are close to those of cars.

Consider the data provided in the rail White Paper (which I would regard as reliable not least because of the high level of accountability expected of civil servants for the content of such official published documents).[28] Domestic air travel involves between 150 and 300 grams of carbon dioxide per passenger kilometre, the private car (assuming 1½ occupants on average) 150g, diesel rail 70–130g, and electric rail 50–100g. Overall, rail performs well from a carbon perspective, but there is scope to do better, for instance through reducing the weight of future train designs. Nevertheless, even if the capacity of the rail system were doubled and all the additional traffic transferred from the roads, this would deliver a reduction in total carbon dioxide emissions of only up to 1 per cent – worthwhile but not decisive, as the White Paper recognizes.

Somewhat paradoxically, environmentalists are enthusiastic about collective transport in the form of buses and trains, but averse to collective transport in the form of air travel. While the Greens have a point, they find it hard to persuade the rest of us to shrink our desire for mobility. Most people are keen on both cars and planes since these get us to where we want more quickly than the alternatives. Let's now turn to aviation. In so doing, we shift our attention from travel that takes place within the day to trips over longer distances which take us away from home overnight. Time remains a constraint, but in ways that are less apparent.

## Fear of flying

Tackling climate change has become a central theme of public policy. The concern is to limit global emissions of carbon dioxide and the other greenhouse gases. The main approach is by introducing some form of charge to reflect the amount of carbon emitted. In addition, we need to foster the development of new and improved energy and transport technologies, as well as tackle market failures and behaviours that prevent the uptake of low-cost reductions of emissions.[29] Transport is the fastest growing sector for energy use and greenhouse gas emissions, and aviation is the fastest expanding subsector within transport. This expansion reflects the attractions of air travel, both the increasing range of destinations on offer and easier affordability in competitive markets with rising personal incomes.

Politicians are in a dilemma. They tiptoe around the conundrum of aviation policy. How do we reconcile the need to limit greenhouse gas emissions with the popularity of ever increasing personal air travel?

Approximately 235 million passengers passed through UK airports in 2006, twice the number of just 12 years before. Freight carried by air also doubled over this period. The total number of passengers transported by air in the EU in 2005 was up by 8.5 per cent on the previous year.[30] This rapid growth in air travel is attributed to both rising incomes amongst travellers and falling fares. Fares paid by UK leisure travellers to 12 other EU countries fell in real terms by 6 per cent per annum on average in the six years to 2003. This was largely the result of competition in the short-haul market instigated by the no-frills budget carriers offering point-to-point services. Consumers now routinely expect low fares for European and domestic travel.[31]

This growth of demand puts pressure on airport capacity, particularly in the south-east of England where proposals for additional runway and terminal capacity have invariably met local resistance. In 2003 the British government published a White Paper entitled 'The Future of Air Transport', setting out a 30-year strategic framework that emphasized the increasing dependence of the economy on air travel. It was argued that the growth in the popularity and importance of air travel was set to continue over the next 30 years such that passenger numbers though British airports could rise to between 400 million and 600 million a year if sufficient capacity were provided. In 2007 these projections were reviewed and the range narrowed to 460–540 million in the absence of airport capacity constraints, with a central case for 495 million (slightly lower if some modest capacity constraints were assumed). This compares with 228 million in 2005. This growth implies an average of just under two return journeys per UK resident in 2030 compared with just under one today, and 58 million visits by foreign residents compared with 21 million today.[32]

The UK government takes the view that the provision of some additional airport capacity is essential if even part of the potential growth in demand is to be accommodated. Failure to provide additional capacity would become a barrier to future economic growth and competitiveness, it is argued. Airports would become more congested, air fares would rise as take-off and landing slots became increasingly sought-after, and much of the future growth in air travel – along with the associated economic growth – could in due course migrate elsewhere. In 2007 the government embarked on a public consultation about adding an extra runway at Heathrow airport.

This expansion of aviation must involve increased emissions of greenhouse gases. The government's latest estimate is that UK aviation carbon dioxide emissions are projected to grow from 37.5 million tonnes (mt) in 2005 to 60mt by 2030. Emissions are then projected to stay more or less steady at that level until 2050, largely due to airport capacity constraints and improved aircraft fuel efficiency. Aviation's share of the UK's total carbon dioxide emissions would rise from 6.4 per cent in 2005 to 20 per cent in 2050. These estimates allow for the effect of a charge for carbon emissions but exclude the effect of other aviation greenhouse gases. As well as carbon dioxide, aircraft engines emit water vapour and nitrogen oxides at altitude which contribute to climate change and which increase the impact by about two-fold. If the effect of other greenhouse gases is taken into account, aviation's share of climate change emissions would increase from 10 per cent currently to 30 per cent in 2050. These projections assume success in achieving the government's objective of a general 60 per cent reduction in carbon dioxide emissions (excluding aviation) by 2050.

The 60 per cent reduction policy was confirmed in the government's Climate Change Programme[33] and is to be put into practice by means of the Climate Change Bill introduced into parliament in late 2007. Carbon emissions from international aviation do not form part of the UK government's existing targets, nor are they covered by the Kyoto Protocol. However, the proposed legislation could be modified after enactment should targets for such emission be agreed internationally. The government is publicly committed to the inclusion of aviation in the EU Emissions Trading Scheme and would prefer global trading arrangements. Inclusion of aviation in such trading arrangements would ensure that growth in passenger numbers would require the airlines to purchase carbon emission permits, the cost of which would feed through into ticket prices.

Present government policy, then, is that aviation's share of Britain's contribution to global warming should be allowed to increase three-fold over the coming half-century while at the same time our overall contribution must be reduced by 60 per cent (or even 80 per cent, based on the latest science and a wish to avoid more than 2°C of warming – in which case aviation's share would rise even higher). Projections by knowledgeable independent analysts confirm the difficulty of fitting future aviation carbon emissions into the overall emissions level sought by the government. One such estimate suggests that the aviation industry would account for between 25 per cent and 50 per cent of the UK's 2050 carbon budget. Another is that with an overall carbon reduction target of 80 per cent by 2050 and continued aviation growth, the rest of the UK economy would need to reduce emissions by 95 per cent.[34]

There is an apparent incoherence here. It is difficult to see how these projected aviation growth rates and carbon emissions can be reconciled with the rest of environmental policy. The government's policy on climate change generally recognizes that present patterns of energy use cannot continue as usual, and that there will need to be substantial changes in technology and behaviour if a 60 per cent reduction in carbon emissions is to be achieved. In contrast, the government's aviation policy combines 'business as usual' projections of demand growth with a 'predict and provide' stance towards airport capacity. At the very least, aviation policy is going to stress-test climate change policy. What might be done to ease the pressures?

## Demand for air travel

The future development of demand for air travel needs critical reconsideration. It is possible that the official forecasts considerably exaggerate the prospects because too little account is taken of crucial changes that are now perhaps emerging. Projecting forward recent trends is understandable, given that it takes a brave forecaster to identify inflexions and turning points. Nevertheless, in the carbon-constrained world in which we now live, business does not always proceed as usual.[35]

Consider first the projections of demand for personal air travel. These are based on econometric modelling for which the main drivers are economic growth, air fares and world trade. A key issue for any rapidly growing market, not least aviation, is the degree to which it is approaching 'maturity'. The growth in demand for products and services can be characterized by three life-cycle phases. First, there is low growth following initial introduction with limited consumer awareness and supply. This is followed by a phase of rapid growth as the product achieves greater market awareness and supply expands to meet the new demand. Finally, slower growth once the product has become established and the market approaches saturation. It is usual for the rate of growth during the middle phase of the life cycle to be faster than the rate of growth of the economy as a whole. Obviously, this situation cannot persist indefinitely, which is why a transition to slower growth is inevitable. It is, however, difficult to predict where UK aviation is at present in this life cycle.

The view implicit in official forecasts is that aviation is a long way from market saturation, given that current usage amounts to just under one return trip a year for each UK resident, which could be judged well short of any maximum. However, this average conceals wide variation. Sixty-two per cent of those asked in the National Travel Survey in 2006 had not made any international flights in last 12 months, 21 per cent had made one flight, and 9 per cent had made three or more. Growth prospects for the aviation sector depend on whether the 60 per cent of non-fliers change their habits. Perhaps they won't, perhaps they don't fancy flying. Given the present low fares to many attractive destinations, it is unlikely that most of these non-fliers have been deterred by the cost. The question then is the appetite of the frequent fliers for yet more trips, bearing in mind the hassle of getting to and from the airports and coping with the many tedious queues. In 2007 it was taking five hours to get from the centre of London to the centre of Frankfurt via Heathrow airport, of which only 90 minutes was in the air.

In the longer term, time constraints would also be expected to limit demand for air travel, particularly for leisure purposes, just as time constrains surface travel, a central theme of this book. For those travellers who commute each day to business by plane – few in Europe, more in the US – this element of travel time has to be fitted into the daily schedule, as for travel generally. But for most of us, a trip by air is a slightly special event, involving significant time away from home, and it is this total amount of time that can constrain our use of aviation. For many frequent business flyers, this constraint already bites. Leisure trips are constrained by the amount of leisure time available to individuals, which is thought to be increasing more slowly than leisure air travel. This implies that air travel for leisure purposes will reach a level at which it is limited to lower growth by a time constraint. There is, of course, scope for individuals to reverse the recent trend of substituting several short breaks for a longer break taking the same amount of time, so saving on flying and its emissions. This is a particular possibility for retired people with a holiday home abroad, for whom current low air fares encourage frequent flying.

The Aviation White Paper made much of the link between air travel and economic growth. Around 25 million foreign visitors coming to Britain each year, two-thirds of whom come by air, contribute to a tourist industry that directly supports more than two million jobs. Businesses coming to Britain are attracted by our good air links, and airports are a magnet for other forms of development. In an increasingly competitive global marketplace, Britain's continuing success depends crucially on the strength of our international transport links. The aviation industry itself makes an important contribution to our economy, directly supporting around 200,000 jobs, and indirectly up to three times as many. That's the official line. But it's less convincing than it seems at first sight.

One important fact not stressed in the White Paper is that only a modest proportion of passengers passing through UK airports are travelling on business. Of the 54 million UK residents who travelled abroad by air in 2006, only 13 per cent were on business. The large majority were taking holidays or visiting family and friends. In the same year, 25 million overseas residents visited Britain by air, of which 27 per cent were on business.[36] Even at Heathrow, almost twice as many international passengers are travelling for leisure purposes as on business trips. Evidently, sufficient airport capacity already exists for continued growth of premium business travel with its economic benefits, if this could be at the expense of non-business flying.

Another source of airport capacity lies in the fact that Britain's airports, Heathrow in particular, are important centres of international air travel. One fifth of all international passengers in the world are on flights to or from Britain, and a quarter of passenger traffic through London's airports comprises people connecting between flights. Three-quarters of these are overseas residents.[37] While some are connecting to UK destinations, many are in transit between other countries, for instance between Europe and the Americas. This represents good business for Britain's airlines. But again this is traffic that could migrate elsewhere without loss to the non-aviation sector of the British economy if our airports were to become busier with passengers who live or stay in the country. This would be to the commercial disadvantage of British carriers, unless they were able to acquire landing slots at airports in Europe.

Business travel tends to be less price sensitive than non-business travel.[38] So if the cost of air travel rose in real terms, contrary to recent trends, then leisure travel would be most affected. A slowdown in the growth of tourism in the UK would not be insupportable for the hospitality industry. Tourist hotspots seem already to be full to their limit during the peak season. And the same applies to many tourist destinations in the countries to which UK residents travel by air, with valued environments coming under increasing stress. When one Sunday newspaper magazine proclaims on its cover that it will disclose 'The 20 best kept travel secrets: where the travel professionals get away from it all', surely we are going too far?[39]

What increases to air fares might arise from incorporating the impact of aviation on climate change? The most recent UK government estimates of demand employ a central assumption that passengers will face an additional cost linked to their emissions charged at £19 per tonne of carbon dioxide, rising at 2 per cent per annum in real terms. However, the projections indicate that demand for air travel is relatively insensitive to variations in the cost of carbon emissions: 495 million passengers per annum in 2030 on the central case, down by 5 million if the cost of carbon goes up 20 per cent, up 5 million if the cost falls by 10 per cent. Other studies support the conclusion that the demand for aviation is relatively insensitive to the cost of flying.[40]

One reason why air travel seems insensitive to changes in cost is that with the relative fall in fares, their proportion of total trip expenses has declined. For instance, it is no longer the case that transport to and from holiday destinations constitutes a major, if not the biggest, part of holiday expenses. A survey of outbound leisure passengers at Stansted airport indicated that the share of air fares in total expenditure on holidays abroad is, on average, somewhere in the range of 25–35 per cent.[41]

We have then a situation in which the real cost of air travel has been falling and demand has been growing vigorously, while the prospects for reversing this trend through taxes or charges related to the carbon and other emissions from aircraft seem modest at best. So we don't yet have a resolution to the conundrum that aviation carbon emissions seem set to become a large, even dominant, part of total UK emissions – unless we are nearer to meeting the underlying demand for air travel than is generally supposed.

## The price of flying

I next consider the possibility that the demand for air travel, particularly non-business demand, could be more sensitive to price than is presently believed (more 'price elastic', as economists would put it). The arrival of the low-cost airlines in the UK market over the past decade and more has certainly reduced fares, but has not affected the overall rate of growth of air travel.[42] The no-frills carriers have grown at the expense of scheduled and charter flights, helped by promotional marketing that seems to offer off-season travel at trivial prices. One interpretation of this development is that without the boost provided by these lower fares, the rate of growth of demand for air travel would have begun to flatten off. So if there were a reversal of the downward trend in air fares, the fall-off in demand might be greater than analysts are currently predicting. We might in fact be nearer market maturity than is generally envisaged.

A further possibility is that the price of carbon will be considerably higher than is presently expected. As I discussed in Chapter 2, the main approach to tackling climate change is through an international system for trading emission permits. The leading development is the European Union Emissions Trading Scheme (EU ETS) which allows permits for carbon emissions to be bought and sold. Businesses which can reduce their emissions through improved efficiency can sell their surplus permits, while those that need more to expand activities can purchase permits at the market price. As in any market, the price at which carbon trades sends signals about the technologies in which it will be best to invest. A key driver of the market price is the overall cap on carbon emissions which for each member state must be consistent with the requirements of the Kyoto Protocol (and its successor). Under this the UK must reduce its greenhouse gas emissions by 12.5 per cent below base year levels over the 2008–12 commitment period. Britain has in fact committed itself to go beyond this target by setting a national goal to reduce carbon dioxide emissions by 20 per cent below 1990 levels by 2010.

At present the EU ETS does not include the aviation sector. However, there is a strong policy impetus to bring aviation in. This is supported by the British government, the European Commission, and much of the aviation industry, as well as by Friends of the Earth.[43] One reason that the industry supports inclusion of their business in the ETS is that this offers the prospect of less restraint on growth than other approaches to limiting the impact of the aviation sector. Analyses sponsored by the European Commission suggest that the initial impact of including aviation in the ETS would be quite small, whether judged by the extra cost of fares, the reduction in demand for flying, or the cost of carbon to other sectors of the economy. This is consistent with the UK government's forecasts, discussed above, that aviation growth is insensitive to the price of carbon.

One reason for the limited impact of carbon trading on aviation is that this sector would have the opportunity to purchase carbon credits from other industry sectors where it is cheaper to 'decarbonize'. Another is that the Kyoto Protocol allows various kinds of investment in carbon-saving technologies to be made in countries that are developing or in transition to full development. Rich countries that fund such investment can get carbon credits to set against their own emissions. It is supposed that the combination of such imported credits, plus credits sold by other sectors of the domestic economy, would be sufficient to permit the aviation sector to continue in business as usual for the next few decades.

Growing demand by aviation for carbon credits would tend to increase their price. Much depends on what happens in other sectors. The price of carbon would be lower, and the headroom for air travel greater, if the electricity generation sector moved strongly towards either nuclear power or renewables or both; if we could deploy technologies for capturing and storing carbon from coal-burning plant; if surface transport could switch from fossil fuels; and if we achieved big efficiency savings in our energy consumption at home and in energy-intensive industries. Conversely, if all these approaches proved to be slow and difficult, then we would find that air travel was becoming much less affordable.

So while in principle bringing aviation into a properly policed international emission trading scheme should ensure that this sector plays its part in overall carbon emission reductions, just how much reduction there will be in the growth of flying is hard to assess at present. More expensive air travel would lead to a change in the balance between business and leisure flying. Business travel is less sensitive to price increases than the holiday trips we pay for out of our own pockets. So business travellers will continue to make their important journeys, though they will restrict themselves somewhat on the less essential trips (and similarly for air freight, with highest value goods prioritized). The global economy as a whole would not suffer appreciably, although there would be lower growth in the tourism and aviation industries than either has been used to in recent years. But neither sector seems at all likely to contract.

Leisure travel by air can be very cheap under current conditions. It would be desirable to send price signals about future costs to the leisure market sooner rather than later. If people are investing in overseas holiday homes on the assumption that cheap air fares will continue indefinitely, it would be sensible to give them an early warning about higher future prices. A similar situation arises when people contemplate taking a job that is an air trip away from their main home, whether on the basis of daily or weekly commuting. To send suitable price signals in advance of the long-run price of carbon working through into ticket prices, various forms of tax or charge are proposed. These include taxing aviation kerosene at the level petrol is taxed, and charging VAT on tickets. The government's preferred option is the Air Passenger Duty, added to each air fare, which was doubled in 2007 to between £10 and £80, depending on the distance and class of travel. The intention in future is to transform this duty into a per aircraft tax, to cover cargo and private planes and to make the rate reflect more closely distances travelled as well as to encourage aircraft to fly at full capacity.

Most people pay the duty at the lowest rate, however, which doesn't have much impact on their decision to fly. And raising charges in this way tends to be unpopular with the public and the airlines, which makes politicians nervous. So the prospects for using taxation to constrain the growth of air travel do not look promising.

Another way in which flying could get a bit more expensive is if more of us make the personal decision to offset the impact of our flights by paying a sum to help fund projects around the world to reduce, avoid or absorb greenhouse gas emissions. This is known as 'carbon offsetting'. For instance, British Airways will calculate your personal emissions by dividing the total fuel used on a journey by the number of passengers on the flight. For my recent holiday in Menorca, BA estimated that my carbon dioxide emissions would amount to 0.3 tonnes, for which they would seek the very modest payment of £2.24 to offset this by investing in projects for renewable energy, energy efficiency and forest restoration. There has been some dubious practice in the use made of carbon-offsetting funds and the government proposes a voluntary code of practice to improve standards.[44] However, whether or not credibility is restored, given both the need for an individual decision and the low payment sought, it seems unlikely that carbon offsetting will have an appreciable impact on the amount of flying.

The expansion of air travel envisaged in the Aviation White Paper – doubling or trebling over the next 30 years – would require a substantial increase in airport capacity, both runways and terminals. The White Paper and subsequent government forecasts envisage that two new runways will be needed in the south-east of England, a second one at Stansted and a third at Heathrow. But even if these are built, flying would still be constrained by airport capacity, which is why current projections show growth of carbon emissions from aviation flattening off after 2030.

## The future of aviation

The Department for Transport wants more runways in the near term while recognizing that airport capacity constrains air travel for its longer term forecasts of carbon emissions from aviation. Even so, aviation's projected share of total UK carbon emissions seems implausibly large. Projections of continued rapid growth of air travel, largely for leisure purposes, imply that consumers will have little difficulty in affording the costs associated with decarbonizing the rest of the economy – major and rapid changes in technology for electricity generation and surface transport, and huge efforts to reduce energy consumption of homes and commercial buildings. This optimistic view might be consistent with the conclusion of the Stern Review of the economics of climate change, that the annual cost of stabilizing the climate would be around 1 per cent of global GDP if we act now. On the other hand, the likely difficulty of securing agreement to the post-Kyoto regime suggests the existence of a widespread perception that the costs could be considerably higher.

The paradox of present official aviation policy is that it implies that we will use a large proportion of the UK's carbon budget for leisure travel by plane. This does not seem to me to be convincing. It would be sensible to hold off building more runways until the long-term impact of the ETS on the growth of aviation becomes clearer. It could work like the housing market. There is high demand for housing in the prosperous parts of Britain. House building is limited by the availability of land with planning permission. We could make more such land available in the green belts around our cities if we chose, but we feel rather protective of the countryside. So there is a tension here between two different needs, and increasing public debate on what to do. The outcome might be a bit of a shift in the balance towards meeting housing need. But we're unlikely to give up the green belts, and so will continue to live with relatively high-priced housing.

In a similar way, if we do not increase runway capacity, the growth of flying would be constrained. A halt to runway expansion pending a clearer vision of the impact of carbon trading on aviation would represent a responsible environmental policy stance. To ensure that flights of highest value secure priority, for instance those for predominantly business travel, it would be desirable that scarce landing and take-off opportunities at airport (known as 'slots') should be allocated in a transparent market-based way. At present slots are held largely on the basis of historic entitlements with subsequent trading in a grey market. But there are strong arguments for allowing open trading in slots, an approach endorsed in the Aviation White Paper.[43] Moreover, if slot trading is allowed across the EU, efficient UK airlines would be able to expand into Europe, even if opportunities in the south-east of England were constrained.

If runway capacity were not allowed to grow, those who live near noisy airport flight paths would be pleased. Because of scarcity, the airlines would be able to charge higher fares. They and the airports would then be able to afford to provide better services for their customers – who surely need this, given the fairly horrible experience that is the norm at most busy airports. More check-in desks, more security channels, and faster throughput, with less hanging around, that's what we want. If there has to be a constraint on the growth of the *quantity* of air travel to limit climate change, then what we need is an improvement of the *quality* of the experience.

If take-off and landing slots are tradable, the profits of the industry would be redistributed, with those carriers facing weakening demand being able to cash in some of their slot entitlements. If the overall profits of the industry are judged to be excessive, then some kind of profits tax might be contemplated, to secure a share of the windfall from higher fares for taxpayers at large. One possibility would be a tax on the value of traded slots, analogous to stamp duty on property transactions. The politically important point is that any tax change would follow the emergence of profits arising from higher air fares, and would not drive the fare increase.

The Department for Transport's stance on runways is similar to its attitude to roads, where it pays lip service to the idea that we can't build our way out of congestion and must limit transport sector carbon emission, while continuing a large road building programme. The Department is comfortable with its traditional role of building infrastructure to meet travel demand, but is not comfortable with the trickier task of managing demand. This stance is understandable but not defensible in a carbon-constrained world.

# 7

# Individual Effort

One important advance in transport thinking in recent years is the idea that we should encourage the 'slow modes' – walking and cycling. Environmentalists, public health advocates and transport professionals can all agree. Walking and cycling are good for health, help reduce congestion and vehicle emissions, and boost social interactions and a sense of community, it is argued.[1]

## Slow modes

There's no doubt that most of us could do with more exercise. Around 60 per cent of men and 70 per cent of women are not physically active enough to benefit their health. Many people are looking for ways to be more physically active, which is important if we are to reverse the rising incidence of obesity. We can fit exercise into the day-to-day routine, in a way that is economical of both money and time, if we are able to walk safely in local streets and have access to more routes designed with cyclists and pedestrians in mind. Nearly a quarter of the trips we make are one mile or less, generally a walkable distance. Another 40 per cent of journeys are within two miles, less than the average length of a cycle trip.[2]

I can vouch for the attractions of regular cycling. Some of this book was written at my desk at home, but much was pulled together at the Centre for Transport Studies, University College London, a 20-minute bike ride away. The morning ride sharpens up the reflexes, mental and physical, as you navigate through and around the sluggish rush-hour traffic. The return in the evening, slightly uphill, provides moderate aerobic exercise. And the shower at the end of that ride sets you up for the evening's activities. Admittedly, rain is a bit of a dampener, in both senses, but it's rarer than you might think in the two fairly short daily time slots. It's not just the health benefits of cycling that I extol. You're independent of the vagaries of public transport and not much affected by traffic congestion, so journey time is predictable. Moreover, for me, and I suspect most cyclists, there is a real pleasure and a sense

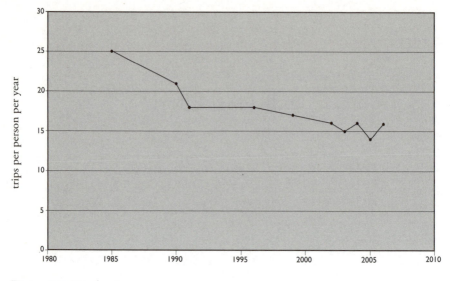

**Figure 7.1** *Bicycle trips per person per year*

*Source*: *National Travel Survey 2005*, Table 3.7; and *National Travel Survey 2006*, Table 3.2

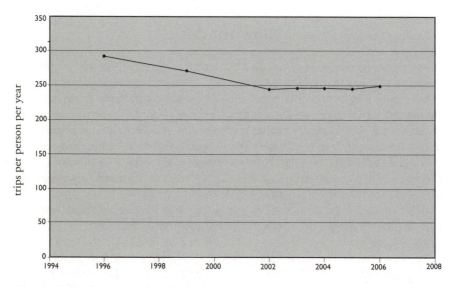

**Figure 7.2** *Walking trips per person per year*

*Source*: *National Travel Survey 2006*, Table 3.2

of virtue in bike-based mobility, where you're using your own efforts to go places, sustainably, with pretty much zero environmental impact.

So why isn't cycling more popular in Britain? Figure 7.1 shows that bicycle riding in Britain has been in slow decline over the past 20 years, albeit with evidence of recent levelling off. This is the case in terms both of the average number of trips made and average distance travelled. Figure 7.2 shows that walking has also declined, rather than increased, over the past ten years, despite government policy supportive of both walking and cycling. For instance, a National Cycling Strategy was announced in 1996 with targets of doubling the number of cycle journeys by 2002 and quadrupling them by 2012 – evidently a total failure.[3]

There is a good reason why these slow modes are proving difficult to boost. The whole history of transport has involved going faster, within the time we allow ourselves for travel, to get access to a greater choice of destinations. So persuading people to opt for these slower forms of travel tends to deprive them of the range of choice to which they have become accustomed. Even the suggestion that you walk to the local shop, rather than take the car, can seem problematic if you're trying to fit too many activities into the 24-hour day of which travel time amounts on average to only a single hour.

The general exercise of choice through mobility has repercussions. Suppose the village shop closes. Access to the services it provided is reduced, as is the opportunity for shopping on foot or by bike. Travel to shops in the nearest town increases, and those without use of a car are disadvantaged. Bad news all round, it seems. However, the reason why the shop closed is that the competing services offered elsewhere are seen by many as preferable – in terms of choice, quality or value for money – even after taking account of the extra travel cost and travel time. So for the majority who can take advantage of car-based mobility, the better accessibility of the village shop is a secondary consideration, as are the loss of walking and cycling opportunities.[4]

Nevertheless, there surely must be potential for increasing walking and cycling. I mentioned Copenhagen in the last chapter as the only European city to have prevented growth in car traffic over last 30 years. Since 1962, when it was decided to make the city centre more attractive for pedestrians and cyclists, cycling has increased by 65 per cent and pedestrian journeys by 25 per cent. However, central Copenhagen is only a small part of Denmark. For the country as a whole, car use dominates, exceeding bicycle use by fifteen-fold (vehicle kilometres).[5]

The cities of the Netherlands are famous for their cyclists. The Dutch make 28 per cent of urban trips by bike, compared with 4 per cent in Britain. Nevertheless, there is extensive interurban travel via a trunk road network which is amongst the densest in the world as well as being overcrowded. In consequence, 48 per cent of all journeys are made by car, only 5 per cent by public transport and 27 per cent by bicycle. For Britain, the roughly comparable figures are 70 per cent, 15 per cent and 2 per cent. The popularity of cycling in the Netherlands is therefore partly at the expense of public transport use, which is not so helpful in relation to the objectives of reducing congestion and vehicle emissions.[6]

Cycling in London has increased markedly in recent years, up by over 80 per cent in 2007 compared with 2000. This is in part the result of substantial investment in cycling facilities by Transport for London – including cycle tracks, parking places and training. Nevertheless, the 400,000 daily bike trips represent less than 2 per cent of the 24 million trips by all transport modes that take place in London each day.[7]

One way of promoting cycling in city centres is to make bikes readily available for rent. Such arrangements can be found in a number of European cities, of which Paris is the most noteworthy. This successful scheme started in July 2007 with 10,000 distinctively designed bikes at 750 locations, with the intent to grow quickly to double those numbers. The high density of locations means that the average distance from a random point to a bike location would be only about 90 metres, so a bike is always close to hand. There is a low subscription price of €1 a day or €29 a year, €150 on a credit card for security deposit, rental is free for first half hour, €1 for the second, then escalating rates to encourage short hires. You never have to worry about someone stealing your bike since once you park at a location it's no longer yours.[8] However, the main impact of such bike schemes seems likely to divert people from public transport, rather than from their cars.

While it is possible to make quite substantial improvements to the historic centre of major cities to make them attractive for residents and visitors, as well as local businesses, those who live and work there tend largely to be self-selected 'urbanites' who are able to take advantage of the facilities close to hand and very often are content not to have a car, using public transport, walking and cycling to get around. But when circumstances change, for instance with the arrival of small children, then the suburbs and the car, or even cars plural, become the more attractive lifestyle. In any event, most people live outside city centres, even in densely populated countries. What are the prospects for reducing car use there?

The UK sustainable transport charity, Sustrans, has ambitious plans to stitch together existing cycle routes and develop new ones into a country-wide network. Twice the original target of 2500 miles to be built by 2000 was achieved and the 10,000-mile mark was reached in 2005. The National Cycle Network now passes within one mile of half the population and as it continues to grow so does its popularity – 230 million trips were made on the network in 2005 alone.[9] Averaged across the whole population, however, this amounts to less than four trips per person per year, out of a total of a thousand trips a year. So while it is very attractive in many respects, the overall impact is pretty modest.

## Soft measures

There are a variety of techniques for influencing people's travel behaviour towards more sustainable options, including the encouragement of school, workplace and individualized travel planning; marketing services such as travel awareness campaigns; car share schemes; supporting car clubs and encouraging teleworking and teleconferencing. In Britain these are branded as 'Smarter Choices', no doubt to help people feel good about opting for them. The potential of changing behaviour is apparent from the fact that at 8.45am on a weekday term-time morning 18 per cent of urban traffic is on the 'school run'.[10]

The evidence base for this promotional activity is a detailed report by Sally Cairns and colleagues of the practical experience of a variety of 'soft' measures aimed at helping people to reduce car use while enhancing the attractiveness of alternatives. One conclusion was that a more intense use of such measures could potentially result in a reduction in peak period urban traffic of about 21 per cent, peak non-urban traffic of about 14 per cent, and a nationwide reduction in all traffic of about 11 per cent. This could reduce congestion substantially, but would attract more car use by other people (the familiar phenomenon of induced traffic) unless other measures were put in place to prevent this. Measures to safeguard the traffic reduction benefits of smarter choice measures include reallocation of road space away from cars in favour of pedestrians, public transport and cyclists; parking controls and traffic calming; and congestion charging or other traffic restraint.[11]

This is one example of a general need to 'lock in' the benefits of any approach to congestion reduction through demand management measures. From the perspective developed in this book, the effect of these soft measures is to divert some drivers away from car use. This will result in less congestion and hence higher speeds, which in turn will permit other drivers to make longer trips within the time they have available for travel. Longer trips mean more traffic, which negates the congestion reduction. The net result is that, without 'locking in', those people influenced by the soft measures make less use of their cars (good for their pockets and their health), while those not so influenced may make more use.[12]

What is not clear is whether those influenced to adopt 'smart choices' end up with less access – because travel by car tends to be quicker door-to-door – and indeed whether such perceived loss of speed is what limits uptake of these soft measures. I suspect that those who can be persuaded to give up car use are those for whom this is practicable at the time, on account for instance of living conveniently close enough to work and not having kids to cart around. But if circumstances change, these same people could be back in their cars, although then there would be others, for whom circumstances changed the opposite way, who could be targeted for the smarter choices treatment.

Prompted by the evidence for the potential benefits of soft measures, the UK Department for Transport in 2005 initiated a programme aimed at influencing people's travel behaviour towards more sustainable options such as walking, cycling, car sharing and public transport. It was recognized that these smarter choices would need to be combined with hard traffic restraint measures, to lock in the benefits. One important initiative is the Sustainable Travel Demonstration Towns, a five-year project which aims to demonstrate the effect that a sustained package of *smarter choices* measures can have when coupled with infrastructure improvements. Darlington, Peterborough and Worcester are the test sites, where 'individualized travel marketing' was a key component. This approach uses marketing techniques to persuade individuals to change their travel behaviour. Results over the first 12–18 months seem encouraging. In one part of Worcester public transport trips were boosted by 14 per cent, walking by 17 per cent, cycling by 32 per cent, and car trips were reduced by 13 per cent. However, even after these changes, car driver trips dominated at 420 per person per year, while bike trips and public transport trips were 30 and 90 respectively. A review of the research findings and case studies covering nearly a quarter of a million targeted households indicated that car trips were reduced by 11 per cent in the targeted population, with walking the main beneficiary.[13]

These favourable outcomes reflect changed behaviour by those experiencing the individualized travel marketing technique. But in the three demonstration towns no measures seem to have been taken to lock in the benefits of less car use by the targeted individuals. It is not known whether there has been any overall change in traffic levels because this was not measured, or at least not reported. It would not be technically easy to measure small reductions in total traffic due to local drivers making fewer short trips, in part because of traffic passing through the town to and from external destinations. So those who are sceptical about the case for soft measures to persuade drivers to drive less have a point. The clincher to justify smarter choices would be evidence of overall lower traffic levels and/or lower carbon emissions – and that we don't have, yet. Part of the problem is how to lock in benefits. If you take away road space by constructing cycle and bus lanes, for instance, you could hope to achieve carbon savings, but not reduced congestion.[14]

Recently, an amiable young man from the local council called at our house, and the others in the street, to persuade us of the possibilities for using the car less. Subsequently he sent a Personalized Travel Planning pack, 'tailored to suit your particular requirements', to give us 'a clearer picture of your local travel alternatives'. This contained two bus maps, three cycle maps, three leaflets about cycling, one local rail timetable, three rail maps, a leaflet about how to pay for public transport, two leaflets about discounts on rail travel, a leaflet about safe travel at night, and a couple of other leaflets. We make rather little use of our car – only about 3000 miles a year – but do use a bicycle and public transport. So there was not much scope to shift our travel behaviour. However, one thing that has indeed changed our driving behaviour a bit has been the introduction of congestion charging in central London during weekday working hours. It is rare that we find it necessary to pay this charge since other modes of travel are better value for money.

This underlines the issue of hard measures (such as the congestion charge) versus soft measures (such as the information pack or individualized travel marketing). Both the researchers, who carried out the 'smart choices' study, and the Department for Transport itself recognize the need for hard measures of traffic restraint to be implemented to 'lock in' the benefits of the soft measures. The question then is which of these is more important. Arguably, it is the hard measures that really matter – they have teeth. The soft measures can be seen as complementary and facilitating, nice but not essential since people would learn to adapt in any event. Soft measures alone certainly seem to be able to change the behaviour of significant numbers of individuals to use travel modes other than the car. However, by freeing up road space, average traffic speeds would be increased. This in turn would permit the majority who choose to continue to use their cars to gain access to a greater choice of destinations in the more-or-less fixed amount of time they have for travel. In any event, for most people concerns about the environment are a weak motivator for changing travel behaviour.[15]

Soft measures alone seem unlikely either to deliver transport policy objectives, or to contribute much to climate change targets. While virtuous in many ways and deserving of support, we need to be careful not to be distracted from the difficult but unavoidable hard measures. What is needed is fairly rigorous evaluation of each and every soft or smart intervention, measuring their impact on traffic levels and carbon emissions. We should not count these particular chickens before they hatch.

# Personal action

Our personal willingness to volunteer, or be persuaded, to change our travel behaviour is part of a wider question concerning the role of the individual in countering climate change. Chris Goodall, author of the recent book *How to Live a Low-carbon Life*, is sceptical of government action to tackle climate change, which he argues has been ineffective. 'The only possible route forward is, therefore, for individual citizens to take action to change their styles of life in order to minimize their own responsibility for emissions.' This is possible because about half of the 12½ tonnes of greenhouse gases that on average we each emit every year arises from the way we run our lives, in our homes and as we travel. Goodall thinks that no institution or market mechanism has any prospect of effective reduction of fossil fuel use. He urges us to use our cars less but goes on: 'I will ignore the appalling possibility that, by reducing congestion, using your car less will encourage others to use theirs more, thus wiping out any benefit from your actions. This kind of economist's logic creates inertia and despair.'[16]

Appalling or not, the logic is not merely theoretical but what is observed when congestion is eased by road widening. I would expect any means of congestion relief to have a similar effect, including the virtuous behaviour of some drivers in giving up their cars. More generally, I myself am sceptical about the likelihood of enough individuals voluntarily changing their lifestyles to make a significant difference to the carbon arising from the transport system. So collective action seems essential. Indeed, new forms of collective action are how we respond to new challenges in a democratic society. No need for inertia or despair. There is of course scope for action by committed individuals to demonstrate to the rest of us what might be practicable and acceptable.

One kind of approach that combines the individual and the collective would be legally binding individual carbon budgets, which would be tradable. This approach has been urged by Mayer Hillman, a persuasive prophet of the future of the planet. Personal carbon trading is based on the concept that each citizen would be allocated an equal 'carbon allowance', which would fall over time as part of cap-and-trade arrangements (described in Chapter 2). These carbon allowances would be surrendered electronically when purchasing fuel and electricity, possibly using existing credit and debit cards. People using less than their share could sell the surplus to people or businesses using more than their allotted share, via a market. In this way, it would provide an incentive for every individual to take steps to reduce the emissions for which they are directly responsible. The Royal Society for Arts is running a pilot project to see how this might work in practice, including in the transport sector. David Miliband, when Secretary of State for the Environment, made a speech drawing attention to the potential advantages of personal carbon trading, promising further official analysis.[17]

One attractive possibility would be to combine the hard measure of personal carbon trading with hard measures to constrain traffic growth. The latter would include congestion charging, parking constraints, traffic calming, speed limitations, and reallocating road space to pedestrians and cyclists. In this way we would bear down on both carbon emissions and congestion, with the 'policy stress' spread over two kinds of instrument. Spreading the stress seems likely to be important since the aim would be to slow, and then very possibly halt or even reverse the long-term trend towards ever greater mobility. This will be tough because reducing mobility reduces choice.

## Mobility and choice

Choice has become a much debated topic in recent years. Do we have too much choice, particularly of consumer goods? Barry Schwartz, in his influential book *The Paradox of Choice*, records a trip to a small US supermarket where he found 285 varieties of cookies, 85 kinds of juices, 95 varieties of crisps, 230 soup offerings, 120 different pasta sauces, 275 varieties of cereal and 175 types of tea bags. Supermarkets today carry more than 30,000 items, and 20,000 new products are introduced each year – and almost all of them are doomed to failure. Schwartz argues that having too many choices produces psychological distress – disappointment and depression. Chris Anderson, in his equally influential book *The Long Tail*, draws attention to the way the internet allows almost unlimited choice, which people do in fact exercise. A book or record store is physically able to stock only a certain range of better-selling titles, which limits sales. An on-line provider can stock everything in print and finds that nearly every title makes sales. Many of these – the 'long tail' of the sales figures – sell in small numbers, handfuls or less a year, but there are so many of them that in aggregate they add up to big business.[18]

There is of course a big difference between books and groceries. You might feel that 285 varieties of biscuits would be more than enough, whereas 285 book titles on the airport bookstall might not be sufficient for you to choose something new and interesting for your journey. For books, music and movies it would be hard to argue for constraining choice on grounds of psychological distress – and indeed these subjects are not found in the index of Barry Schwartz's book. As for other consumer goods, we'll see if there is a reaction by the customers against excessive choice. I'd be doubtful myself.

Internet shopping allows us the maximum possible choice of high-value compact items like books and electronic arts, as well as fairly extensive choice of consumer goods, groceries and so on that can be delivered to our door by post or by white van. Moreover, if such means of purchase are substitutes for shopping by car, then the distance travelled per shopping load could in theory be reduced by 70 per cent or more. However, I would expect that less time spent travelling to the shops would be offset by more time spent travelling to other destinations, given the constant average travel time. This is particularly to be expected when people who feel short of time use the internet to shop rather than go shopping in person. So I would not be optimistic about home-delivered shopping as a great saver of traffic.[19]

The more important point is that internet shopping could sustain choice of consumer goods at a time when carbon and congestion concerns may well limit our physical mobility. I'll take up the relationship between information and telecommunications technologies and physical transport in the next chapter.

# Ageing population

The relationship between choice and mobility is important also for another aspect of modern living – ageing, both individually and for the population as a whole. As we get older, disabilities of various kinds become commoner. These may affect walking, vision, hearing and cognitive function. We may suffer from single such disabilities, and indeed some have the misfortune to be afflicted from an early age as a result of an accident of birth or genetic inheritance. Others may be hit in mid-life by illness or injury. In later life multiple minor disabilities are common – relatively small losses of ambulation, vision and hearing perhaps, which in combination pose a significant challenge to getting about. The population of the earth is ageing as life expectancy increases. In Britain and many other developed countries, this phenomenon will be exacerbated by the ageing of the baby boomers, the numerically larger generation born after the Second World War who will be coming up to retirement in the next decade or two.

Mobility – being able to get around to do the things you want – is important for quality of life not just in old age but throughout the life course. Mobility is not just about being able to visit friends and family and reach desired destinations. There are also psychological benefits of movement, of getting out and about, to which the good feelings from much leisure travel contribute. For country walks and bike rides, sailing, boating, skiing and so forth, the journeying contributes substantially to the overall benefits of the trip, in addition to the pleasures to be found at the destination. The exercise benefits of walking and cycling also contribute to this class of 'destination-independent' benefits of travel, as does involvement in the local community and support networks helped by encountering neighbours face to face.[20]

All these benefits of mobility are at risk of being lost in later life on account of increasing frailty. Consequently, there are quite a number of policies in place to promote the mobility of older and disabled people. In Britain, undoubtedly the most popular is free off-peak travel on local buses (in London this extends to the Underground and rail travel). There is extensive anecdotal evidence that this offering is well used and promotes mobility, at least for those fit enough to use public transport. A variety of measures are in place to counter the effects of age-associated disabilities that hinder mobility, including low-floor buses, subsidized taxis and community transport schemes. Disability discrimination legislation promotes access to public transport vehicles for older people and people with disabilities. The motor car is of increasing importance in later life, particularly for those with disabilities, and a variety of design and technological approaches are being brought to bear to maintain the mobility of older people. These various efforts undoubtedly enhance the mobility of older people. But it is hard to judge to what extent all reasonable needs are being met.[21]

Accommodating people with disabilities by the transport system has generally been seen as an 'add-on' to mainstream policy and practice. My colleague Professor Nick Tyler argues persuasively for an inclusive approach. Nick is the Chadwick Professor of Civil Engineering at University College London. Edwin Chadwick was a social reformer whose report in 1842 entitled 'The Sanitary Conditions of the Labouring Population' was an influential call for public health reform, including provision of a constant supply of fresh clean water, toilets in every house, and a system of carrying sewage away. While civil engineers tend to be best known for the construction of massive structures such as bridges and dams, there is also a tradition of what used to be called 'municipal engineering'. This aspect is concerned with mundane matters such as sewers and the elements that go to make a public transport system, including bus stops, the design of which is the subject of a book by Nick Tyler (there is more to this than is apparent at first thought).

A person's business card is a mini-biography. Nick Tyler's includes the standard credentials of a university professor (MSc, PhD), plus a couple to be expected of a senior civil engineer (CEng and FICE, Chartered Engineer and Fellow of the Institute of Civil Engineers). But there is one other that indicates an unusual pedigree: ARCM, Associate of the Royal College of Music. Nick started out as a professional oboist. When work was short he supplemented his income by driving for a logistics and distribution firm that then offered him management training. This led him to undertake a master's degree in transport planning and management, and then to take a research job at UCL concerning bus systems in Brazil. Subsequently he set up the Accessibility Research Group which aims to understand how people are disabled by poor design of the transport system, so that they can be provided with accessible systems that enable them to achieve their potential.

As befits a renaissance man, Nick Tyler quotes philosophers such as Rousseau and Rawls in discussion of what society owes to the individuals that constitute it. He argues that transport is the means by which society coheres, people meet and carry out daily activities, and freedom of choice and independent living are made real. Taking account of justice and fairness, we should aim for an inclusive transport system, as far as possible. We should focus on the design of public transport, especially the bus, because this tends to be the default system, for instance for those no longer able to drive a car.[22]

Earlier thinking about disability focused on medical aspects. If the deficiency could be remedied through a surgical or medical intervention, all well and good. Otherwise the disability would have to be borne. However, younger people with disabilities that could not be fixed were reluctant to accept that nothing could be done for them. They argued that the real problem was that people were disabled because society had not learnt to accommodate them. This led to legislation that gives disabled people rights in a variety of areas including access to goods, facilities and services, and that requires public bodies to promote equality of opportunity for disabled people. It also allows the government to set minimum standards so that disabled people can use public transport easily. This societal focus on disability, following on from the earlier medical focus, represents real progress. But we need to move on and now focus on the individual, Nick Tyler argues.

Individuals have certain capabilities. As I write, I am recovering from a sprained ankle, so my ambulatory capabilities are reduced somewhat. I am cautious when crossing a busy road because I know that I am not as agile as I would be usually. I expect to recover from this particular disability, but I know that at some point in later life I'm likely to suffer from a chronic disability of some kind that will limit my functioning as a pedestrian, public transport user or driver.

As well as the capabilities of the individual, what is also important are the capabilities demanded of them by the environment in which they function. If I am able to walk only slowly because of my sprained ankle, then what becomes important is the time allowed for me to get across a pedestrian crossing equipped with traffic signals. Too little time, and I may not feel confident about using that crossing. If facilities are designed for the average user – or worse, for the fit young person like the typical designer of such facilities – older and disabled people will tend to be excluded unnecessarily. The maxim of inclusive design, coined by the geriatrician, the late Bernard Issacs, is 'Design for the young and you exclude the old; design for the old and you include the young.'

A typical journey involves a number of stages: a walk to the bus stop; a wait for the bus; boarding the bus and finding a seat; the bus journey itself; recognizing when you're about to reach your destination; getting off the bus; and so on. When we're fit and making a regular journey, all this is taken for granted. When we have some degree of disability, or are making a new journey, all of these stages must be managed successfully – hence the importance of good design at bus stops. Every link in the journey chain must be possible. If the individual has doubts about the feasibility of any particular link, they may decide not to make the trip.

To make progress with such an individualized approach to travel, we need a better understanding of human capability. Nick Tyler has constructed a unique resource, the Pedestrian Accessibility and Movement Environment Laboratory (PAMELA for short). This 80 square metre facility can model various street features such as 'dropped kerbs', as well as the layout, surface material, colour and texture, gradients, step heights and the positions of obstacles; and also the effects of different lighting levels, acoustic situations and wet weather. The new laboratory will give us a much better understanding of what people of all ages and disabilities are able to manage. This in turn will provide a better basis for the specification and design of that part of the world through which we walk.[23]

An inclusive approach to the design of the transport system is not justified solely on account of the needs of older people, which we all will become in due course (we hope). Transport problems can be a significant barrier to social inclusion more widely. People may be restricted in getting access to jobs and services on account of low incomes, buses that do not run to the right places at the right times or do not run frequently enough. Women are far and away the prime users of public transport, especially of buses, and their particular needs and aspirations must be taken into account. Women and men can be inhibited by anxieties about safety, crime and antisocial behaviour, which for instance deter many from waiting on an untended train platform after dark. Efforts are being made to tackle limitations of access and concerns about security.[24] These need to be seen as part of the larger project of ensuring a high-quality transport system, as I shall discuss in Chapter 9.

# 8

# Technology Futures

In this chapter I shall discuss the way in which new technologies might help us cope with the two big problems that look likely to limit human mobility: carbon and congestion. There is considerable scope for technological advances to alleviate other problems experienced in the transport sector, including accidents, noise and air pollutants, and indeed many advances which are likely to help with the big problems will be beneficial for these other concerns. However, given constraints on space and the reader's patience, I will not consider these other problems further. I'll first discuss how the carbon footprint of transport might be reduced, and then how technology could help tackle traffic congestion.

Consider the road vehicles which dominate modern transport and which meet most of our travel needs. One approach is to improve efficiency and so reduce consumption of oil-derived fuels and hence carbon dioxide emissions per mile travelled. A second approach is to switch, partially or wholly, to fuels other than fossil fuels. There is a lot going on in both areas. The account that follows is broad brush, emphasizing principles and skipping over much of the detail.

## Efficiency and electricity

One well established means of improving fuel consumption of internal combustion engines is to switch from petrol to diesel. Diesel engines are typically 30–40 per cent more efficient than petrol engines. Modern diesels are quieter and cleaner than the earlier generation, taking advantage of low sulphur fuel, advances in direct fuel injection that improve combustion, turbocharger technology and durable particulate filters on the exhaust. Forty-five per cent of newly registered cars in Europe are diesel-engined. Of the 33 million vehicles on the roads of Britain in 2006, ten million were diesels. In the US stringent emission regulations, and a past reputation for being dirty, noisy and smoky, have inhibited diesel sales, but Volkswagen is promoting diesel-powered cars that comply with emission standards in all 50 states.[1]

An innovation that has attracted much attention in recent years is the hybrid petrol-electric car. This is equipped with both an electric motor and an internal combustion engine, one supplementing the other, and can take a variety of forms. The most familiar type involves an electric motor/generator, linked to large batteries, that supplements the internal combustion engine by providing boost during acceleration and recovers power during braking. The engine charges the batteries. Either the petrol engine or the electric motor, or both, can power the vehicle, although with solely electric power the range is very small on account of low battery capacity. Because of the electric motor, the petrol engine can be smaller than it would be for a standard vehicle of the same size. This, plus regenerative braking, are the sources of fuel efficiency. The Toyota Prius, launched in 1997, is claimed to consume about half as much petrol as a US car of similar size. Good sales have been spurred by rising petrol prices, celebrity endorsements and winning awards such as European Car of the Year in 2005.[2]

In the US some enthusiasts are modifying the Prius to make it rechargeable from mains electricity. This involves replacing the standard nickel-metal hydride battery with a higher capacity lithium-ion unit, as well as changing the control software to prevent the petrol engine kicking in until needed to secure higher speeds. It is claimed that a range of as much as 60 miles can be obtained on the battery alone at freeway speeds (which would meet most people's daily driving needs), as well as fuel consumption of 100mpg on long trips. In the US, cheap night-time electricity could reduce cost per mile by 75 per cent compared with petrol, a relative benefit that would be greater in Europe with its higher petrol taxes. Such 'plug-in' hybrids are favoured by those who are keen to reduce dependency on imported oil.[3]

Pure electric cars have not seemed attractive to the main car manufacturers on account of the limited mileage possible on a fully charged battery, even though some drivers were enthusiastic about both the performance and zero emissions of the GM EV1 car in California in the 1990s. However, in the US the Tesla Roadster, a lightweight electric sports car, currently claims 245 miles per charge and 0 to 60 mph in less than four seconds. In London, a small Indian-built electric car, marketed as the G-Wiz, is currently gaining adherents as a city runabout, helped by its exemption as an electric vehicle from the congestion charge, although there are some anxieties about the crash-test performance of this very light vehicle.[4]

The range of a purely electric car is dependent on battery technology, where the key factors are density of energy storage, rate of charging, weight, durability and cost. The chemical reactions taking place within a battery are complex, with secondary reactions taking place in addition to the primary reactions involved in electricity generation. Batteries therefore need to be selected for particular circumstances, making necessary compromises between desirable characteristics. Research on battery technology has been neglected in favour of fuel cells (see below), with uncertain prospects for big advances that could make battery-powered cars a mass market reality. Nanotechnology techniques seem promising as a means of increasing the surface area of the electrodes and hence the capacity and rate of charging. What is required are batteries with stored energy density several times current levels, with much faster charging.[5]

Perhaps the best means to ensure adequate range for vehicles with an electric drive is to adopted another version of hybrid technology, this time where electricity drives the car at all times, as for the purely electric car. The main charging is overnight from grid electricity, but a small efficient petrol engine operates when necessary to charge the battery. In 2007 General Motors announced the Chevrolet Volt concept car of this design, intended to drive for 40 miles with no petrol use, and with a range of 600–700 miles based on the petrol in the tank. The absence of gears and transmission keeps down both weight and cost. In late 2007 full page ads appeared in the classier US magazines to promote this attractively designed car – 'A daily commute without a drop of gas' – even though it was as yet unavailable for purchase.[6]

This idea – of a vehicle in which the main propulsion is an electric motor powered from batteries which are charged by an internal combustion engine – is not new. Submarines have operated in this mode for decades, and nowadays there are both rail locomotives and large trucks for surface mining powered by a diesel-fuelled generator beyond which everything is electric. The extension of this technology to road vehicles has come about because of advances in transistor technology which allow large electric currents to be controlled, thus permitting the substitution of lighter electric drives for heavier mechanical drives. This reduces power requirements and thus carbon emissions. Where grid electricity can be used for overnight charging, there is further potential for reducing carbon emissions, depending on the source of the electricity – nuclear and renewables being particularly favourable in this context.[7]

Weight reduction generally is a good way to reduce fuel consumption and carbon emissions. The first Volkswagen Golf Mark 1 GTi in 1981 weighed 900kg, whereas its current equivalent weighs nearly 1400kg. This car could be nearly half a tonne lighter without impairing its basic ability to transport four people in reasonable comfort. In broad terms, a weight reduction of about 10 per cent decreases carbon dioxide emissions by about 7 per cent. But the public seem reluctant to forgo those features that add weight – air conditioning, electrically adjusted windows and seats, in-car entertainment systems, safety reinforcement to the body structure, and so forth. Some manufacturers have developed lightweight aluminium body construction, including Audi and Jaguar. However, the Audi A2 lightweight aluminium body diesel flopped and was withdrawn in 2005 – it had perhaps been launched prematurely. The new Mazda 2 small hatchback is almost 100kg lighter than outgoing models, a reversal of trend, due to thinner stronger steel and general weight reduction all round; fuel consumption is claimed as 15 per cent lower and carbon dioxide emissions down by 18 per cent. Despite such attractions, clean cars comprise only a very small proportion of total sales. Less than 5 per cent of cars sold emit no more than 120g carbon dioxide per kilometre (g/km), and demand continues to grow for heavy powerful cars like SUVs.[8]

Stripping out non-essential components is an approach that is being adopted to manufacture small cheap basic cars for the markets of developing countries, especially Asia. Renault launched the Logan model in 2004 as a low-cost global car for emerging markets. It sells in India at £5000, although this is not cheap by Indian standards. Renault is reportedly studying a £1500 car for Indian markets, while Tata Motors is building a mass market car, known as the Nano, to be sold for 100,000 rupees or £1200, available in late 2008.[9]

Amory Lovins, a visionary and persuasive energy specialist, goes further than the auto industry by proposing to double the efficiency of using oil, for which the most important enabling technology is ultra-light vehicle design using advanced composite materials or lightweight steel. He argues that the extra cost would be repaid from fuel saving in about three years.[10]

To achieve the greatest reductions in carbon emissions from road transport without fundamentally changing the size, comfort or performance characteristics of the vehicle, or of the fuel supply system, we might look to a diesel-electric hybrid built of lightweight materials that could be charged from mains electricity where that electricity is from nuclear or renewable sources. One constraint, however, is that batteries of sufficient size to provide a typical daily mileage contribute a considerable weight, offsetting the benefits of lightweight construction.

## Biofuels

An alternative approach to reducing carbon emissions from standard vehicles would be to use suitable biofuels, rather than oil from fossil sources. Plants use the energy of the sun to power the process known as photosynthesis. Carbon dioxide in the atmosphere is converted to carbohydrate that largely forms the growing plant. Such plant carbohydrate can be converted to a liquid fuel, known as a biofuel, which can power a conventional internal combustion engine. The carbon dioxide taken from the atmosphere by photosynthesis offsets the carbon dioxide emitted by the vehicle. In principle, this sequence could be envisaged as 'carbon neutral', meaning that there is no net release of carbon dioxide to the atmosphere. In effect, the sun's energy is employed to drive the vehicle.

Biofuels are liquids and therefore a natural alternative to oil for transport. They work with existing engine technologies. Biofuels are broadly of two types: ethanol (alcohol) and diesel equivalents (made from various kinds of oilseeds). Up to 10 per cent ethanol can be blended with petrol for use in standard vehicles. In Brazil, where ethanol from sugarcane is economically attractive, 75 per cent of cars sold are modified somewhat to use 85 per cent ethanol plus 15 per cent gasoline. Ethanol is the main example of a 'first generation' biofuel, which prompts a number of anxieties. Fossil fuel derived energy may be needed to grow, harvest and convert crops to biofuel – fertilizer, tractors, processing etc. This is a particular problem with ethanol made by fermentation of starch derived from corn (maize) in the US, but much less of a problem in Brazil. The need to use fossil fuels for biofuel production means that greenhouse gas emissions may only be 20–50 per cent lower than for vehicles running on oil derived fuels – far from being carbon neutral. First generation biofuels are controversial because they are made from crops that would otherwise be used for food – sugar and starch crops such as sugar cane, beet, corn and wheat, and oilseeds. Use of these is criticized for forcing up food prices or for encouraging deforestation when plantations of oil palm are established. Ploughing up virgin land releases carbon stored in plants and soils, which can outweigh the carbon-saving benefits of biofuels grown on such land. Production costs may be high, up to three times that of oil-based fuels. Government support is then needed but this can lead to market distortions caused by tax credits, import duties, farm support programmes, trade barriers and subsidies, as happens particularly in the US and the EU. Ethanol subsidies in the US have encouraged farmers to switch to maize from other crops. In 2007 biofuels took a third of the maize harvest. An SUV fuel tank filled with ethanol uses as much maize as would feed a person for a year.[11]

A 'second generation' of biofuels are derived from non-food crops grown on land unsuitable for food crops. One example that is attracting investment in India and elsewhere is jatropha, in the form of nuts from a hardy tree which can be processed to yield a biodiesel fuel. Jatropha grows on arid soil, and so doesn't compete with food crops, and requires no chemical fertilizers or pesticides. Another example is miscanthus grass, a fast-growing Asian grass that can be grown in Britain to 3–4 metres in height. Initially this would be combusted as fuel but might be converted to liquid fuel in long run.[12] Other second generation biofuels might be made from waste products such as straw and other cellulosic material from food crops, wood waste, municipal waste and vegetable oil and animal fat wastes. Generally, these second generation biofuels need further development to achieve both suitable fuel quality and acceptable cost. One necessary area for technical development is enzymic treatments that allow cellulose and other hardy plant material to be broken down to constituent chemicals.[13]

The long-term potential of biofuels depends on land availability and on competing uses, principally for food crops and for solid biomass. Major land use changes such as deforestation and draining of peat bogs can completely negate the carbon savings from biofuels. Nevertheless, Professor Ricardo Hausmann, of Harvard University's Center for International Development, expects that technology will deliver biofuels competitive with fossil energy at current prices (Brazil's ethanol is there now). He takes an optimistic view, seeing the world as full of underutilized good quality land not being cultivated, which would allow biofuel output in the same ballpark as oil production today. This would cap the price of oil at the marginal cost of bioenergy. The impact on land prices and food prices would depend on whether biofuels were made from food crops or from wastes and non-food crops on non-food land.[14]

Other estimates of the technical potential for biofuels are more modest but far from insubstantial. Studies commissioned by the Department for Transport put the potential in the EU as equivalent to 20–30 per cent of road transport fuel use in 2030. The International Energy Agency suggests that biofuels could meet 25 per cent of transport demand by 2050. Current policy is that by 2010, 5 per cent of road transport fuel in Britain should be from renewable sources. A target of 10 per cent has been set for the EU for 2020, subject to the biofuels being sustainable and the second generation becoming available. The commercial attractiveness of biofuels may depend on avoiding competition with food. Such competition would drive up food and land prices and undermine the returns from biofuel investment.[15]

While there are many uncertainties at present – not surprising for a fairly new area of technological and commercial activity – in the longer term there is little doubt that we shall have to reorient much of our liquid fuel and chemical industry away from oil – going back to the future, as one expert puts it. At the beginning of the 20th century, many industrial materials such as dyes, solvents and synthetic fibres were made from trees and agricultural crops. By the late 1960s, most of these bio-based chemical products had been displaced by petroleum derivatives. The challenge today is to develop crops with a range of desirable physical and chemical characteristics while increasing biomass yields by a factor of two, for instance by manipulating the genes involved in photosynthesis to increase the initial capture of light energy, which at present is less than 2 per cent of that falling on the plant.[16]

# Hydrogen

Only two of the 92 elements – carbon and hydrogen – burn readily yet in a controllable manner in a reaction that releases heat without too many side effects. The gas hydrogen combusts by reacting with oxygen in air to yield heat and water vapour. The energy in the form of heat, like the energy from combusting oil, can be used to power an internal combustion engine. The only emission is water. No carbon is involved in this process. So in principle, a transport system based on hydrogen would be attractive since it would not in itself contribute to climate change (although the source of the hydrogen would need to be considered). Moreover, hydrogen can be used more efficiently to power a 'fuel cell' which provides electricity for an electric drive system. A fuel cell is an electrochemical device, a bit like a battery, but rather than store electricity, it generates electricity from an external supply of fuel together with an 'oxidant'. A hydrogen cell uses hydrogen as fuel and oxygen as oxidant.

Trials of buses powered by hydrogen fuel cells are taking place in a number of cities around the world, including London. Nevertheless, there are many barriers to be overcome before this technology could be in widespread use. First, there is the need to develop cost-effective, durable, safe and environmentally acceptable fuel cell systems suitable for cars. Second is the need to store sufficient hydrogen on board the vehicle to provide adequate range. Hydrogen as compressed gas or in liquid form has a low energy density compared with oil-based fuels (car-based mobility has only been possible because of the exceptionally high energy density of petrol and diesel fuel). Current fuel cell lifetimes are much too short and costs are an order of magnitude too high. On-board hydrogen storage is inadequate for commercially viable cars. The prospects for hydrogen-fuelled buses are better because there is more space for fuel tanks, which can be filled at the depots.[17]

A further requirement is to develop a hydrogen generation and distribution system sufficiently extensive to encourage motorists to consider switching. As a transitional measure, it is possible to make hydrogen locally at filling stations from feed stocks such as methanol or natural gas. But in the long run the aim would be to generate hydrogen by the electrolysis of water using electricity from conventional nuclear power plant, from nuclear fission if that ever becomes feasible, from renewable sources, or perhaps from processes in which solar energy is converted directly into hydrogen. The US National Research Council considers that there is the potential for replacing all gasoline with hydrogen over the next half-century and for eliminating almost all carbon dioxide and pollutants from vehicle emissions. But because of the extensive research and development required, there is expected to be only minor progress over next 25 years. A detailed study of technological potential commissioned by the UK government concluded that hydrogen could provide carbon dioxide reductions for road transport by 2030 with costs close to or lower than those for conventional fuels and engines.[18]

Could enough hydrogen be produced to meet transport needs? One estimate of the scope for meeting all the energy needs of the US from solar energy using photovoltaic technology suggests that an area of land about 100 miles square (10,000 square miles) would be needed, which is less than one quarter of the area already covered by roads and streets. A more pessimistic estimate for the UK is that hydrogen to meet all transport needs would require new nuclear power sources similar in amount to the present total electricity generation capacity, or, alternatively, an area for wind turbines larger than the area of Wales. It seems that the task of producing enough hydrogen at an acceptable price would not be easy, but that it would be premature to be too pessimistic about this technology at the present early stage.[19]

## Decarbonization

Technically, it should be possible to 'decarbonize' the surface transport system (see below for aviation). This could be very largely achieved through the further commercial development of 'plug-in' hybrid vehicles, where average daily mileage can be achieved on an overnight charge of the batteries from the electricity socket, with the small petrol or diesel engine available to keep the batteries charged for longer trips. If batteries of higher capacity could be manufactured, then the need for liquid fuel would be diminished, perhaps even eliminated. In any event, biofuel from sustainable sources could meet this need.

The alternative route to decarbonization is by means of hydrogen fuel cells. This, however, requires both a major change in vehicle technology – the fuel cell – and a new fuel manufacture and delivery infrastructure. Transitional steps are possible, including using hydrogen in conventional internal combustion engines, and generating hydrogen from fossil fuel sources. The car manufacturer BMW advertises limited availability of an existing internal combustion engined car to run on hydrogen as an alternative to gasoline. The distance possible on a single tank of hydrogen is low (123 miles) however, and it is reported that half the tank's content can evaporate in nine days. Honda has announced 'limited marketing' of a hydrogen fuel-cell car with a range of up to 270 miles, which sounds more promising.[20]

A comprehensive review of technology options has been carried out recently for the UK government by Professor Julia King. She has drawn the optimistic conclusion that within ten years we could achieve 30 per cent reduction in carbon emissions using cars of the kind we drive today, while in the medium term to 2030 we could have a 50 per cent per kilometre reduction using battery-electric vehicles plus biofuels. For the long term, zero carbon electricity or hydrogen are a probability, to help meet the challenge of achieving 90 per cent reductions in carbon per kilometre.[21]

In terms of technology, the transport sector is, however, extremely conservative. The essentials of the motor car have remained unchanged for 100 years since the first mass-produced vehicle, the Model T Ford, was manufactured in 1908 – an internal combustion engine powered by an oil-derived liquid fuel, driving four rubber-tyred road wheels on a tarmac surface via a mechanical drive train, in the charge of an amateur driver. Of course, all these components have been developed and refined over the years to yield the modern automobile which is comfortable and reliable, increasingly safe and efficient, and available in a wide range of styles and specifications to meet the desires of the purchaser. The large production volumes of mass market cars allows development costs to be spread and production costs to be reduced through continuous incremental improvement.

Switching to new kinds of technology, whether engine or fuel, makes people nervous, both manufacturers and motorists. The risks are substantial. The need to develop new technologies to secure high efficiency and reliability imposes substantial costs which need to be recovered, one way or another. The costs of developing a dead-end technology have to be written off, damaging the balance sheet. Barriers to innovation include uncertainty about likely strength of policy for transport sector carbon dioxide reduction; limited regulatory requirement for carbon emission reductions; uncertainty about consumer demand; increased costs of low carbon technologies; the low profitability of many vehicle manufacturers; and the need to manage a large number of diverse and interrelated technologies.[22]

In the long run, inclusion of transport within the EU Emissions Trading Scheme should set a price for carbon emissions that will make low-carbon transport modes more attractive. As discussed earlier, the price of carbon will depend on developments in the wider energy economy, in particular which carbon-saving technologies prove to be most practicable and cost-effective.

Stephen Pacala and Robert Socolow of Princeton University have made an influential proposal for 'solving the climate and carbon problem for the next half century'. They propose a range of measures that would stabilize atmospheric carbon dioxide at 500ppm, rather less than double the pre-industrial level, by restraining annual carbon emissions to the current seven billion tonnes of carbon a year for the next 50 years. Without intervention, carbon emissions would double to some 14 billion tonnes by the 2050s. What therefore is needed is, say, seven new technologies each of which could build up to yield one billion tonnes a year of carbon saving over this period. Pacala and Socolow identify 15 technologies, each of which has this necessary potential. The four relevant to transport are: doubled fuel economy of cars; half the mileage travelled by car; wind power to generate hydrogen for fuel-cell cars; and substantial biofuels for vehicles.[23] All these seem feasible except halving the distance travelled by car, which would substantially reduce choice of jobs, homes, shopping, education, leisure and so forth. However, the essence of both the emissions trading and new technologies approaches is that the most cost-effective actions should be taken across the whole range of innovations, not singling transport out for special treatment.

Pending the full impact of carbon pricing as driven by emissions trading or other mechanism, we have in place a number of modest measures aimed at promoting low-carbon road transport. These include linking vehicle excise duty in the UK to the level of carbon emissions to encourage both manufacturers to produce cleaner cars and drivers to choose the least polluting cars; company car taxation that depends on carbon emissions of the vehicle; some local authorities levying charges for on-street parking that depend on the vehicle's emissions performance; and in London a congestion charging regime which, it is proposed, should allow the lowest carbon emitting vehicles free use but charge the most emitting cars £25 a day. One particular challenge arises from the so-called 'grey vehicle fleets', cars owned by individuals but used for work purposes, with mileage reimbursed at generous rates approved by the tax authorities that allow users to make a profit, and hence encourage more driving.

The European Commission proposes to reduce the carbon dioxide emissions of average new cars sold in Europe to 130g/km by 2012, with a further 10g saved from such measures as more efficient tyres, air-conditioning and biofuels. The Commission plans to legislate in 2008, following the limited success of a previous voluntary scheme. Engine size, and hence carbon emissions, varies from market to market as a matter of culture. Average capacity in the US is 3.4 litres, whereas for Britain and Germany the figure is 1.8, France 1.7 and Italy 1.6 litres. There is no inherent difficulty in making cars that emit only 130g/km, provided they are small with limited acceleration. So manufacturers that specialize in large, powerful and profitable models would have a hard time in complying with such regulations.[24]

The UK Commission for Integrated Transport has proposed that the various measures mentioned above should be tightened up, including EU-wide average emissions for new cars of 100g/km by 2020. This Commission would also like to see fuel duty raised to offset fuel cost savings through improved vehicle technology, purchasing and driving. It also advocates behavioural changes aimed at reducing carbon emissions such as the promotion of 'eco-driving' techniques and enforcing the 70mph speed limit on motorways and dual carriageway roads.[25]

Governments can help the development and deployment of new technologies through support of research and through procurement. The UK Department for Transport has a Low Carbon Vehicle Procurement Programme which will fund the initial phase of procurement of a lower-carbon van. Currently there is no such model available on the mass UK market, despite the fact that technology options exist for improving the carbon performance of vans. The intention is that public sector organizations should use their combined purchasing power to secure desirable environmental outcomes, demonstrate leadership on greening vehicles fleets, and have a wider impact on the market.[26]

A question that is crucial to reducing carbon emissions from transport is the relative importance of behavioural change and technological progress. The Commission for Integrated Transport argues that promotion of such behavioural change could be more cost-effective in reducing carbon than technological developments of vehicles and fuels, but it recognizes that this depends on millions of separate decisions by individuals, with little guarantee of consistent and sustained behavioural adaptation (unless enforced, as in the case of speed limits). My own view is that behavioural change, unless enforceable, will not be easy because of the reduction of choice that would commonly be involved. And what's not easy is unlikely to be cost-effective.

I'll conclude this section with a fairly brief comment on the prospects for lower carbon aviation. Designing aircraft able to take off with a full load of passengers and fuel and fly safely between continents is a demanding task that has depended on the availability of oil-derived kerosene with high energy density. Substituting bioderived kerosene would in principle be possible, and hydrogen might ultimately be applicable to aviation. However, the relative infrequency of new airplane and engine development, together with safety concerns, mean that progress to lower carbon technology is likely to be slow. There may be scope for reduction in carbon emissions of up to 50 per cent per passenger-kilometre through better air traffic management and more efficient airframes and engines – possibly involving fairly radical redesign. Nevertheless, aviation seems set to be the sector for which oil-based fuel will have the highest intrinsic value, notwithstanding the impact of carbon pricing.[27, 28]

# Remedies for congestion

Congestion is the second big problem for which we might look for help to technological advances. I'll focus on roads, although traffic congestion also arises elsewhere. Congested skies near airports will benefit from developments in air traffic control technologies, as well as policy initiatives such as the Single European Sky aimed at overcoming the effects of fragmented European national air traffic management regimes.[29] On the railways congestion can also be a difficulty, particularly at busy city-centre terminals – not just the crowds of passengers but also the number of trains seeking to load and discharge passengers at peak times. The general problem is that of excess demand in relation to the capacity of the system. Where access is controlled, as with planes and trains, demand can be managed, but because the system is working at or close to maximum capacity, incidents of one kind or another can cause significant delays. In the case of roads, vehicle access is not generally controlled and the sheer weight of traffic results in slower and variable speeds and stop–start driving.

I'll discuss first alternatives to the car, as one means for coping with congestion, and then possibilities for managing the road network more effectively.

In Britain in recent years, use of the railways has increased markedly – up 40 per cent over the last ten years after half a century of decline. In part this is a response to congestion on the road network. Future development of the railways will help reduce road congestion and relieve overcrowding on trains and at stations. There are two distinct kinds of technological development for the rail system: to seek higher speeds; and to increase capacity, enhance comfort and improve efficiency at existing speeds.

High-speed rail travel was pioneered in France with the TGV (*Train à Grande Vitesse*) which operates at 200mph on purpose-built track without sharp curves. The one British track of this class is the Channel Tunnel Rail Link, now known as High Speed 1, which opened in November 2007. Rail enthusiasts are keen for more such high-speed rail lines to be developed, in part to provide a lower carbon alternative to domestic aviation. However, in Britain, particularly in the crowded south-east, it is not easy to find land for the new tracks that are needed. High land values are one of the reasons why the cost of high-speed rail construction in Britain appears to be much greater than in other countries. Moreover, as Sir Rod Eddington observed in his report on transport for the British government, the carbon reduction benefits from a zero-carbon high-speed rail link between London and Scotland that took all present air passengers would only yield a net carbon saving of 0.2 per cent of the UK's annual carbon emissions, this at relatively high cost. Eddington took the view that in broad terms the UK transport system provides the right connections in the right places to support the journeys that matter to economic performance, and he was sceptical about those high-speed rail options that rely on untested technologies.[30]

From the perspective I have been developing in this book, it is clear that higher speed rail would encourage people to go farther in the time they have available for travel, in particular to commute for longer distances. This would have environmental consequences, both higher carbon emissions and pressure for housing development on greenfield sites. There is an argument for running faster trains along existing tracks so that rail travel could be competitive in journey time with domestic aviation, thus making savings in carbon emissions. But this benefit would be offset by the extra commuting and other travel that would result.

A sustainable railway would provide more efficiency and capacity at current speeds, to reduce present overcrowding and allow future growth in passenger numbers. Improvements in signalling technology allow more trains to be run safely on existing tracks. Radio-based in-cab signalling, as used in the TGV, should permit the number of trains on the West Coast Main Line out of London to be increased from 14 to 20 an hour. At present trains on this route are kept more than six miles apart when travelling at 125mph, but this is capable of reduction to two miles, the safe braking distance. Other sensible proposals in the government's recent Railways White Paper include lengthening trains and platforms, adding station and track capacity at pinch-points in the network, multitracking existing lines, as well as reducing the weight of rolling stock, hence cutting energy use, carbon emissions and track damage.[31] Generally, the need is to take fullest advantage of the transport corridors that the railways have inherited, while ensuring that their use continues to be broadly acceptable to those living nearby. Electrification of the rail routes that still use diesel trains would be a sensible investment for the long term, allowing use of non-fossil fuel electricity.

Beyond the existing steel-wheel-on-steel-rail technology there is 'maglev' technology – magnetic levitation – in which the train floats over a special track by means of repulsive electromagnetic force. This could operate at around 300mph, allowing a London to Glasgow trip that would compete with air on journey time. While maglev has been in development around the world for some years, only one short commercial route operates, between Shanghai and its airport. Costs for this technology seem high, as does energy consumption and noise, and it seems unlikely that maglev will be developed in Britain.

Another technology using dedicated tracks is bus rapid transit, which I discussed in Chapter 6. One example of this is the guided busway currently under construction which uses a disused railway line to link St Ives to Cambridge, with travel on normal roads through the city centre. This will be the longest such system in Europe, with over 25km of guideway.[32]

A rather different track-based technology, in this case designed to operate in urban areas at lower speeds, is designated 'personal rapid transit'. The example under active development in Britain is known as ULTra (urban light transport) and involves battery/electric-powered driverless vehicles with four seats, available on demand to passengers, designed to travel at 25mph on narrow concrete track which would be elevated in city centres.[33]

The ULTra system was conceived as an environmentally acceptable urban transport solution by Martin Lowson, a former chief scientist at Westland Helicopters and subsequently professor of aerospace engineering at Bristol University. The concept involves passengers being able to travel non-stop between any pair of 'stations', with the need for a local bus service eliminated and car use reduced. I was pleased to be able to help provide some R&D funding for an early stage of this project when I was chief scientist at the Department of Transport. I recall suggesting that, rather than trying to find a city centre for a pilot scheme, some self-contained environment such as an airport might be better to demonstrate the technology. I'm not sure whether I had any influence, but an ULTra system is under construction at Heathrow airport to link a passenger car park to the new Terminal 5. The link comprises 18 vehicles on 4.2km of track, and is due to open in summer 2008. The demonstration will provide an important test of the technical and commercial feasibility of this mode of transport for niche markets, as well as allowing judgement to be made about prospects for city-centre use.[34]

Road traffic congestion is a problem in two dimensions. Might we take advantage of the space in the third dimension? The ULTra system envisages elevated tracks above city roads. Before he gave up on helicopters, Martin Lowson had designed the rotor system used to set the absolute world speed record. It has long been envisaged that helicopters could provide mobility, at least for some. Aldous Huxley, in his novel *Brave New World*, described how, at the end of the working day, executives would go from their offices up to the roof to pick up their personal helicopters, rather than down to the basement garage as now. 'The summer afternoon was drowsy with the hum of passing helicopters…' At the time the novel was published, in 1932, that seemed a reasonable prospect.

Today, the place with the most extensive helicopter service is São Paulo, the largest city in Brazil and South America, which has experienced rapid growth in helicopter use for both within and beyond the urban area. In June 2004, the civil aviation authority in São Paulo began to implement the world's first dedicated air traffic control system for helicopter urban flights. Over 400 helicopters operate within the metropolitan area, making it possibly the largest civilian helicopter base in the world. Use of helicopters by the wealthy is prompted by traffic congestion, inadequate public transport, anxieties about violence on the streets and a desire for an expensive status symbol. The noise of helicopters is experienced by the protesting middle classes who live in the neighbourhoods with helipads. Helicopter accidents very often involve celebrities, which gains them widespread media coverage.[35]

Away from population centres, there are examples of successful helicopter services, for instance bringing racegoers to the Cheltenham Gold Cup meeting, albeit at upwards of £750 a seat. Noise is the main problem here as elsewhere, with landings fitted in between races so as not to frighten the horses. In contrast, the authorities have shut down one of the biggest helicopter landing pads in the Gulf of Saint-Tropez area on account of noise disturbance. Noise reduction through improved technology would allow greater use of helicopters, but the prospects for substantial improvements do not seem promising. In any event, helicopters use a lot of energy to stay in the air and emit a lot of carbon. So a breakthrough in noise reduction technology would be a mixed blessing.[36]

Going downwards in the third dimension takes us into tunnels. Although humans are not burrowing creatures, we seem to be fairly happy in tunnels. Alice started her adventures in Wonderland by following the White Rabbit into a hole that became a tunnel. Roads and railways in tunnels in principle allow additional capacity where surface traffic is congested. Road tunnels have limited prospects – best used in an area of environmental sensitivity – because if the capacity is new, rather than replacing an existing surface road, then congestion is likely where the traffic has to rejoin the surface flow. Underground rail is of course attractive as a means to service conurbations. But tunnels are expensive and sometimes prone to cost overruns. Boston's Central Artery/Tunnel project (the 'Big Dig') was completed five years late and vastly over budget, while the Jubilee Line extension to London's Docklands, opened two years late with a large cost overrun. On the other hand, the Channel Tunnel Rail Link, involving over 30km of tunnels, was built to time and budget. There is some scope for cost reduction in tunnelling technology, and whatever the cost of construction, tunnels rarely become disused or are regretted.

## Congestion relief through intelligent technologies

Conventional transport technologies are ponderous. They change very slowly, in part because of the interdependence of the different elements – engines, fuels, track, control, guidance – and in part because of the huge investment needed in infrastructure, manufacturing, research and development. It is simply too difficult and expensive to effect fast change. In contrast, information and telecommunications technologies – ITC for short – are remarkably agile, with innovation and new products brought to market at a spectacular pace. Could the ITC technologies, current and future, help solve some of the transport sector problems?[37]

The first question is whether telecommunications could substitute for some travel, particularly for trips connected with work – cutting down on visits to clients or working from home by taking advantage of broadband connections. Until now, the evidence for telecoms replacing travel has been unpersuasive. Indeed, the argument might go the other way in that travel increasingly depends on telecoms to make the arrangements. Some years ago it was estimated that it took 10,000 phone calls to get a passenger airliner off the ground (nowadays much of this would be in the form of emails).[38] The availability of very cheap international telecoms facilitates international air travel for both commercial and family business. 'VFF' (visiting family and friends) is the fastest growing purpose category for international aviation, and the 'transnational family' is increasingly common. More generally, it seems that much of impact of ITC is to modify travel patterns. We do not know how much substitution and how much stimulation of travel is taking place. What research is uncovering is the complexity of the interactions of telecommunications with the already complex phenomena of human activity and travel behaviour.[39] For the future, there are prospects for some substitution of business travel by the latest version of videoconferencing, known as *telepresence*, where big improvements in the technology create the illusion that people are in same room. Still relatively expensive, it is suggested that it can pay for itself by keeping travel bills down, with claims of a 20 per cent cut in travel expenditure and reductions in carbon emissions.[40] However, much depends on the appetite for travel on the part of executives, their need to make personal contact, and the desire of their firms to make cash and carbon savings.

A further question to which we lack a clear answer is whether those who take advantage of ITC to travel less for work purposes compensate by travelling more for other purposes. Another question is whether the space on the transport system freed up by some people travelling less is occupied by others travelling more. This is what would be expected given that average travel time is constant. So teleworking, working from home rather than going to the office, may not yield any overall travel saving. In the longer term, location decisions may change, with people willing to live farther from their places of work, thus making fewer but longer trips.[41]

The other big application of ITC technologies to transport is to improve safety, efficiency and comfort. I've previously mentioned improved signalling on the railways and the scope for more effective air traffic control, in both cases utilizing advances in technology to improve the use of the available space and enhancing safety. Here I'll focus on road vehicles, for which the application of ITC technologies is variously known as 'intelligent transport systems' or 'transport telematics'.

There is a variety of applications aimed at making driving safer and more comfortable. These make their commercial entry at the top end of the vehicle manufacturer's product range. As customer experience is gained and the potential for cost reduction through volume production achieved, the applications move down the range to lower priced models. Current and prospective applications for which motorists might be willing to pay include parking assistance using a device that senses the distance to the car behind and sends an audible warning or employs a rear-facing video camera; 'tracker' transponders that locate a vehicle in the event of theft; adaptive cruise control to maintain a constant distance behind the car you are following, even if it slows down; and lane-keeping assistance using a device that recognizes the white lines on the road surface and gives you the feeling that you are driving in a trough.[42]

Other telematics applications might be desirable for wider reasons of safety, although adoption would probably require legislation. One would be arrangements for automatic collision warning-mitigation-avoidance, where questions of driver responsibility arise. A second is the so-called 'intelligent speed adaptation', which involves external control over the vehicle's speed using satnav location (see below), together with a digital map database that includes speed limits, linked to the vehicle's accelerator that resists attempts to exceed the speed limit.

A further class of telematics applications helps the road network manager control traffic flows more effectively. These include a variety of means for collecting and analysing data, including taking advantage of the mobile phones carried by drivers in vehicles (anonymously to protect privacy) to estimate routes and speeds of traffic, this to help forecast future real-time traffic flows. Such flow data can be used to advise motorists of the optimum speed on congested roads, since as speeds are reduced the safe distance between vehicles reduces and the chances of flow breakdown (leading to stop–start driving) are lessened. This approach to what is known as 'active traffic management' is employed on a number of busy sections of British motorways. A complementary approach is 'ramp metering' where the movement of vehicles on the ramp or feeder road is controlled by signals in order to minimize flow breakdown on the motorway. This has long been used in the US and has now been adopted in Britain.[43]

For the future, there are further possibilities for packing more vehicles into a given amount of road space. 'Cooperative active cruise control' involves vehicles exchanging braking and acceleration data so as to be able to reduce the distance between them without compromising safety. Beyond that, there have been trials in the US of 'platooning' in which some ten vehicles travel together, each aware of all the others, without normal driver involvement. The attraction of this approach is that normally only around 5 per cent of a lane is occupied at any one time, so there is considerable existing capacity that might be usable. Research suggests that a platoon of trucks has reduced levels of aerodynamic drag, reduced emissions, better fuel economy, and enables road capacity to be doubled from 800 trucks an hour to 1500. There is continuing research and development driven by a military requirement for autonomous vehicles that keep soldiers out of dangerous situations, and this may have spin-offs for the road transport sector. However, full automation is likely to require dedicated lanes, which would be a constraint. Automation may in any event not be suitable on the UK's road network because the junctions are closely spaced and there would therefore be many short-distance journeys with traffic switching between automated and manual modes. There could be safety risks and there is also the problem of managing higher traffic flows away from the dedicated lanes to other roads with less capacity.[44]

Returning from possible futures to the present day, the most pervasive ITC application in the transport sector is satellite navigation. The number of 'satnav' systems in use on Britain's roads is thought to exceed four million, having doubled in two years, and of such significance as to be included in the basket of goods and services on which the retail price index is based. The popularity of this location and navigation device is such that large-volume production from specialist manufactures has enabled costs to be driven down to mass market prices, made possible by the availability of flash memory of sufficient capacity to store a detailed digital road map of a continent on a single memory card. This system allows trips to be planned, modifications made en route, and time of arrival estimated.

Satnav systems are popular with haulage firms. Half of UK fleets are equipped to track vehicles in real time, thus saving fuel, finding more efficient routes, avoiding traffic hold-ups, and so gaining competitive advantage in service provision. Nevertheless, satnav systems are not without their difficulties. Heavy lorries can find themselves misdirected down unsuitable country lanes or caught under low bridges. Villages can find themselves blighted as 'rat runs'. However, it seems likely that the suppliers of digital maps will modify these to recognize physical and legal restrictions as well as warnings of steep hills, sharp curves and such. More generally, it should be entirely feasible for arrangements to be made, whether voluntary or obligatory, to reconcile the interests of drivers, the providers of satnav equipment and local authorities representing inhabitants who may be affected by new traffic flows.[45]

## Plan B

Satnav has more potential benefit than has yet been recognized, in my view. It could be the basis for 'Plan B' – what is to be done to tackle congestion if and when national road pricing proves not to be acceptable, for the reasons I set out in Chapter 5.

The main argument for road pricing, according to the economists, is to reduce time wasted by drivers in slow moving or stationary traffic by pricing a proportion of motorists off the network at times of peak usage. A secondary benefit lies in the improved reliability of journey time. The time-saving argument is mistaken, for the reasons I discussed in Chapter 5. Congestion certainly slows traffic, but the effect is to reduce access, given that average travel time is constant.

To see how to tackle the problem of congestion, we need to identify what in fact is detrimental. People's perception of detriment seems to be greater than their actual experience. Around a quarter of respondents to a recent UK survey say that they experience congestion all or most of their time on their most frequent road journeys. But people see congestion as less of a problem for themselves than for their region and for the whole country.[46] I suspect this is because we have first-hand experience that congestion is self-limiting and that the proverbial 'gridlock' is a very rare event indeed.

What seems to bother travellers more than stop–start driving is the uncertainty of journey times. Longer journey times on account of slower speeds do not appear to be much of a concern. A similar worry arises with freight deliveries, for which predictability seems more important than speed.[47] Hence if traffic congestion is in prospect, drivers either start out earlier and risk having time to spare if all goes smoothly, or they allow just enough time for the trip and risk being late for their appointments. Accordingly, a direct approach to dealing with the main detriment arising from congestion would be to provide drivers with good predictive information about journey times, so that they could better plan and manage their trips. This seems increasing feasible as the relevant technologies rapidly develop.

Type 'Seattle traffic' into Google and you'll get to a web page of the Washington State Department of Transportation which shows current traffic conditions in the Seattle area. Now click on 'Real-time Travel Times' and you'll find a list of the main freeways in the area, the length of each section, the average travel time per section according to the time of day, and the current travel time. As I write, it's 8.00am on a wet Monday morning and current times are mostly above the average, some well above. For instance, Bellevue to Seattle is an 11-mile stretch with an average travel time of 19 minutes, now recording 25 minutes. A friend who has an hour commute in this area tells me that he decides when to set out on his homeward journey in the light of this real-time travel data. He'll postpone leaving until he can keep his trip time below an acceptable figure. By doing this he both reduces the uncertainty of his own journey time and removes one car from the peak traffic flow. The former is the main private benefit from road pricing, and the latter is the main public benefit – both achieved with current technology and without charging drivers a penny.

So what we need to do is to collect more and better traffic information, use this to make short-term predictions about flows, and supply this to a whole variety of outlets from which all kinds of travellers can benefit. As well as the computer in home and office, there are the satnav devices, both in the vehicle and as part of a personal digital assistant or a mobile phone. And there are web-based journey planners, such as the Department for Transport's *Transport Direct* (for both car and public transport trips) or the Transport for London *Journey Planner* (limited to public transport). At present, these navigation devices and planners mostly use historic patterns of traffic to forecast journey times, although efforts are increasingly being devoted to incorporate real-time information.

It doesn't take much to imagine a navigation device that provides optimized routes and reasonably reliable journey time predictions based on real-time current and forecast traffic information. The traveller would be advised on the best route and would have assurance about arrival time. There would be a variety of ways in which such a device might be used. You could trade off a briefer commute at off-peak hours against a preference for working standard office hours. You might plan a trip under congested traffic conditions, including route and departure time. You could decide choice of shopping destination in the light of the expected journey time. Businesses could achieve enhanced efficiency for a road-based delivery or service operations.

Navigation devices that provide the best route in the light of expected traffic conditions and predict journey times (which might be termed 'predictive navigation') would have an additional benefit if widely adopted – to help optimize the efficient use of the road network by making clear the alternatives to using the system at times of peak usage. The effect would be similar to the effect of road pricing in that some trips would be shifted in time, while others would be abandoned. With road pricing, those displaced at peak are travellers least able to afford the charge. With predictive navigation those displaced are travellers who can trade off arrival time convenience against overall journey time. This trade-off reflects values of time as perceived by the individual traveller. Road pricing, in contrast, involves standard charges which, as regards economic efficiency, would be too low for drivers with above average incomes and too high for those below average. In terms of economic principles, therefore, predictive navigation is not necessarily inferior to road pricing.

In terms of practicalities and acceptability, predictive navigation would have much to recommend it, compared with road pricing. Uptake would not be obligatory, but at the choice of the driver, who bears the cost of the in-vehicle navigation device and the subscription to the traffic information service (although the latter might be fully- or part-funded by highway authorities in the interest of system-wide efficiency). Early adopters gain advantage from optimal routing, to the extent that such is feasible under congested conditions. As the majority of drivers become equipped, the network increasingly benefits from modified travel behaviour, and these users have assurance about journey times. There is no need to standardize the in-vehicle devices, other than to agree a protocol for the interface with the traffic information stream. There are no privacy concerns, and no low-income motorists penalized by the charging regime when making an unavoidable car journey to work. Public expenditure would be quite modest – perhaps mainly for gathering, processing and disseminating traffic information.

One particular advantage of predictive navigation is the attraction of what marketing people term 'the offering'. In return for clearly specified charges, the benefits are route optimization (in principle attractive if hard to evaluate) and assured journey times (attractive and easy to evaluate). In contrast, national road pricing involves charges which may not be clear at the outset of a trip, particularly for an unfamiliar route, and uncertain benefits – some reduction in congestion and an improvement in journey time reliability, in relation to whatever would have been the case in the absence of road pricing.

Predictive navigation does not yet quite exist. But efforts are being made to provide real-time traffic information of the kind that could provide input to in-vehicle route guidance devices. Authorities responsible for road networks are generating traffic information for drivers. In Britain, for instance, the Highways Agency, which manages the trunk road system, is making information about traffic conditions in real time available to the home or office PC desktop, and has arranged for its roadside variable message signs to display predicted journey times. City authorities that operate urban traffic management and control systems are likewise exploring the practicalities of providing real-time information to drivers. And the suppliers of satnav systems are gearing up to take advantage of traffic information to improve their offerings. Inrix, a US supplier of traffic information, claims a technology, based on Bayesian statistics developed at Microsoft Research, which can be used to estimate traffic flow patterns every 15 minutes up to a year into the future. In Britain, Trafficmaster offers what is described as an intelligent route-finding service that uses satellite navigation and live traffic information to find best routes and guide drivers around congestion.[48]

Predictive navigation goes with the grain of technological developments, consumer choice and public acceptability. The main uncertainty concerns the ability to provide sufficiently accurate near-term forecasting of traffic conditions to ensure consumer satisfaction with the service. What is now needed is collaboration between the manufacturers of navigation devices, gatherers of traffic information and the network authorities. The aim would be to take full advantage of real-time traffic data to inform the guidance offered to drivers, and to develop predictive algorithms that allow near-term forecasting of road conditions – based on current flows, historic experience, weather forecasts and knowledge of planned public events and road maintenance. Road works are claimed to have the greatest single impact on journey time variability, which is helpful since their location and timing should be readily identifiable.[49]

One particular service that would be welcomed by drivers is reliable information on parking. You can't make a journey by car unless you're able to park at your destination – hence the attractiveness of supermarkets and stores with parking. In the early days of motoring there was plenty of road space for those rich enough to own a car and you could park on the street at your convenience. Today, it's only in movies that the robbers can park outside the bank.

In fact, every private car journey involves two parking acts and, for homes without off-street parking, finding space on the street is a growing problem, not least because cars spend most of their time parked (variously estimated at over 80 per cent or 95 per cent). Seventeen per cent of people in England report finding it difficult to park outside their home. In the future more cars will be owned in urban areas that are fully 'parked up' for most of day and night. Parking availability on the street increases the value of property, although three-quarters of garages are used for storage. Front gardens are increasingly paved over for parking – nearly half in the north-east of England, 20–30 per cent in most other regions, although only 14 per cent in London.[50]

Seeking parking space in cities wastes fuel and adds to carbon emissions. We cruise around in a mobile queue of cars waiting for curb space vacancies, but no one can see how many cars there are in the queue because of the other cars that are en route to a destination. Studies suggest that up to three-quarters of the cars in congested downtown areas of US and UK cities are looking for parking. In England

30 per cent of motorists say they have given up and gone home because they couldn't find a space on at least one occasion, and a similar proportion have waited at least 20 minutes to find a space.[51] Predictive navigation should be able to provide accurate information about off-street parking availability plus in-vehicle guidance to a designated, pre-booked space, perhaps paid for via a mobile phone.

Although the road network and its population of driver and vehicles is highly complex, the availability of modern computing power should allow progress to be made in providing useful traffic forecasts, just as weather forecasting has improved over the years. There is one helpful distinction between traffic and the weather. The former is to some extent capable of modification by the network managers through traffic signals and other means. For instance, over half the traffic signals in London can have their timings adjusted from a central control centre to cope with changing traffic conditions. On the motorway system, I've previously noted that a number of traffic management techniques are being introduced, including variable speed limits and ramp metering. As predictive navigation becomes available, the main aim of these traffic management techniques should be to smooth flows and thus improve the accuracy of forecasting. Dealing quickly with traffic accidents and breakdowns would be important for the same reason.

At this stage, it's hard to be precise about the scale of benefits from predictive navigation. But for my money, it seems far more attractive than any system for national road pricing. It would be worth the Department for Transport lending some support for development and demonstration, not least because it could complement, and not conflict with, the road pricing approach that it currently prefers.

*9*

# Travelling Hopefully

---

We live in an era of mass expectations of ever increasing individual mobility. Growth of personal mobility has accompanied industrialization. Two hundred years ago, only a minority ventured more than a few miles from their place of birth and only the better-off regularly travelled any distance. Then came the successive developments of the steam engine, the internal combustion engine and the gas turbine, together with the corresponding rail, road and aviation infrastructure. Now we currently travel annually on average about 7000 miles a year in Britain, even before international air travel is taken into account. These technological innovations have made possible faster travel speeds and thereby greater distances, and have democratized both everyday and long-distance travel.

## Mobility for the masses

The car is the dominant transport mode in all developed countries. In the beginning, the motor car was a hand-crafted horseless carriage, usually chauffeur-driven. Then came the Model T Ford, the first mass-produced automobile, of which 15 million were manufactured between 1908 and 1927. Productivity improvements, based on the moving assembly line, meant that by 1912 this car had become the first to cost less than the average annual wage. Henry Ford doubled the pay of his workers in 1914 to reduce labour force turnover. This enabled autoworkers to purchase the cars they themselves produced. So began the era of mass motorization. Similarly, not so long ago air travel was only for the relatively rich. Now, two billion passengers crowd British airports each year, a thousand-fold increase over 50 years.

Conventional projections of transport demand point to continued future growth of road travel, a continuation of the historic steady increase in both numbers of vehicles and distance travelled. The British Department for Transport projects increases of about 30 per cent for both traffic and congestion by 2025 compared with 2003.[1] Such projections reflect belief in a tenacious link between economic growth and traffic growth. As we get richer, we can increasingly afford the costs of motoring and of air travel. Technological advances and competitive markets are tending to reduce these costs in real terms. When we acquire cars, we travel greater distances. Acquisition of the second or third car by the household permits more travel, particularly by women.

This additional travel arises because people find that they can improve their quality of life though mobility, despite the time spent in congested traffic – time made increasingly acceptable in more comfortable cars equipped with in-car entertainment and navigation aids. We can seek employment within a wide area without the domestic upheaval of moving house, and can reconcile employment opportunities for ourselves and others in our household through car-based mobility. The decline of trade union membership in the private sector is a consequence of a labour market where employees are no longer limited to working for the small number of employers in the immediate locality of home or on a convenient public transport route. There is now less need for a union to counter the bargaining power of the local employers at the mine, mill or factory. The travel-to-work area enlarges as the workers get in their cars to seek out employers who most value their services, wherever located within acceptable travelling time. Development of individual skills and expertise is encouraged in a labour market in which physical mobility facilitates social mobility. Increasing everyday travel promotes the shift from a class society to something nearer a meritocracy.

Most of us have chosen lives in which increasing personal mobility – very largely by car – feels as though it improves our quality of life, despite the negative aspects of road traffic. The same car-based mobility is being sought in developing countries as per capita incomes increase, reflecting the attractions of door-to-door convenience and the status and autonomy associated with the private motor vehicle. The global motor industry, fiercely competitive and driven largely by short-term objectives, effectively promotes car ownership to a receptive audience of actual and potential users. Innovation drives down prices while improving quality, thus enhancing the attraction of the product. It's hard to stand out against the trend. Adult cyclists tend to be mostly middle-class fitness fans or environmentalists. What the workers want, and can increasingly afford, is a proper set of wheels.

The road builders also have a natural interest in car-based mobility. Ministries of transport have seen it as a core function to channel tax revenues from ministries of finance to the construction companies and have devised methodologies for economic appraisal to justify this transfer. The main economic benefit is held to be the travel time saved by motorists through new road construction, the aggregate of quite small time savings made by a very large number of individual travellers.

In the face of the undoubted attractions of motorized mobility promoted by powerful commercial interests, why are we concerned about the growth of travel? Critics of car-based mass-mobility draw attention to a number of disadvantages. John Adams recognizes that mobility is liberating and empowering, but in his critique of what he terms 'hypermobility', he highlights unwelcome aspects including suburban sprawl, polarization of society between the mobility-rich and the mobility have-nots, greater dangers for those not in cars, and more obesity. He supposes that a more mobile world would have less cultural variety, would be more anonymous and less convivial, would be more crime-ridden and less democratic. Lynn Sloman argues that cars have come to dominate our culture and our daily lives. Cars are the ultimate mixed blessing, hogging the roads, closing local shops and services, lessening social contact, making us fat, causing death and injury, and killing the planet. George Monbiot believes that the growth in driving is one of the primary reasons for the libertarianism now sweeping through parts of the rich world. When you drive, society becomes an obstacle.[2]

Some social scientists suggest that increasing mobility results in a lack of connections, commitment and emotional nearness, and can undermine communities. Social networks are individualized, so there is a proliferation of weak ties while strong ties are increasingly few and short-lived. Weak ties seem suitable for mobile lifestyles – they represent routes while strong ties imply roots. Robert Putnam argues that we are spending more time alone in the car, and while many see this as a time for quiet relaxation, the car and the commute are demonstrably bad for community life. He suggests that suburban sprawl detracts from 'social capital' (the concept he has championed). On the other hand, there is a counter-argument that travel can indeed generate social capital – people keep in touch though recurrent long-distance communication and intermittent physical reunion.[3]

More generally, there is growing interest in the idea of 'slowness'. This started with the 'Slow Food' movement, founded 20 years ago in Italy by Carlo Petrini, which emphasizes leisurely dining based on fresh local produce and traditional artisanal techniques from sustainable farming. The concept of 'slow' has been extended to other aspects of living, although seemingly with little focus on travel.[4] Yet slow travel can be very agreeable, witness the popularity of cruises in all their varied forms. My own taste is to sail at an average speed of about five knots around the isles off the west coast of Scotland, after a slow overnight train journey on the London to Glasgow sleeper followed by the spectacularly scenic but slow trip up the West Highland Line to the port of Oban.

These arguments against car-based mobility and for a more measured pace of life, however attractive and virtuous, have made little impact on society, thus far at least. Most people cram activities into daily life, aided by ready access to the car and other fast modes of transport. Moreover, the car has very particular attractions, over and above as a means of getting from A to B.

In your car you inhabit a personal, private space, a home from home moving through external environments, in which, as well as travelling, you can conduct acts of business, romance, family, friendship and so on. Unlike public transport, the car facilitates a domestic mode of dwelling where, as at home, you can fill the space with music or voices. But cars are for driving, and different personality types satisfy their need for car-based mobility in different ways, some with considerable enthusiasm for the act of driving. Sigmund Freud explained the pleasures of motoring as echoes of the pleasures of early childhood. Toddlers delight in independent movement, running away from their parents when out walking in the park. At other times, they gain comfort in a passive way from being cradled in their mothers' arms. Car-owning adults can relive the thrill of the chase while insulated in a soft cocoon, Freud suggested.[5]

Whatever the reasons, cars and motoring are enormously popular. In developed countries, the proportion of men licensed to drive is as least as high as the proportion able to read. In Britain, 90 per cent of men between aged 40 and 60 hold a driving licence (and three-quarters of women), and for many driving is likely to be more pleasurable than reading. The BBC TV 'petrol-heads' programme, *Top Gear*, presented by Jeremy Clarkson, is seen by more than six million viewers in Britain and shown in 100 countries around world. Witness too the popularity of motoring magazines, the top five in Britain having a combined circulation of over half a million. Formula One motor racing attracts very large television audiences, around 500 million viewers worldwide over the course of a season.[6]

We need to face up to the implications of the historic and cultural trend towards increasing mobility through the personal motor car. There are two generally accepted reasons why we should be concerned about the continued growth in individual travel. First, anxiety that traffic congestion will get steadily worse, ending in frequent gridlock. Second, we worry about the environmental consequences of unconstrained road traffic and aviation growth, particularly global warming. To see what must be done, recall the key arguments from earlier chapters.

## Travel in a nutshell

The amount of time that people spend travelling is limited by the 24 hours of the day and all the other activities that we need to fit in. It turns out that on average people spend about an hour a day in motion. For the same reason, the number of journeys we make is also limited – about a thousand a year on average. And it also turns out that the proportion of average household expenditure devoted to travel stays pretty constant over the years. The big increase in personal mobility over the past century and more is the result of travelling at higher speeds. Average daily distances travelled have increased substantially, reflecting mainly the longer journeys that can be made comfortably by modern cars on improved roads, all within acceptable limits of personal daily travel time. One key driver of change in the transport sector of the economy is technological progress. While genuinely innovative technologies are quite rare, steady refinement is the norm, permitting higher average speeds at lower cost. The second source of change is the growth of personal incomes that makes faster travel increasingly affordable.

All this is about the past. What of the future? If we adopt that favourite device of the strategists, the 'business-as-usual' scenario, we can project into the future three constants: travel time, number of trips and expenditure on travel (as a proportion of household expenditure). We can assume that incomes continue to grow as they have in the past – perhaps a doubling in real terms over the next 30 years. We might also assume that motoring and aviation costs hold steady. And we could further suppose continued incremental refinement of current transport technologies. Where would such a business-as-usual scenario lead? One possible outcome is that we would attempt to travel yet faster and farther. But then we would run up against the two big limitations to future human mobility: carbon and congestion.

Contrast the historic growth of travel with the historic growth of communications. For a long time, the latter depended on the former, as messages and letters were delivered by hand through a journey chain involving physical transport. Then came the telegraph, followed by the telephone, radio and television, and then the internet. The link with the transport system was broken. We now have the prospect of information and entertainment virtually without limit, as costs plummet and bandwidth expands. As for any problems with electronic congestion, carbon emissions or safety, well, there's nothing that can't be fixed. Bandwidth may be a constraint on some kinds of download at present. The huge 'server farms' that make the internet possible can use a lot of electricity. And there are some residual concerns about the health impact of mobile phone radio frequency emissions. But these are nuisances rather than real impediments.

There is an important distinction between 'weightless' and 'physical' technologies in respect of meeting consumer expectations at times of peak demand. For instance, while demand at popular sporting and entertainment venues can commonly be such that each seat could be filled many times over, there is no limit to the size of the television audience for such events. Transport is of course a 'live event' and a realistic view of transport options needs to take this into account. In general, we cannot hope to meet unconstrained travel demand at times of peak usage, which means that congestion is a natural and unavoidable phenomenon in transport systems.

## Congestion: A concise account

So, what is to be done about congestion? First, recognize that it has always been a feature of busy city centres, ever since Roman times. It's inconvenient but not disastrous. The proverbial 'gridlock' rarely if ever occurs. In theory, traffic backing up from intersections in a close-spaced network of intersecting roads could lock up, as the tail from one intersection reaches back to the previous one. But with modern computer-coordinated traffic signals, this can be avoided. Overall, congestion is self-limiting since those with the least need to travel at peak times decide to set out at other times or travel by rail when that is a possibility. Congestion charging, as used successfully in central London, can reduce the level of congestion. But it would need very high charges to eliminate it altogether, charges which would be very unpopular and economically inefficient. London-type congestion charging can best be viewed as a charge on motorists for occupying road space while on the move, analogous to the charge for roadside parking, the proceeds from which are used to subsidize public transport and which helpfully lessens congestion. Plans to modify the scheme to encourage low-carbon vehicles make clear the aim of using charging to achieve a number of desirable behavioural changes.[7]

In city centres, road construction is very difficult or impossible. Beyond the cities the traditional remedy for congestion has been to build new roads or widen existing ones. But this is no solution to the problem of congestion. Adding road space results in faster traffic speeds. This allows motorists access to more distant destinations in the limited time they have for travel (which is good because it enlarges choice), but adds to the detriments, carbon emissions, accidents and so forth (which is bad), without making significant difference to congestion, because the effect of extra road space is offset by the greater distance needed between faster vehicles. As has been rightly said by many ministers of transport, 'we cannot build our way out of congestion'. This is why the investment in new and improved roads in Britain running at £5 billion a year is poor value for money.

One answer to the problem of congestion outside city centres is road pricing. The economists are keen on charging for road use to deter those motorists whose need to travel at times of peak use is least, or who least can afford to pay. The success of congestion charging in central London is seen as encouraging. There is, however, a crucial difference between city centres, with their dense networks of public transport, and the suburbs and beyond where car use is so extensive. Fewer than 10 per cent of those commuting into the original central charging zone in London travel by car, whereas for Britain as a whole 70 per cent of journeys to work are by car. So the impact of London congestion charging falls on a small minority of drivers, mostly better off, while non-drivers benefit from improved public transport. But any form of national road pricing would hit the pockets of lower income motorists for whom public transport options will usually be more limited. Moreover, national road pricing would be technically difficult and expensive to implement, as I explained in Chapter 5.

What's the alternative to road pricing? If you ask drivers why congestion is a problem, they say that the main concern is uncertainty about journey time. So what needs to be done is to provide drivers with predictive information about how long their trip should take, available at both their home and office computers before setting out, and on their mobile phones and in-car navigation devices while travelling. 'Predictive navigation', as this might be called, would provide the best route in the light of prevailing traffic conditions as well as the expected time of arrival. This would reduce anxiety about arrival time. It would also allow planning the departure time to avoid the worst of the traffic. In this respect predictive navigation would function like road pricing by reducing congestion at peak times. But predictive navigation would go with the grain of many current technological developments, as well as being voluntarily adopted and paid for by those most able to benefit. It's not clear yet what impact predictive navigation would have on the quality of the journey, nor indeed how effective predictive traffic forecasting would be. But in my view it would be worth quite a bit of effort to research and develop this approach since it is so much more attractive than general road pricing.

## Carbon in brief

Greenhouse gas emissions, principally carbon dioxide, are the other big problem for the future of mobility. Transport sector emissions could be reduced by new technologies or by changing people's travel behaviour. But first, what is the objective?

I would argue, along with many others, that there is no need to treat transport in isolation and reduce this sector's emissions by 60 per cent or 80 per cent by 2050, or whatever is the necessary reduction to avoid dangerous climate change. Such targets should apply to the totality of greenhouse gas emissions from all areas of activity. There is nothing special about carbon emissions from transport – except for the potency of aircraft emissions into the upper atmosphere, which of course must be factored in to requirements to be expected from the aviation industry. Let us suppose that international negotiations lead to agreement that all the developed and major developing counties adopt 'contraction-and-convergence' as a broad principle, together with 'cap-and-trade' as the means to implement this. That is, there would be a global cap on annual greenhouse gas emissions, which would be set to decline year after year until a safe level is reached. Consistent with this cap, allocations of permissible emissions would be made to individual countries, reflecting their existing emissions and state of economic development. Over time per capita emissions would converge to a common level. And trading in emission permits would take place, as in the European Union Emissions Trading Scheme.

Such arrangements, outlined in briefest possible form above, are certain to require huge diplomatic effort to put in place, and the timescale may cover many years. But if the adverse effects of climate change, including evidence of ice cap melting, become apparent on an increasing scale, the impetus to achieve a successful outcome would grow. Possibly alternative mechanisms would be considered and perhaps adopted: for instance reliance on carbon taxes – I have no objection to this if the necessary impact on reducing emissions can be achieved. It is, however, possible that no agreement internationally will be achieved, in which case we will all need to grapple with far greater problems than the efficient functioning of our transport system.

So for the purposes of this book, I'm assuming that we will progress to an international trading system for carbon emissions (to cover the other greenhouse gases as well), which would include all significant transport sources. The outcome would be a traded price for carbon that would favour zero- and low-carbon energy sources and transport technologies, and would penalize carbon emissions from fossil fuels. The level and rate of increase in the carbon price would depend on how individuals and businesses respond. If there is a big effort to adopt what seem likely to be cost-effective technologies to improve the efficiency of energy use in the home and at work, and to switch to electricity generation from coal to renewable or nuclear sources (or to capture and store carbon dioxide from coal-fired plant), then there would be headroom for continued use of oil-based fuels in the transport sector at modest extra cost. But if it turns out to be difficult to achieve such carbon savings, then the price of carbon would be higher and would impact more substantially on transport use.

It's not just what happens in Britain or even Europe. As the developing countries, including China and India, develop their economies and as their populations seek the benefits of car-based mobility and of flying, their carbon emissions will rise. If these are to be accommodated within an overall cap that declines over time, then the cost of carbon is likely to rise, and opportunities may shrink for the developed countries to buy carbon credits from the developing countries since they would need their allocation of credits to cope with their own emissions. There are therefore good arguments that we should plan for a future of rising carbon prices in which transport technologies that avoid using oil-based fuels will become increasingly commercially viable.[8] This implies higher cost travel, given the need to finance the development and deployment of new, low-carbon technologies, but that should not be a big problem for most people. We've been in the habit of spending a fairly fixed proportion of our household expenditure on travel, a proportion that could rise somewhat in the future provided the increase takes place sufficiently slowly for people to have time to adapt. But there could be difficulties for those on low incomes, a transport equivalent of 'fuel poverty' which is said to occur when a household needs to spend more than 10 per cent of its income on fuel use in order to heat the home to an adequate standard of warmth. This equity issue will be of increasing political significance as carbon prices rise.

There are a number of routes to low-carbon transport. More efficient versions of existing technologies would get us some way. But such gains tend to be offset by desires for bigger, heavier vehicles which use more fuel. So we need to think in terms of a step change downwards in emissions from new transport technologies, including electric vehicles using electricity from zero-carbon generation, hydrogen as an energy carrier derived from zero-carbon sources, and biofuels derived from plants that capture atmospheric carbon dioxide as they grow. There are prospects for all these approaches, but at present they are mostly higher cost than existing oil-based motive power even at current high oil prices. These high costs reflect the relatively early stages of development of the technologies, before long-run economies are discovered under the pressure of competition, as the famous learning curve is traversed downwards. How to give the development of these technologies more impetus I discuss below.

## Behavioural change in brief

The other approach to reducing transport carbon emissions would be to change people's behaviour, particularly to reduce car use. This would also cut congestion. There are quite a lot of possibilities that are actively canvassed and some pilot schemes that seem encouraging. These include: promoting the 'slow modes' – walking and cycling; more attractive public transport; car sharing and car clubs; personalized travel planning that suggests alternatives to car use; and enforcing speed limits. These are virtuous ideas which deserve to succeed. But we should be wary of counting carbon savings before they have been well and truly demonstrated.

Regrettably, there are a number of reasons for scepticism. First, the car is dominant, and walking and cycling have been in long-term decline. Efforts to boost their use start from a low base, so even a doubling would make limited impact. Second, walking, cycling and buses are generally slower than the car, door to door, so switching from the car tends to limit distance travelled and hence choice of destinations, given that travel time is a limiting constraint on mobility. The reason why we use our cars for short journeys where we could more healthily walk or cycle is that we are short of time. Third, persuading some people not to use their cars helps reduce congestion (which is good) but in effect frees up road space for others to make longer trips (not so good). The effect is similar to widening a road. To retain the carbon- and congestion-reducing benefits of getting some people out of their cars, we need to lock them in somehow, which is not easy.

Another way that is advocated to reduce the need to travel is through land use planning that fosters the convenient location of homes, workplaces, shopping and leisure facilities and so forth, in contrast to the usual pattern of suburbanization and car-based travel to most of the places you need to reach. The question that arises is whether, if people live close to where they work, they will travel less as a result, or whether because a certain amount of daily travel meets a basic human need, they would compensate for less travelling to work by more travelling to other places – and if so in what way? More walking would be fine, more car travel not so.

While I would like to see more walking and cycling, more use of public transport, and less car use, it does seem to me that we are pushing uphill and should not count these chickens until they hatch. The one switch away from the car that goes with the grain of how we live is the increasing use being made of the rail system.

## Seven sustainable policies for transport

We all make individual decisions about how, when and to where we travel. These decisions affect other travellers, especially at times of peak demand. Transport policy is the collective attempt, working through our political institutions, to achieve outcomes with the biggest general benefit.

However, the key current policies of transport ministries, such as the British Department for Transport, are incoherent and counterproductive. There is a dedication to a major road building programme which yields little benefit, and certainly no relief of traffic congestion, for the reason which any reader who has reached this far will understand. The justification for road building is based on defective cost–benefit analysis which supposes that travellers seek to save travel time, whereas in fact what they benefit from is the extra access. The models by which transport planners try to forecast future travel demand are based on idealized rational behaviour rather than authentic behaviour as observed in the real world. Road pricing at national level is sometimes seen as the best answer to congestion, sometimes as a policy only for the very long term, but in any event would be unpopular and disappointing in outcome. And the impact of constraints on carbon emissions is not taken sufficiently into account in forward thinking, so that airport expansion is proposed to meet demand arising from extraordinarily cheap air fares for leisure travel. All these 'policies' are set out in a succession of entirely unmemorable White Papers, ten-year plans and the like, which have minimal practical impact.

So, what better policies might we envisage? Let me offer seven suggestions, focusing on the situation in Britain, though much of this could apply to other developed countries.

First, an economically advanced country such as Britain already has a well developed transport system. Most people have considerable choice through access based on mobility. Improvements in access might still be made, but it is important to understand what is happening in order to avoid unintended consequences. Industry and trade associations are under no obligation to see the bigger picture and commonly urge simple-minded expansions to the transport system which appeal to the generality of their membership. Nor should we be swayed by facile international comparisons. A recent independent study concluded that Britain compares favourably with its European counterparts across a range of transport outcomes, and that we had some clear strengths, as well as some weaknesses that need to be addressed. Robert Wright, the well-informed transport correspondent of the *Financial Times*, has challenged the common assumption that transport in Britain is run badly – for instance, while the French have impressive high-speed trains, their regional rail services have been allowed to deteriorate.[9]

We do not therefore need any wholesale expansion or transformation of the transport system. Indeed, we should be parsimonious in adding to surface transport infrastructure. The aim is to improve access, not to save time. Decisions should be made based on comparisons of the cost-effectiveness of the full range of solutions to particular problems of access. An intended new urban development, for instance, must allow its inhabitants access to the jobs they are likely to seek, to schools, hospitals, shops and so on. Suitable transport must be put in place even as the buildings are going up. The population of Britain is projected to increase from 60 million now to about 70 million by 2030. This implies a need for housing to accommodate the increased number of households and for transport infrastructure to support such housing. If most of this population growth is to be accommodated in existing cities and towns where there is little scope for road construction, then substantial investment in public transport would be needed to service the increased urban population density.

Second, we should be austere in making provision for the growth of aviation for leisure travel. We should not sanction new runways until we are clear that their capacity will be useable in the long run in a world in which carbon constraints bite hard. In the meantime, arrangements are needed to permit the airlines to trade the rights they have to take-off and landing slots at busy airports. This would allow economically valuable business travel to claim priority over leisure travel, and would encourage efficient airlines to build their international businesses at the expense of less efficient carriers.

Third, we must recognize that whatever the intention, if the impact of investment in the transport system is to increase speed, people will end up travelling farther, with a bigger environmental footprint. So we should generally avoid increasing the speed of travel unless there is a good reason to improve access. An example: a new bypass around a town or village is motivated by the wish to reduce the impact of traffic on the community. But this new road is likely to be a faster road and so longer trips result and hence more traffic is generated. We need bypasses that provide the environmental benefit without speeding up the traffic.

Fourth, in a carbon-constrained world, individuals and businesses will adapt to limitations on physical transport by making better use of information and telecoms technologies. These technologies have substantial potential and need to be fostered, both to substitute for travel and to provide predictive information about future traffic and travel conditions. A parsimonious approach to the construction of new road and aviation infrastructure will mean that the growth of traffic will 'decouple' from the growth of the economy. Over the past 30 years or so the earlier strong link between energy consumption and economic growth has weakened, as the structure of the developed economies has shifted from manufacturing to services. Transport demand growth too has been slowing relative to economic growth since the early 1990s. Central London demonstrates that a dynamic economy need not be car-dependent.

The development of information and telecommunication technologies will allow individuals to make better decisions when they exercise choice about when and how to travel, as well as providing reassurance about time of arrival. Because we live in close mutual proximity and tend to be active at similar times, we must accept that traffic congestion is inevitable, a shared experience that has to be lived with. We could manage busy lives more effectively, however, if we had better information about travel conditions and the performance of the transport system.

Fifth, rail travel is expanding and should be encouraged, by using advanced signal technology to run more frequent services on established routes, as well as longer trains. This would relieve overcrowding. Light rail, trams and underground services in cities are a good thing, despite their seemingly high cost. Rail can substitute for cars, save carbon and can allow more people to commute to city centres where the economic benefits of working in close proximity to suppliers, customers and competitors are increasingly recognized. Expansion of the rail system should be at current train speeds. Higher speed trains on new track are expensive to build and operate, and would result in people commuting ever longer distances.

When I started writing this book, I had not expected to end up endorsing substantially more expenditure on the railways, which are responsible for only 7 per cent of all personal travel (passenger kilometres), compared with 85 per cent by car and van. I don't use trains a lot, I'm not a railways buff, and I didn't have a big model train set as a boy. But the case for rail is that it can serve dense urban areas effectively with a high enough quality service to get drivers out of their cars. This is environmentally a better option in terms not only of carbon but of noise and local pollutants. Moreover, international experience shows that a good city centre needs track-based transport.

The argument for rail is part of a more general argument for focusing more on the *quality* of the transport system and less on the *quantity* of travel. In recent years the average distance travelled within Britain has held steady at about 7000 miles a year and the average number of overseas trips by air has been about one per person per year. Arguably, we should rest content with that, and should bend our efforts to improving the quality of our journeys. The development of the motor car over the past century shows what quality improvement is achievable – a prime example of the success of incremental innovation driven by competition, which has led to hugely improved standards of comfort and mechanical reliability, as well as to lower real costs. This is what the public transport system needs to emulate through close attention to the needs of travellers, high quality engineering and innovative approaches.

So, sixth on my list of policies, we now need to extend such high quality standards to the public and collective elements of the transport system – including not least the ill-managed airports in the London area. Quality improvement is particularly relevant to a further constraint on human mobility – beyond carbon and congestion – that is becoming of increasing importance as the population ages. Human frailty limits our travel in later life, and earlier if we have a disability. To make a journey, every link must be manageable in the chain that starts and finishes at home. The past designers of our historic transport structures, particular the railways, neglected the needs of travellers with limited mobility. We now have a much better recognition of what needs to be done for them, though this is far from being put fully into practice. A high quality transport system maximizes use by older people, our future selves.

Seventh and last, we need to accelerate the introduction of low- and zero-carbon transport technologies, to sustain the degree of mobility to which we have become accustomed. One approach would be to anticipate a future high traded price of carbon by interim measures – 'green taxes' and the like – that send quite strong signals about the commercial prospects for low-carbon technologies. The most promising approach in the near term would be to sustain a cultural shift to smaller cars. Europeans drive smaller cars than Americans without feeling deprived of mobility. Smallness can be promoted, both through regulations about carbon emissions from new cars and through fiscal measures. Taxation on fossil-derived oil fuels needs to be increased steadily. To counter the unpopularity of increased pump prices the extra revenue should be earmarked to reduce other taxation, so most people would feel no worse off but would be motivated to buy a rather smaller car. In London, it has been proposed to modify the congestion charging scheme by subjecting vehicles with the highest carbon emissions to a charge of three times the standard rate to enter the charging zone. A further measure would be to enforce the legal speed limit on motorways in the interest of safety, fuel economy, constraining journey lengths and encouraging use of smaller-engined cars (less need for high acceleration up the slip road to enter the traffic stream). If smoking can be banned in public places, legal speed limits on motorways and elsewhere could be enforced, not least through the knowledge that accumulating too many penalty points leads to loss of the driving licence.

For the longer term, governments should fund the development and procurement of promising low- and zero-carbon technologies, sharing the burden internationally with like-minded governments. While civil servants in transport and industry departments tend to be reluctant to pick technological 'winners', their counterparts in defence ministries know this cannot be avoided. The government could fund, for example, the development and procurement of a hydrogen supply system for road-based public transport and for public service vehicles. If hydrogen proved in due course to be commercially viable for road vehicles generally, the outlets would be expandable to compete with petrol and diesel at the pump.

The budgetary consequences of these seven policy proposals would be a substantial switch from spending on road construction to spending on rail and low-carbon transport technologies. The mission of the Department for Transport would be to maintain mobility while leading the task of decarbonizing the transport system.

## The science of human mobility

I've been rather sceptical about the prospects for changing human behaviour in a direction that reduces the distance that we travel. This is because of the clear trend towards increasing personal mobility, common to all societies as they develop economically. Mobility is very attractive both for the choices it permits at the destinations we can reach, and for the intrinsic satisfaction of travelling – travelling for fun, one might say for short. It would therefore be a real challenge to change the behaviour of those of us in developed countries who have become used to having considerable choice and fun through travel. It would also be hard to deny these opportunities to people in developing countries as they become able to afford car- and plane-based mobility. And as well as mobility, there are all the other uses of energy that would be needed for the good health and well-being of the world's population, including the three billion extra inhabitants of the planet that are expected to be among us by mid-century. All this suggests that we face formidable problems in limiting travel and other forms of energy use, even for the excellent reason of avoiding dangerous climate change.

So an important question is whether there is scope for limiting the growth of mobility, even reducing it. People certainly do change basic kinds of behaviour. We have seen what is known as the 'demographic transition' in which family size has shrunk dramatically as parents realized that having more and more children did not improve the prospects for the family as a whole. Might we now envisage a 'mobility transition' based on a recognition that our quality of life does not depend on being able to access yet another supermarket, commute ever longer distances, or holiday on ever more remote beaches?

It's hard to answer such questions at present, in part because 'human mobility' as a subject for enquiry has barely got going. There are researchers like me in the field of 'transport studies', roughly the ground covered by this book. There are psychologists who study the behaviour of people on the move, very largely in relation to safety. Some social scientists are attempting to develop an area of discourse designated 'mobilities', which covers topics such as tourism, migration, transport and social exclusion, and trans-national social networks. They argue that social science has generally focused on static aspects of society and has largely ignored the importance of the movement of people for work and family life, for leisure and pleasure, and for politics and protest. In particular, the huge impact of the car has been neglected. One potential attraction of this 'new mobilities paradigm' is the potential to address the origins of the demand for travel, which conventional transport researchers and economists tend to take as a given.[10]

This 'mobilities' initiative amongst the social scientists may increase our under-standing of the underlying social and individual determinants of human mobility. At present, however, the approach seems somewhat limited by a reluctance to engage with economic aspects of travel behaviour, and there are barriers to comprehension to those not in the field that can arise from the use of 'post-modern' language.[11] More important, there is also the question of the nature of the findings from studies grounded in the mobilities perspective. My own scientific upbringing has fostered the rather simple view that the aim of science is to generate reliable knowledge – know-ledge that can be relied on when applied in the world at large. The more conceptual kind of social science seems to find difficulty in generating knowledge that is reliable and thus useful in practice. Nevertheless, ideas prompted by such studies can stimu-late practical thinking. The study of nomads, people always on the move but slowly, relics of our evolutionary past, could be suggestive, as could be consideration of those who have adopted static lifestyles, monks for instance. Pilgrimage, common amongst the world's religions, is another topic of potential significance. How mobility relates to happiness may also be a fruitful theme. Evolutionary approaches to psychology and brain function suggest that natural selection has led to modern humans having brains composed of different mental modules or programmes that are specialized for solving adaptive ancestral problems. Some of these relate to mobility, including mental maps for large territories, a sense of danger, habitat selection and foraging. However, no mind module has apparently been suggested for mobility as such – a possible fertile topic for consideration.[12]

When submitting a paper to a scientific journal, it is common for the author to be asked to provide a few 'keywords' which can be used to help identify papers in the subject index of the journal's contents. The keywords distil the paper's content. For this book, four keywords suggest themselves, in two pairs: Choice and Fun, Carbon and Congestion. More choice of activities is what has driven our ever increasing mobility. Fun from travel – being out and about, using our skills, exercising and so forth – underpins both daily mobility and longer trips. What constrains mobility is congestion, and increasingly for the future, carbon emissions.

We need to understand these four key aspects of travel and transport better if the problems we face are to be tackled successfully. The most challenging topics for research are the behavioural aspects of travel, understanding the motivations of choice and fun with a view to influencing people to change in ways that would help solve global problems. In what ways does human quality of life and indeed happiness depend on mobility? How much choice of destination do we need – both day-to-day and longer distance leisure travel? How much such choice could be met without physical travel, by means of information and telecoms technologies? What are the important aspects of the fun that we get from travelling? Why do we feel good when on the move? How much of this could be met from walking or cycling or other low-carbon modes? Social scientists have a great opportunity to illuminate these aspects of human behaviour in ways that would be practically useful.

# Epilogue

Travel is not the only manifestation of human mobility. Children playing actively are often in motion. Children and adults indulge in sports, which involve not only movement but also competition. Another ubiquitous kind of human mobility is dance, which seems to have been an important part of ceremony, rituals, celebrations and entertainment since the earliest human civilizations. The historian William Hardy McNeill has asked whether something as simple and seemingly natural as falling into step could have marked us for evolutionary success. He suggests that coordinated rhythmic movement – and the shared feelings it evokes – has been a powerful force in holding human groups together.[13]

Our propensity to dance must surely be driven by some element from our evolutionary origins, perhaps connecting mobility with a feeling of well-being, the pairing which motivated humankind to populate nearly all the land of the planet. In dancing, moving with our fellows, we recapture an elemental spirit. Poussin's famous painting, *A Dance to the Music of Time*, which hangs in the Wallace Collection in London, depicts the Seasons, hand in hand and facing outwards, treading in rhythm in intricate measure to the notes of the lyre. A contemporary counterpart of this circular dance is the *Rueda de Casino*, where couples dance to the rhythmically complex music of the Cuban salsa, moving on to new partners around the circle to the commands of the *cantante*, meeting again at full circuit your own partner, in my case Monica to whom this book is dedicated, as we devote a weekly evening to this curiously fulfilling pastime, whose satisfactions require some explaining to our less mobile friends. We are sensing perhaps some earlier phase of existence, gratifying a deep human need to move in synchrony with others of the tribe, motion in time, retreating and approaching, change and repetition, individual display within the group – feelings that may not be wholly inapplicable to the problems we now face, were we to act on the maxim: travel less, dance more.

# Endnotes

## Chapter I

1 The data regarding personal travel cited here and elsewhere are taken from the excellent compilations of the Department for Transport, including the annual publications *Transport Trends*, *Transport Statistics for Great Britain*, and the *National Travel Survey*. The latest editions can be found at www.dft.gov. uk/pgr/statistics

2 Survey findings from *Transport Trends 2006*.

3 Cann (2001); Goldstein and Chikhi (2002); Mellars (2006).

4 Heinrich (2002); Bramble and Lieberman (2004); Stone and Lurquin (2007).

5 Jones (2000), p312.

6 Serbin et al (2001).

7 Alexander and Hines (2002).

8 Sack (1986); Marchetti (1994).

9 The most recent data on travel time in Britain can be found in the *National Travel Survey 2006*, published by the Department for Transport, 2007. For a discussion of some methodological issues see Metz (2008).

10 For discussion of the variation of travel time see Metz (2005).

11 For discussion of international data compilations of travel time see Metz (2008). See also Eurostat (2007) 'Passenger mobility in Europe', *Statistics in Focus*, issue number 87/2007.

12 www.surveyarchive.org/zahavi.html; Zahavi and Talvitie (1980).

13 British data in Figure 1.3 taken from *Family Spending 2006 edition*, published by National Statistics (there have been some changes over the years in the classification of certain elements of travel expenditure, such as vehicle tax and insurance, which limit comparisons over long time periods). For international data on travel expenditure see Schafer and Victor (2000) and also Metz (2005).

14 See Schafer (2000) for international data on time use. *The Time Use Survey*

*2005: How we spend our time* (authors Lader, D., Short, S. and Gurshuny, J., published by National Statistics, 2006) records average travel time in Britain as 87 minutes a day, significantly higher than that from the Department for Transport's *National Travel Survey*. At least part of the explanation is that the *Time Use Survey* covers people over the age of 16 only, whereas the *National Travel Survey* also includes children – who on average travel less.

15   There is a small literature that discusses the tempo of life in different towns and countries, although this has not been related to travel behaviour; see Bornstein and Bornstein (1976), Levine (2006) and Shaw (2001). See also Griffiths (1999) for a discursive and original argument about how people experience time.

16   *National Travel Survey 2006.*

17   The mistaken idea that increasing access to a car results in more journeys being made is well established in transport thinking. It was probably first described by John Wootton who later became a distinguished director of the Transport Research Laboratory. The methodological error, which is well understood in epidemiology, arises from assuming that an effect seen at any one time in a cross-section of society allows an inference to be drawn about how this effect will change over time. To study the latter, longitudinal data are needed in which change over time is explicitly investigated. See Wootton (1999) and Wootton and Pick (1967). The fundamental relationship is a positive correlation between socio-economic status and travel behaviour.

18   Phil Goodwin, Inaugural Lecture as professor of transport policy at University College, 23 October 1997. To be found at http://www.cts.ucl.ac.uk/tsu/pbginau. htm

19   The findings of Goodwin and his team, then at the Transport Studies Unit, Oxford University, are included in the report prepared for the RAC Foundation for Motoring and the Environment in 1995 entitled 'Car Dependency'. See also Dargay and Hanly (2007).

20   Metz (2002).

21   Dobbs (2005); and a report by the Centre for Research in Social Policy (2006) 'Evidence base review of mobility: Choices and barriers for different social groups', www.dft.gov.uk/pgr/scienceresearch/social/evidence_base_review_on_mobility

22   Data from *Transport Trends 2006 edition*.

## Chapter 2

1   See Woodcock et al (2007) for a recent overview; also Fletcher and McMichael (1997).

2   *Transport Statistics for Great Britain 2007 edition*; Department for Transport (2007) 'Tomorrow's roads – safer for everyone: The second three year review (the Government's road safety strategy and casualty reduction targets for 2010)', www.dft.gov.uk/pgr/roadsafety/strategytargetsperformance/2ndreview/

3   Department for Transport (2006) *Road Casualties Great Britain: 2005*.

4   Commission for Global Road Safety (2007) 'Make roads safe: A new priority for sustainable development', London. This report is co-authored by Kate McMahon

who had been in charge of Department for Transport's road safety research, which I had regarded as the department's best run research programme.

5   Boseley, S. (2007) 'International aid swells road deaths', *The Guardian*, 23 April.

6   Cavill et al (2006).

7   Attributed to Professor Sir George Alberti, former president of the International Diabetes Federation.

8   Department for Environment, Food and Rural Affairs (2005), Air Quality Expert Group, 'Particulate matter in the United Kingdom'.

9   Holmen and Niemeier (2003).

10  National Statistics (2007) News release, 'Inequalities in life expectancy at 65 in UK', 28 November.

11  AEA Technology (2006) 'London low emission zone health impact assessment – final report', published by Transport for London.

12  Allowance is also made for the flow of costs and benefits over time, adjusting for the changing value of money over time – known as 'discounted cash flow'.

13  The UK Department for Transport's *Transport Analysis Guidance* is probably the most comprehensive available for the appraisal of new infrastructure. See www. webtag.org.uk; unit 3.3 deals with the valuation of environmental aspects.

14  Rothengatter (2003).

15  Watts et al (2006). See also *The Idiot's Guide to Highway Maintenance* at www. highwaysmaintence.com/noise.htm

16  Intergovernmental Panel on Climate Change (2007) 'Summary for policy makers', in *Climate Change 2007: The physical science basis*. Contribution of working group 1 to the fourth assessment report of the Intergovernmental Panel on Climate Change, Cambridge University Press.

17  Hansen et al (1981); Burroughs (2007).

18  IPCC (2007) 'Summary for policy makers of the synthesis report of the IPCC fourth assessment report', 17 November, http://www.ipcc.ch/pdf/assessment-report/ar4/syr/ar4_syr_spm.pdf

19  *The Economist* (2007) 'A special report on business and climate change', 2 June.

20  Department for Environment, Food and Rural Affairs (2006) 'Climate change: The UK programme 2006'; Climate Change Bill published and introduced to parliament 14 November 2007.

21  See Lawson (1992) for his career as a minister. In November 2006 Lord Lawson delivered a lecture to the Centre for Policy Studies entitled 'The economics and politics of climate change: An appeal to reason', which expressed considerable scepticism about the science of climate change and the just-published Stern report. He was a co-author of a paper taking issue with Stern's economic analysis (Byatt et al, 2006), which was rebutted by Dietz et al (2007). Lawson is quoted in *The Observer* on 15 May 2007 as no longer disputing the science but arguing that the conventional economic view – urgent action needed now to help future generations – is unfair to present developing countries like China.

22  Barry, R. (2007) 'Carbon trading', *Prospect*, July, pp14–15; *The Economist* (2007) 'Doffing the cap', 16 June; Palmer (2006); Office of Climate Change

(2007) 'Analysis paper on EU Emissions Trading Scheme Review options', at
www.occ.gov.uk/publications/index.htm

23   MacKenzie, D. (2007) 'The political economy of carbon trading', *London Review of Books*, 5 April, pp29–31.

24   Stern (2006).

25   See Note 20.

26   Department for Transport (2007) *Road Transport and the EU Emissions Trading Scheme*; Watters, H. and Tight, M. (2007) 'Designing an emissions trading scheme suitable for surface transport', Commission for Integrated Transport, at www.cfit.gov.uk/docs/2007/climatechange/index.htm

27   Hitchin, R. (2007) 'Decarbonising buildings', *Ingenia*, issue 31, June, Royal Academy of Engineering.

28   Harvey, F. (2007) 'Planet's enemies on the patio', *Financial Times*, 19–20 May, p9.

# Chapter 3

1   van Tilburg (2007).

2   Wachs (2002); Creswell (1958) *Architectural Review*, December, quoted in Jacobs (1961).

3   McCrae, H. (2002) 'Congestion is wonderful: It is a sign of wealth, and a progressive tax', *The Independent*, 27 February.

4   For an historical introduction see Mackie et al (2003).

5   The critique, outlined in this section, of the standard approach to justifying expenditure on roads and other aspects of current transport economic analysis is taken from my paper entitled 'The myth of travel time saving' (Metz, 2008) where full references to the published literature can be found. The approach builds on previous arguments; see Metz (2004b).

6   Standing Advisory Committee on Trunk Road Assessment (1994) 'Trunk roads and the generation of traffic', HMSO, London.

7   Eddington (2006), see especially summary report, para 1.23, and vol 4, para 1.48; Goodwin, P. (2006) 'Induced traffic again. And again. And again'. *Local Transport Today*, 24 August; Parliamentary answer on 27 March 2006 (Column 634W House of Commons Hansard): Dr Stephen Ladyman, the Minister of State for Transport, said that some 90 per cent of road schemes over the last ten years had been appraised using a fixed trip matrix (i.e. trip origins and destinations were assumed to be unchanged after the improved road had opened, implying zero induced traffic). There are other problems with the Eddington report, beyond the neglect of induced traffic, as Eddington himself recognized. He identified a 'conundrum' in the form of a lack of transport projects in urban areas which might have been expected to offer very high returns; see Metz (2007a) for discussion.

8   Flyvbjerg (2004).

9   Metz (2007b).

10   Highways Agency (2006) 'A34 Newbury bypass "five years after" evaluation (1998–

2003)', www.highways.gov.uk/roads/documents/Newbury_Bypass_Five_Years_After_1.pdf

11 Metz (2006c); Amundsen and Elvik (2004).
12 Competition Commission (2000) 'Supermarkets: A report on the supply of groceries from multiple stores in the United Kingdom', Cm 4842.
13 There is one situation in which the access achieved through personal travel would not necessarily involve diminishing marginal utility. There are locations of a unique nature or special value, which are either scarce in some absolute or socially imposed way, or subject to congestion or crowding through more intense use. Unlike supermarkets, they cannot be replicated. Examples include historic sites, waterfront properties, and premiership football stadiums. Higher speeds allow access to a greater number of such distinctive locations. However, the benefits of such enhanced access are offset by increased crowding, as others with similar interests take advantage of the improved transport infrastructure (Hirsch, 1977).
14 Hupkes (1982); Metz (2000); Mokhtarian and Salomon (2001); Choo, Collantes and Mokhtarian (2005); Mokhtarian (2005).
15 Society of Motor Manufacturers and Traders (2006) 'Annual $CO_2$ report – 2006 market'.
16 Lyons and Urry (2005); Lyons, G. (2005) Report on workshop 'Travel time use – developing a research agenda', Department for Transport, 22 September 2005, to be found at www.dft.gov.uk/pgr/economics/rdg/
17 Agglomeration and other benefits to business of transport infrastructure are an important theme of the Eddington (2006) report.
18 Goodwin, P. (2005) 'The remarkable consistency of travel time', *Local Transport Today*, 8 August.
19 Metz (2007b); Campaign to Protect Rural England and Countryside Agency (2006) 'Beyond transport infrastructure: Lessons for the future from recent road projects', www.cpre.org.uk/library/results/transport
20 See at www.dft.gov.uk/pgr/economics/rdg/: (a) 'Audit of the LASER 3 model'; (b) 'Report on workshop for variable demand modelling: A new direction', 28 September 2006.
21 Mullainathan and Thaler (2000); Camerer and Loewenstein (2004). There is a developing body of transport studies which questions utility maximization as the basis for decisions by travellers (see Avineri and Prashker (2005) for a recent discussion).
22 Camerer at al (1997); Mathew (2006).

# Chapter 4

1 Schafer and Victor (2000).
2 For a good account of recent developments in China and India see Pucher et al (2007).
3 Skeer and Wang (2007).
4 Zhao and Wu (2007).

5   See Note 3.

6   Sperling et al (2005).

7   Iyer and Badami (2007); CNN-IBM TV channel website on 27 January 2007 reported a poll of 'middle class' Indians.

8   Singh (2006).

9   UN World Population Prospects 2006 revision; Collier (2007).

10  Pucher et al (2007).

11  Charoentrakulpeeti et al (2006).

12  Government of Hong Kong Special Administrative Region, Transport Department: *Annual Transport Digest 2006*, and *Annual Traffic Census 2003*.

13  Metz (2007a).

14  He et al (2005); Skeer and Wang (2007).

15  Singh (2006).

16  Wright and Fulton (2005).

17  A number of studies have assumed constant travel time and expenditure as the basis for long-term energy and carbon projections, including Schafer (1998), Schafer and Victor (1999, 2000), Azar et al (2003), and Zhang et al (2007).

18  Tapio et al (2007).

19  Rajan (2006).

20  Maugeri (2006).

21  BP Statistical Review of World Energy 2007.

22  Department of Trade and Industry (2007) 'Energy white paper: Meeting the energy challenge', Cm 7124, chapter 4.

23  Deffeyes (2005); Strahan (2007).

24  Cambridge Energy Research Associates (2006) 'Why the peak oil theory falls down', press release 14 November, www.cera.com; Leggett (2006).

25  Witze, A. (2007) 'That's oil folks...' *Nature*, vol 444, pp14–17.

26  Shah (2004); Brower (2006); Simon, B. (2007) 'Alberta oil sands frenzy slows to a more sustainable pace', *Financial Times*, 8 May; Kolbert, E. (2007) 'Unconventional crude: Canada's synthetic fuels boom', *The New Yorker*, 12 November, pp46–51.

27  Jaccard (2005).

28  Stern (2006), chapter 7; Leggett (2006) draws a similar conclusion.

29  See the International Energy Agency's publications on energy security at www.iea.org

30  For cost data see: Confederation of Passenger Transport, 'Cost index' at www.cpt-uk.org; International Air Transport Association 'Economic Briefing, airline fuel and labour cost share June 2007', www.iata.org; *Transport Statistics for Great Britain 2007 edition*, table 3.3.

# Chapter 5

1   Department for Transport (2007) *Transport Trends 2006 edition*, Trend 1.7b; Nichols, M. (2007) 'Review of Highways Agency's major roads programme: A report to the Secretary of State', 14 March; www.dft.gov.uk/pgr/roads/

nicholsreport/nicholsreport; Vidal, J. and Milmo, D. (2007) 'Are these the world's costliest roadworks?' *The Guardian*, 31 July.

2   See Metz (2004a) for a fuller treatment of the argument in this section and for references. See also Metz (2006b).

3   Stopher (2004).

4   Metz (2007b).

5   Richards (2006).

6   Eddington (2006).

7   Commission for Integrated Transport (2006) 'World review of road pricing, phases 1 and 2 reports', London; it was reported in *Local Transport Today* (6 December 2007) that the Dutch government had announced plans to introduced distance-based road user charging starting in 2011–12.

8   Department for Transport (2004) 'Feasibility study of road pricing in the UK', annex C.

9   Vigor, A. (2006) 'Germany delivers the goods', *Transport Times*, 13 January.

10   See Note 8.

11   Supernak, J. (2005) 'HOT lanes on Interstate 15 in San Diego: Technology, impacts and equity issues', PIARC Seminar on Road Pricing, Financing, Regulation and Equity, Cancun, Mexico.

12   www.91expresslanes.com/generalinfo/tollpolicy.asp

13   Kelly (2006).

14   See Note 7.

15   Transport for London (2007) 'Central London congestion charging impact monitoring, fifth annual report', table 6.2.

16   Deloitte Consulting (2004) 'Report on implementation feasibility of DfT road pricing scenarios and proposed business architecture', Department for Transport, London.

17   Transport for London (2007) 'Central London congestion charging impact monitoring, fifth annual report'.

18   Nash et al (2004).

19   Santos and Bhakar (2006); Evans, R. (2007) 'Central London congestion charging scheme: Ex-post evaluation of the quantified impacts of the original scheme', Transport for London.

20   Marsden (2002).

21   Bonsall and Kelly (2005).

22   Department for Transport (2004) 'Feasibility study of road pricing in the UK', annex E. In 2007 the Department for Transport stated that road pricing schemes should promote social inclusion and accessibility and issued guidance to local authorities considering such schemes, based on a review of available evidence; see www.dft.gov.uk/pgr/scienceresearch/social/socialanddistributionimpacts/

23   Metz (2005).

24   Jones (2003).

25   House of Commons Transport Committee (2005) 'Road pricing: The next step', seventh report of session 2004–05.

26   Bird, J. (2006) 'The Stockholm syndrome', *Whitehall and Westminster World*, London, 24 October.

27   Saunders (2005).
28   Lyons, G., Dudley, G., Slater, E. and Parkhurst, G. (2004) 'Evidence-based review: Attitudes to road pricing', Centre for Transport and Society, University of the West of England, Bristol; Bird, J. and Vigor, A. (2006) 'Charging forward: Public attitudes towards road pricing', Institute for Public Policy Research, London; Bird, J. and Morris, J. (2006) 'Steering through change: Winning the debate on road pricing', Institute for Public Policy Research, London.
29   Department for Transport (2007) *Road Statistics 2006: Traffic, Speeds and Congestion*, figure 1.4a, www.dft.gov.uk/pgr/statistics/ datatablespublications/roadstraffic/speedscongestion/
30   Grayling (2004).
31   Most of the rail system in the US is used exclusively for freight transport, but this is an unusual circumstance. In Britain, there is an inconspicuous pipeline system that reduces the need for oil product transport by road and rail tankers.
32   Eddington (2006), vol 1, para 2.7, and vol 2, para 1.6.
33   See Metz (2004a) for earlier references.
34   Eddington (2006) notes that just-in-time practices have reduced the inventory: output ratio in UK over the past 20 years by 20 per cent.
35   Eddington (2006), executive summary, para 7; Wilson, J. and Tighe, C. (2007) 'Yorkshire sees off rivals as ideal location for "supersheds"', *Financial Times*, 3 December; *Transport Trends 2006 edition* (Department for Transport).
36   Quarmby (1989).
37   Rigby, E. (2006) 'Boots takes action to freshen up its brand', *Financial Times*, 16 March.

# Chapter 6

1   UN Population Fund (2007) 'State of world population 2007: Unleashing the potential of urban growth', www.unfpa.org/swp/swpmain.htm
2   Glaeser and Kahn (2003); Bruegmann (2005).
3   Rogers and Power (2000); Katz (2002).
4   Rogers, R. (chair) (1999) 'Towards an urban renaissance', a report of the Urban Task Force, Department for the Environment, Transport and the Regions; Department for the Environment, Transport and the Regions (2000) 'Our towns and cities: The future – delivering an urban renaissance'; Hutton, W. (2000), forword to Rogers and Power (2000).
5   Gehl and Gemzoe (2000); Rogers and Power (2000). For a general discussion of the effect of pedestrianization on trade see Goodwin (2003).
6   Brehany (1999).
7   Agglomeration is an important theme of the Eddington (2006) report, from which the Lancashire example is taken. See also Metz (2007a).
8   Heartfield, J. (2006) 'Farewell to the city?' www.spiked-online.com/Articles/ 0000000CAFFC.htm
9   Bruegmann (2005).
10   Echenique, M. and Homewood, R. (2003) 'The future of suburbs and exurbs',

a report prepared for the Independent Transport Commission; Independent Transport Commission (2004) 'Suburban future', www.trg.soton.ac.uk/itc/reports.htm

11   Brehany (1999), Echenique and Saint (2001).

12   MVA (2002) 'South and West Yorkshire motorway box multi-modal study', conducted for the Government Office for Yorkshire and The Humber, www.gos.gov.uk/goyh/transp/rts/swmms/

13   Burdett, R., Travers, T., Czischke, D., Rode, P. and Moser, B. (2004) 'Density and urban neighbourhoods in London', Enterprise LSE Cities, www.lse.ac.uk/collections/cities/pdf/LSEDensityReport.pdf

14   Headicar (2003).

15   Caldwell, C. (2007) 'Urban sprawl and a waste of energy', *Financial Times*, 27/8 January.

16   Newman and Kenworthy (2007); see also Newman and Kenworthy (1989).

17   Sperling and Clausen (2002).

18   Heathcote, E. (2006) 'Living for the modern city' [interview with Ricky Burdett, director of LSE's cities programme], *Financial Times*, 21 August.

19   Commission for Integrated Transport (2005) 'World cities research', www.cfit.gov.uk/docs/2005/index.htm; Ott (1995).

20   See Note 17.

21   BRT-UK (2007) 'Buses as rapid transit: A transport revolution in waiting', www.brtuk.org; Eastman, C. (2006) 'It's time for local authorities to seriously consider the advantages of bus rapid transit systems', *Local Transport Today*, 9 November.

22   Commission for Integrated Transport (2007) 'Moving forward: Better transport for city regions', www.cfit.gov.uk/docs/2007/index.htm; Department for Transport (2006) 'Putting passengers first: The Government's proposals for a modernised national framework for bus services', www.dft.gov.uk/pgr/regional/buses/secputtingpassengersfirst/; Transport for London (2006) 'Transport 2025: Transport vision for a growing world city', www.tfl.gov.uk/assets/downloads/corporate/T2025-new.pdf

23   Transport for London (2006) 'London Travel Report 2006', www.tfl.gov.uk/assets/downloads/corporate/London-Travel-Report-2006-final.pdf

24   Department for Transport (2007) 'Delivering a sustainable railway', Cm7176.

25   Quarmby, D. (2007) 'The railways should invigorate the re-shaping of Britain's towns and cities', *Local Transport Today*, 16 August.

26   There has been debate about the value for money of Crossrail, including whether it connects the most appropriate destinations along its corridor, see for instance Kay, J. (2007) 'London deserves something better than Crossrail', *Financial Times*, 3 October.

27   Steer, J. (2007) 'White Paper's evidence against high-speed rail doesn't survive close scrutiny', *Local Transport Today*, 16 August.

28   Department for Transport (2007) 'Delivering a sustainable railway', Cm7176, fig 11.1, p113 for carbon comparisons; see also Kemp, R. (2007) 'Traction energy metrics', research project T618, Rail Safety and Standards Board, London.

29   This general approach is that of the Stern (2006) review.

30   *Transport Statistics for Great Britain 2007 edition*; Eurostat (2007) 'Air transport in Europe 2005'.

31   Njegovan (2006).

32   Department for Transport (2003) 'The future of air transport'; Department for Transport (2007) 'UK air passenger demand and $CO_2$ forecasts', November.

33   Department for Environment, Food and Rural Affairs (2006) 'Climate change: The UK programme 2006'.

34   Bows and Anderson (2007); Institute of Public Policy Research (2007) '80% challenge: Delivering a low-carbon UK'. See also the extensive analysis by Cairns and Newson (2006).

35   For a critique of air passenger forecasts see Riddington (2006).

36   National Statistics (2007) 'Travel trends 2006: Data from the International Passenger Survey', www.statistics.gov.uk/downloads/theme_transport/TravelTrends2006.pdf

37   Civil Aviation Authority (2006) 'CAA passenger survey report 2005', www.caa.co.uk/docs/81/2005CAAPaxSurveyReport.pdf

38   Cairns and Newson (2006).

39   www.tourismconcern.org.uk/; Hickman (2007); *The Observer Magazine*, 14 October 2007.

40   Olsthoorn (2001); Tol (2007); Civil Aviation Authority (2003) 'The future development of air transport in the UK'.

41   See Note 30.

42   Civil Aviation Authority (2006) 'No-frills carriers: Revolution or evolution? A study by the Civil Aviation Authority', CAP 770, www.caa.co.uk/docs/33/CAP770.pdf

43   House of Lords European Union Committee (2006) 'Including the aviation sector in the European Union Emissions Trading Scheme', www.publications.parliament.uk/pa/ld200506/ldselect/ldeucom/107/107.pdf; International Civil Aviation Organization (2007) 'Report on voluntary emissions trading for aviation', www.icao.int/icao/en/env/vets_report.pdf; Commission of the European Communities (2006) 'Impact assessment of the inclusion of aviation activities in the scheme for greenhouse gas emission allowance trading within the Community', SEC (2006) 1684, www.ec.europa.eu/environment/climat/pdf/aviation/sec_2006_1684_en.pdf

44   Harvey, F. and Fidler, S. (2007) 'Industry caught in carbon "smokescreen"', *Financial Times*, 25 April; Department for Environment, Food and Rural Affairs (2007) 'Establishing a voluntary code of best practice for the provision of carbon offsetting to UK customers', www.defra.gov.uk/corporate/consult/carbonoffsetting-cop/index.htm

45   Civil Aviation Authority (2006) 'Reforming slot allocation in Europe: Making the most of a valuable resource', www.caa.co.uk/docs/589/ERG_slots_doc.pdf; Done, K. (2007) 'Takeoff jigsaw falling into place at Heathrow', *Financial Times*, 26 October.

# Chapter 7

1 For a review of policy towards walking and cycling see Page (2005). See also Amato (2004) for a history of walking.

2 Department of Health (2004) 'Choosing health: Making healthier choices easier', Public Health White Paper, Cm6374; Department for Transport (2004) 'Walking and cycling: An action plan', www.dft.gov.uk/pgr/sustainable/walking/

3 For an uncritical post-mortem of the National Cycling Strategy see Department for Transport (2005) 'Delivery of the National Cycling Strategy: A review', www.dft.gov.uk/pgr/sustainable/cycling/deliveryofthenationalcycling5738

4 Metz (2006a).

5 Danish Ministry of Transport and Energy (2005) 'Key figures for transport 2005', www.trm.dk/sw58031.asp

6 Pucher and Dijkstra (2003); Bovy (2001); Ministerie van Verkeer en Waterstaat (2007) 'Cycling in the Netherlands', Den Haag.

7 Transport for London: Annual Report and Accounts, 2006–07; *London Travel Report 2006.*

8 Goodwin, P. (2007) 'It's finally time to take the bike seriously', *Local Transport Today*, 30 August.

9 www.sustrans.org.uk

10 *National Travel Survey 2006*, table 4.6.

11 Cairns, S., Sloman, L., Newson, C., Anable, J., Kirkbride, A. and Goodwin, P. (2004) 'Smarter Choices: Changing the way we travel', Department for Transport, www.dft.gov.uk/pgr/sustainable/smarterchoices/ctwwt/

12 The Department for Transport has recognized the need, in principle at least, to 'lock in' the congestion-reduction benefits of both road widening and 'Smarter Choices' (see Department for Transport (2003) 'Managing our roads', para 96, www.dft.gov.uk/pgr/roads/network/policy/managingourroadsprintver.pdf); see also Department for Transport (2005) 'Making smarter choices work', www.dft.gov.uk/pgr/sustainable/smarterchoices/makingwork/. However, little if anything is done in practice to secure this objective.

13 Department for Transport (2005) 'Making smarter choices work', www.dft.gov.uk/pgr/sustainable/smarterchoices/makingwork/; Socialdata (2007) 'Worcester: Sustainable travel demonstration town: Interim evaluation of ITM programme', report for Worcestershire County Council; Department for Transport (2007) 'Making personal travel planning work', research report by Integrated Transport Planning Ltd, www.dft.gov.uk/pgr/sustainable/travelplans/ptp/makingptpworkresearch (accompanying case studies include initial findings from the three sustainable travel demonstration towns).

14 The argument for 'locking in' the benefits of congestion reduction seems first to have been put forward by Denvil Coombe who recommended that new road capacity should not be provided without some means for controlling the additional traffic that would be induced by the new capacity. The preferred mechanism was area-wide road user charging. However, as I point out in Chapter 5, road user charging itself would give rise to induced traffic. That leaves physical measures to lock in widening benefits, such as ramp metering and lanes limited to high occupancy vehicles (common in the US).

15   Richardson, J., Harrison, G. and Parkhurst, G. (2007) 'Public understanding of sustainable transport', a report to the Department for Environment, Food and Rural Affairs.

16   Goodall (2007).

17   Hillman (2004); Starkey, R. and Anderson, K. (2005) 'Domestic tradable quotas: A policy instrument for reducing greenhouse gas emissions from energy use', technical report 39, Tyndall Centre for Climate Change Research; RSAcarbonlimited, www.rsacarbonlimited.org; speech by the Rt Hon David Miliband MP – 'The great stink: Towards an environmental contract', at the Audit Commission annual lecture, 19 July 2006, www.defra.gov.uk/corporate/ministers/speeches/david-miliband/dm060719.htm

18   Schwartz (2004); Anderson (2007).

19   I concede that Cairns et al (see note 11 above) cite evidence to show that the substitution of cars by delivery vehicles does have a substantial impact.

20   Metz (2000); Metz and Underwood (2005); Knight, T., Dixon, J., Warrener, M. and Webster, S. (2007) 'Understanding the travel needs, behaviour and aspirations of people in later life', prepared for the Department for Transport, http://www.dft.gov.uk/pgr/scienceresearch/social/

21   Metz (2003); Department for Transport (2001) 'Older people: Their transport needs and requirements', www.dft.gov.uk/pgr/inclusion/older/; European Conference of Ministers of Transport (1998) Round Table 112, 'Transport and the ageing of the population', OECD, Paris.

22   Tyler (2002); Tyler (2006).

23   www.cts.ucl.ac.uk/arg/pamela2/

24   Social Exclusion Unit (2003) 'Making the connections: Final report on transport and social exclusion', Office of the Deputy Prime Minister, London; Department for Transport (2006) 'Tackling crime on public transport', www.dft.gov.uk/pgr/crime/; Department for Transport (2000) 'Public transport gender audit evidence base', www.dft.gov.uk/pgr/inclusion/women/

# Chapter 8

1   Carson and Vaitheeswaran (2007), chapter 8; this book is a lively and well informed account of current developments from two technology writers for *The Economist*; Simon, B. (2007) 'VW cleans up diesel's grimy US image', *Financial Times*, 4 May.

2   *The Economist* (2004) 'Why the future is hybrid', *Technology Quarterly*, 4 December.

3   *The Economist* (2006) 'Plug and play', 28 January; *The Economist* (2006) 'Plugging into the future', 10 June.

4   See the 2006 film: *Who killed the electric car?*, written and directed by Chris Paine (Sony Picture Classics); www.teslamotors.com; *The Economist* (2007) 'Charging around the city', 2 June.

5   Berndt (2003); Cookson, C. (2005) 'Research into better batteries has gone flat', *Financial Times*, 8 February; *The Economist* (2005) 'Building a better battery', *Technology Quarterly*, 17 September; King (2007).

6  Simon, B. (2007) 'GM eyes electric car initiative', *Financial Times*, 13 August.

7  Huber, P. and Mills, M. (2005) 'The end of M.E.?' *ME Magazine*, May issue.

8  Griffiths, J. (2007) 'Their loss is the planet's gain', *Financial Times*, 29 June; Reed, J. (2007) 'Eco-friendly sales in a slow lane', *Financial Times*, 27 September; Reed, J. (2007) 'Prius loses ground to other cars', *Financial Times*, 26 September.

9  Reed, J. and Yee, A. (2007) 'Thrills without frills', *Financial Times*, 25 June; Johnson, J. (2008) 'One-lakh car takes populist road', *Financial Times*, 11 January.

10 Lovins (2004); www.oilendgame.com; see also E4Tech (2007) 'Review of the UK innovation system for low carbon road transport technologies', Department for Transport, www.dft.gov.uk/pgr/scienceresearch/technology/lctis/e4techlc.pdf

11 See Worldwatch Institute (2007) for a comprehensive account of biofuels for transport; International Energy Agency (2004) 'Biofuels for transport', OECD, Paris; Wolf, M. (2007) 'Biofuels: An everyday story of special interests and subsidies', *Financial Times*, 31 October; *The Economist* (2007) 'The end of cheap food', 8 December.

12 Strahan (2007); Fairless (2007).

13 Worldwatch Institute (2007), chapter 5.

14 Hausmann, R. (2007) 'Biofuels can match oil production', *Financial Times*, 7 November.

15 E4Tech (2007) 'Review of the UK innovation system for low carbon road transport technologies', Department for Transport, www.dft.gov.uk/pgr/scienceresearch/technology/lctis/e4techlc.pdf; E4Tech (2006) 'UK carbon reduction potential from technologies in the transport sector', Department for Transport, www.berr.gov.uk/files/file31647.pdf; International Energy Agency (2004) 'Biofuels for transport', OECD, Paris; Worldwatch Institute (2007), chapter 6; Department for Environment, Food and Rural Affairs (2007) 'Biofuels-risk and opportunities', www.defra.gov.uk/farm/crops/industrial/energy/energy2.htm

16 Ragauskas et al (2007).

17 National Research Council and National Academy of Engineering (2004) *The Hydrogen Economy*, The National Academies Press, Washington; Busby (2005); www.ballard.com

18 E4Tech (2004) 'A strategic framework for hydrogen development in the UK', report for the DTI, www.berr.gov.uk/files/file26737.pdf

19 Turner (1999); Strahan (2007), chapter 4.

20 www.bmwgroup.com/cleanenergy/; www.world.honda.com/FuelCell/

21 See King (2007), which is concerned with technology options; Part 2 of this report, published in March 2008, made policy recommendations that were endorsed by the government. See also Carson and Vaitheeswaran (2007) for an optimistic view.

22 E4Tech (2007) 'Review of the UK innovation system for low carbon road transport technologies', Department for Transport, www.dft.gov.uk/pgr/scienceresearch/technology/lctis/e4techlc.pdf; Department for Transport

(2007) 'Low Carbon Transport Innovation Strategy', www.dft.gov.uk/pgr/scienceresearch/technology/lctis/; see also House of Commons Transport Committee seventeenth report session 2003–04, November 2004, 'Cars of the future'.

23   Pacala and Socolow (2004); see also Hickman and Banister (2007) who address the behavioural and technological options available to achieve a 60 per cent reduction in UK transport carbon emissions by 2030.

24   www.ec.europa.eu/environment/co2/co2_home.htm; *The Economist* (2007) 'Collision course', 22 December.

25   Commission for Integrated Transport (2007) 'Transport and climate change', www.cfit.gov.uk/docs/2007/climatechange/index.htm (see also at the same website the supporting document prepared by Anable and Bristow, particularly the full discussion about enforcing speed limits). Others have argued for enforcement of the official 70mph speed limit as a means of reducing carbon emissions, see UK Energy Research Centre (2006) 'Quick hits: Limiting speed', Environmental Change Institute, Oxford University; see also Transport 2000 (2006) 'Driving up carbon emissions from road transport: An analysis of current government projections', a report by Steer Davies Gleave.

26   Department for Transport (2007) 'Low carbon vehicle procurement programme: Initial programme plans', www.dft.gov.uk/pgr/scienceresearch/technology/lowcarbonvehicleprocurementprog

27   See Note 18.

28   Kleiner, K. (2007); Department for Transport (2007) 'Low carbon transport innovation strategy', www.dft.gov.uk/pgr/scienceresearch/technology/lctis/

29   www.eurocontrol.int

30   Glover (2007); Commission for Integrated Transport (2004) 'High-speed rail: International comparisons', www.cfit.gov.uk/docs/2004/hsr/research/index.htm; Eddington (2006), fig 4.11 in vol 3; para 7 of Executive Summary; vol 3, para 4.168 et seq.

31   Department for Transport (2007) 'Rail technical strategy', www.dft.gov.uk/about/strategy/whitepapers/whitepapercm7176/railwhitepapertechnicalstrategy/pdfrailtechstrategyrts1; Department for Transport (2007) 'Delivering a sustainable railway', Cm7176.

32   www.cambridgeshire.gov.uk/transport/guided

33   Lowson (2002).

34   Fowler, D. (2007) 'Personal touch', *Transport Times*, September, pp41–42; *The Economist* (2007) 'Beyond the stagecoach', *Technology Quarterly*, 10 March; www.atsltd.co.uk

35   Cwerner (2006).

36   Blitz, R. (2007) 'Helicopter services prove a winner at Cheltenham', *Financial Times*, 10–11 March; Jones, A. (2007) 'Saint-Tropez rich brought down to earth as helicopter faces chop', *Financial Times*, 11–12 August.

37   A rather different perspective from that developed in the present book can be found in 'Technology forward look', prepared for the Office of Science and Technology's 'Intelligent Infrastructure Systems' Foresight project, www.foresight.gov.uk/Previous_Projects/Intelligent_Infrastructure_Systems/Index.html

38  Button (2001).
39  Salomon (2000); Mokhtarian and Salomon (2002); Choo, Mokhtarian and Salomon (2005); Choo and Mokhtarian (2007); Kwan et al (2007).
40  *The Economist* (2007) 'Far away yet strangely personal', 25 August.
41  Banister and Stead (2004).
42  Bishop (2005); Miles and Walker (2006).
43  www.itisholdings.com; Chowdhury and Sadek (2003); Heijligers (2007).
44  Transport Committee (2004) seventeenth report 2003–04: 'Cars of the future', House of Commons, November.
45  Jaggi, R. (2007) 'The spy is out of the cab', *Financial Times*, 9 May; Thomas, R. (2007) 'Navigating the stormy waters of route choice in a world of satnav', *Local Transport Today*, 13 September, pp12–15.
46  Department for Transport (2007) 'Public attitudes to congestion and road pricing', www.dft.gov.uk/pgr/statistics/datatablespublications/trsnstatsatt/; Bird, J. and Morris, J. (2006) 'Steering through change: Winning the debate on road pricing', Institute for Public Policy Research, London
47  Department for Transport (2001) 'Perceptions of and attitudes to congestion', www.dft.gov.uk/pgr/statistics/datatablespublications/trsnstatsatt/earlierreports/; Bird, J. and Vigor, A. (2006) 'Charging forward: Public attitudes towards road pricing', Institute for Public Policy Research, London; Richards (2006), p23.
48  *The Economist* (2005) 'No jam tomorrow?' *Technology Quarterly*, 17 September; www.inrix.com; www.trafficmaster.co.uk
49  Trafficmaster and RAC foundation (2007) 'Congestion report: volume 1', www.racfoundation.org/files/CongestionIndex.pdf
50  Ison and Rye (2006); Alexander (2005).
51  RAC Foundation (2004) 'Motoring towards 2050: Parking in transport policy', www.racfoundation.org/files/parking%20final%20report.pdf

## Chapter 9

1  Department for Transport (2007) 'Road traffic forecasts for England', www.dft.gov.uk/pgr/economics/ntm/071023_AnnualForecast07.pdf
2  Adams, J. (2000) 'Hypermobility', *Prospect*, March, pp27–31; Sloman (2006); Monbiot (2006).
3  Larsen, Axhausen and Urry (2006); see also Larsen, Urry and Axhausen (2006); Putnam (2000).
4  Honoré, C. (2005).
5  Lyons and Urry (2005); Anable (2005); Choo and Mokhtarian (2004); Freud, S., 'Formulations on the two principles of mental functioning', *Sigmund Freud Standard Edition*, vol XII, The Hogarth Press, London (1958) (1st edn published 1911), cited by Wright and Curtis (2005).
6  For a history of motoring see Brandon (2002); for the cultural impact of cars see Wollen and Kerr (2002); see also Offer (2006) for consumer attraction and eventual disillusionment with American cars of the 1950s.

7    Livingstone, K. (2007) 'We will not fritter away congestion charging gains', *Transport Times*, October, p23.

8    For a discussion of the complex questions of the present and future price of carbon, see Price et al (2007).

9    Commission for Integrated Transport (2007) 'Are we there yet? A comparison of transport in Europe', www.cfit.gov.uk/docs/2007/ebp/index.htm; Wright, R. (2007) 'Let's hear it for Britain's much-slandered transport system', *Financial Times*, 7–8 April.

10   Sheller and Urry (2006); Peters (2006); Featherstone (2004); see also two papers from 'Intelligent Infrastructure Systems' Foresight project: Stradling, S. (2006) 'Moving around: Some aspects of the psychology of transport'; Lyons, G. and Urry, J. (2006) 'Foresight: The place of social science in examining the future role of transport'; http://www.foresight.gov.uk/Previous_Projects/Intelligent_Infrastructure_Systems/Reports_and_Publications/Intelligent_Infrastructure_Futures/Index.html

11   As an example of a language barrier, consider: 'Through a dialogue between the anthropology of nomadism and philosophy of nomadology, the article then seeks to integrate tropes of fluidity, rootlessness and aesthetic reflexivity into an ideal-type of postidentitarian mobility (neo-nomadism), a device for investigating the cultural effects of hypermobility on self, identity and sociality.' Taken from D'Andrea (2006).

12   Pinker (1998); Tooby and Cosmides (2005).

13   McNeill (1995).

# References

The references listed here comprise authored books and articles in journals. In the endnotes to each chapter are to be found other references, including government and other reports, statistical sources, newspaper and magazine articles, and websites. Generally, websites were most recently accessed in December 2007.

Alexander, D. (2005) 'The environmental importance of front gardens – can planning help?', *Town and Country Planning*, December, pp364–366

Alexander, G. M. and Hines, M. (2002) 'Sex differences in response to toys in non-human primates', *Evolution and Human Behaviour*, vol 23, no 6, pp467–479

Amato, J. (2004) *On Foot – A History of Walking*, New York University Press, New York

Amundsen, A. and Elvik, R. (2004) 'Effects on road safety of new urban arterial roads', *Accident Analysis and Prevention*, vol 36, no 1, pp115–123

Anable, J. (2005) '"Complacent Car Addicts" or "Aspiring Environmentalists"? Identifying travel behaviour segments using attitude theory', *Transport Policy*, vol 12, no 1, pp65–78

Anderson, C. (2007) *The Long Tail*, Random House Business Books, London

Avineri, E. and Prashker, J. (2005) 'Sensitivity to travel time variability: Travellers' learning perspective', *Transportation Research Part C*, vol 13, no 2, pp157–183

Azar, C., Lindgren, K. and Andersson, B. (2003) 'Global energy scenarios meeting stringent $CO_2$ constraints – cost-effective fuel choices in the transportation sector', *Energy Policy*, vol 31, no 10, pp961–976

Banister, D. and Stead, D. (2004) 'Impact of information and communications technologies on transport', *Transport Reviews*, vol 24, no 5, pp611–632

Berndt, D. (2003) 'Electrochemical energy storage', in Kiehne H. (ed) *Battery Technology Handbook*, second edition, Marcel Dekker, New York

Bishop, R. (2005) *Intelligent Vehicle Technology and Trends*, Artech House, Boston, MA

Bonsall, P. and Kelly, C. (2005) 'Road user charging and social exclusion: The impact of congestion charges on at-risk groups', *Transport Policy*, vol 12, no 5, pp406–418

Bornstein, M. and Bornstein, H. (1976) 'Evidence that the pace of walking in towns and cities increases with population/size', *Nature*, vol 259, pp557–559

Bovy, P. (2001) 'Traffic flooding the low countries: How the Dutch cope with motorway congestion', *Transport Reviews*, vol 21, no 1, pp89–116

Bows, A. and Anderson, K. (2007) 'Policy clash: Can projected aviation growth be reconciled with the UK Government's 60% carbon-reduction target?' *Transport Policy*, vol 14, no 2, pp103–110

Bramble, D. and Lieberman, D. (2004) 'Endurance running and the evolution of Homo', *Nature*, vol 432, pp345–352

Brandon, R. (2002) *Automobile: How the Car Changed Life*, Macmillan, London

Brehany, M. (ed) (1999) *The People: Where Will They Work?*, Town and Country Planning Association, London

Brower, D. (2006) 'In search of the key', *Petroleum Economist*, vol 73, no 9, pp14–19

Bruegmann, R. (2005) *Sprawl: A Compact History*, University of Chicago Press, Chicago

Burroughs, W. (2007) *Climate Change: A Multidisciplinary Approach*, second edition, Cambridge University Press, Cambridge

Busby, R. (2005) *Hydrogen and Fuel Cells: A Comprehensive Guide*, PennWell, Tulsa, OK

Button, K. (2001) 'Economics of transport networks', in Button, K. and Hensher, D. (eds) *Handbook of Transport Systems and Traffic Control*, Pergamon, Amsterdam, pp61–75

Byatt, I., Castles, I., Goklany, I., Henderson, D., Lawson, N., McKitrick, R., Morris, J., Peacock, A., Robinson, C. and Skidelsky, R. (2006) 'The Stern Review: A dual critique. Part II – economic aspects', *World Economics*, vol 7, no 4, pp199–229

Cairns, S. and Newson, C. (2006) *Predict and Decide: Aviation, Climate Change and UK Policy*, Environmental Change Institute, University of Oxford

Camerer, C., Babcock, L., Loewenstein, G. and Thaler, R. (1997) 'Labor supply of New York City cabdrivers: One day at a time', *The Quarterly Journal of Economics*, vol 112, no 2, pp407–441

Camerer, C. and Loewenstein, G. (2004) 'Behavioural economics: Past, present and future', in Camerer, C., Loewenstein, G. and Rabin, M. (eds) *Advances in Behavioural Economics*, Princeton University Press, Princeton, NJ

Cann, R. (2001) 'Genetic clues to dispersal in human populations: Retracing the past from the present', *Science*, vol 291, pp1742–1748

Carson, I. and Vaitheeswaran, V. (2007) *Zoom: The Global Race to Fuel the Car of the Future*, Twelve, New York

Cavill, D., Kahlmeier, S. and Racioppi, S. (eds) (2006) *Physical Activity and Health in Europe: Evidence for Action*, WHO Europe, Copenhagen

Charoentrakulpeeti, W., Sajor, E. and Zimmermann, W. (2006) 'Middle-class travel patterns, predispositions and attitudes, and present-day transport policy in Bangkok, Thailand', *Transport Reviews*, vol 26, no 6, pp693–712

Choo, S., Collantes, G. and Mokhtarian, P. (2005) 'Wanting to travel, more or less: Exploring the determinants of the deficit and surfeit of personal travel', *Transportation*, vol 32, no 2, pp135–164

Choo, S. and Mokhtarian, P. (2004) 'What type of vehicle do people drive?' *Transportation Research Part A*, vol 38, no 3, pp201–222

Choo, S. and Mokhtarian, P. (2007) 'Telecommunications and travel demand and supply: Aggregate structural equation models for the US', *Transportation Research Part A*, vol 41, no 1, pp4–18

Choo, S., Mokhtarian, P. and Salomon, I. (2005) 'Does telecommuting reduce vehicle-miles travelled?', *Transportation*, vol 32, no 1, pp37–64

Chowdhury, M. and Sadek, A. (2003) *Fundamentals of Intelligent Transport Systems Planning*, Artech House, Boston, MA

Collier, P. (2007) *The Bottom Billion*, Oxford University Press, New York

Cwerner, S. (2006) 'Vertical flight and urban mobilities: The promise and reality of helicopter travel', *Mobilities*, vol 1, no 2, pp191–215

D'Andrea, A. (2006) 'Neo-nomadism: A theory of post-identitarian mobility in the global age', *Mobilities*, vol 1, no1, pp95–119

Dargay, J. and Hanly, M. (2007) 'Volatility of car ownership, commuting mode and time in the UK', *Transportation Research Part A*, vol 41, no 10, pp934–948

Deffeyes, K. (2005) *Beyond Oil: The View From Hubbert's Peak*, Hill and Wang, New York

Dietz, S., Hope, C., Stern, N. and Zenghelis, D. (2007) 'Reflections on the Stern Review (1): A robust case for strong action to reduce the risks of climate change', *World Economics*, vol 8, no 1, pp121–168

Dobbs, L. (2005) 'Wedded to the car: Women, employment and the importance of private transport', *Transport Policy*, vol 12, no 3, pp266–278

Echenique, M. and Saint, A. (2001) 'Introduction', in Echenique, M. and Saint, A. (eds) *Cities for the New Millennium*, Spon, London

Eddington, R. (2006) 'The Eddington transport study: Transport's role in sustaining the UK's productivity and competitiveness', HM Treasury, London

Fairless, D. (2007) 'Biofuel: The little shrub that could – maybe', *Nature*, vol 449, pp652–655

Featherstone, M. (2004) 'Automobilities: An introduction', *Theory, Culture and Society*, vol 21, nos 4-5, pp1–14 (introduction to a special issue)

Fletcher, T. and McMichael, A. (1997) *Health at the Crossroads: Transport Policy and Urban Health*, Wiley, Chichester

Flyvbjerg, B. (2004) 'Procedures for dealing with optimism bias in transport planning', guidance document prepared for the British Department for Transport (http://flyvbjerg.plan.aau.dk/0406DfT-UK%20OptBiasASPUBL.pdf)

Gehl, J. and Gemzoe, L. (2000) *New City Spaces*, The Danish Architectural Press, Copenhagen

Glaeser, E. and Kahn, M. (2003) 'Sprawl and urban growth', discussion paper number 2004, Harvard Institute of Economic Research, Cambridge, MA

Glover, M. (2007) 'High Speed 1', *Ingenia*, Royal Academy of Engineering, issue 32, September, pp16–24

Goldstein, D. and Chikhi, L. (2002) 'Human migration and population structure', *Annual Revue of Genomics and Human Genetics,* vol 3, pp129–152

Goodall, C. (2007) *How to Live a Low-carbon Life*, Earthscan, London

Goodwin, P. (2003) 'Unintended effects of policies', in Hensher, D. and Button, K. (eds) *Handbook of Transport and the Environment*, Elsevier, Amsterdam, pp603–613

Grayling, T. (2004) 'Whatever happened to integrated transport?' *The Political Quarterly,* vol 75, no 1, pp26–33

Griffiths, J. (1999) *Pip Pip: A Sideways Look at Time*, Flamingo, London

Hansen, J., Johnson, D., Lacis, A., Lebedeff, S., Lee, P., Rind, D. and Russell, G. (1981) 'Climate impact of increasing atmospheric carbon dioxide', *Science*, vol 213, pp957–966

He, K., Huo, H., Zhang, Q., He, D., An, F., Wang, M. and Walsh, M. (2005) 'Oil consumption and $CO_2$ emissions in China's road transport: Current status, future trends, and policy implications', *Energy Policy*, vol 33, no 12, pp1499–1507

Headicar, P. (2003) 'Land use planning and the management of transport demand', pp205-224, in Hine, J. and Preston, J. (eds) *Integrated Futures and Transport Choices*, Ashgate, Aldershot

Heijligers, B. (2007) 'Wide-area network: An evaluation of probe sources for real-time traffic information', *Traffic Technology International*, Aug/Sept, pp56–62

Heinrich, B. (2002) *Why We Run: A Natural History*, Harper Collins, New York

Hickman, L. (2007) *The Final Call*, Guardian Books, London

Hickman, R. and Banister, D. (2007) 'Looking over the horizon: Transport and reduced $CO_2$ emissions in the UK by 2030', *Transport Policy*, vol 14, no 5, pp377–387

Hillman, M. (2004) *How We Can Save the Planet*, Penguin Books, London

Hirsch, F. (1977) *Social Limits to Growth*, Routledge and Kegan Paul, London

Holmen, B. and Niemeier, D. (2003) 'Air quality', in Hensher, D. and Button, K. (eds) *Handbook of Transport and the Environment*, Elsevier, Oxford, pp61–79

Honoré, C. (2005) *In Praise of Slow*, Orion Books, London

Hupkes, G. (1982) 'The law of constant travel times and trip rates', *Futures*, vol 14, no 1, pp38–46

Ison, S. and Rye, T. (2006) 'Parking', *Transport Policy*, vol 13, no 6, pp445-446 (editorial introduction to a special issue)

Iyer, N. and Badami, M. (2007) 'Two-wheeled motor vehicle technology in India: Evolution, prospects and issues', *Energy Policy*, vol 35, no 8, pp4319–4331

Jaccard, M. (2005) *Sustainable Fossil Fuels*, Cambridge University Press, Cambridge

Jacobs, J. (1961) *The Death and Life of Great American Cities*, Jonathan Cape, London

Jones, P. (2003) 'Acceptability of road user charging: Meeting the challenge', in Schade, J. and Schlag, B. (eds) *Acceptability of Transport Pricing Strategies,* Elsevier, Amsterdam

Jones, S. (2000) *The Language of the Genes* (revised edition), Flamingo, London

Katz, B. (2002) 'Smart growth: The future of the American metropolis?', paper 58, Centre for Analysis of Urban Exclusion, London School of Economics

Kelly, F. (2006) 'Road pricing: Addressing congestion, pollution and the financing of Britain's roads', *Ingenia*, Royal Academy of Engineering, issue 29, December, pp34–40

King, J. (2007) *The King Review of Low Carbon Cars. Part 1: The Potential for CO₂ Reduction*, HM Treasury, London

Kleiner, K. (2007) 'Civil aviation faces green challenge', *Nature*, vol 448, pp120–121

Kwan, M., Dijst, M. and Schwanen, T. (2007) 'The interaction between ICT and human-activity travel behaviour', *Transportation Research Part A*, vol 41, no 2, pp121–124

Larsen, J., Axhausen, K. and Urry, J. (2006) 'Geographies of social networks: Meetings, travel and communications', *Mobilities*, vol 1, no 2, pp 261–283

Larsen, J., Urry, J. and Axhausen, K. (2006) *Mobilities, Networks, Geographies*, Ashgate, Aldershot

Lawson, N. (1992) *The View From No. 11: Memoirs of a Tory Radical*, Bantam Press, London

Leggett, J. (2006) *Half Gone: Oil, Gas, Hot Air and the Global Energy Crisis*, Portobello Books, London

Levine, R. (2006) *A Geography of Time*, Oneworld, Oxford

Lovins, A. (2004) *Winning the Oil End Game*, Rocky Mountain Institute/Earthscan, London

Lowson, M. (2002) 'Engineering the ULTra system', *Ingenia*, Royal Academy of Engineering, issue 13, August, pp6–12

Lyons, G. and Urry, J. (2005) 'Travel time use in the information age', *Transportation Research Part A*, vol 39, nos 2–3, pp257–276

Mackie, P., Fowkes, A., Wardman, A., Whelan, G., Nellthorp, J. and Bates, J. (2003) 'Value of travel time savings in the UK: Summary report', report to Department for Transport (www.dft.gov.uk/pgr/economics/rdg/valueoftraveltimesavingsinth3130 )

Marchetti, C. (1994) 'Anthropological invariants in travel behaviour', *Technological Forecasting and Social Change*, vol 47, no 1, pp75–88

Marsden, G. (2002) 'Fuel taxes and the environmental–economy trade off', in Lyons, G. and Chatterjee, K. (eds) *Transport Lessons From the Fuel Tax Protests of 2000*, Ashgate, Aldershot

Mathew, B. (2006) *Taxi!: Cabs and Capitalism in New York City*, New Press, New York

Maugeri, L. (2006) 'Two cheers for expensive oil', *Foreign Affairs*, vol 85, no 2, pp149–163

McNeill, W. (1995) *Keeping Together in Time: Dance and Drill in Human History*, Harvard University Press, Cambridge, MA

Mellars, P. (2006) 'Going east: New genetic and archaeological perspectives on the modern human colonisation of Eurasia', *Science*, vol 313, pp796–800

Metz, D. (2000) 'Mobility of older people and their quality of life', *Transport Policy*, vol 7, no 2, pp149–152

Metz, D. (2002) 'The limitations of transport policy', *Transport Reviews*, vol 22, no 2, pp134–145

Metz, D. (2003) 'Transport policy for an ageing population', *Transport Reviews*, vol 23, no 4, pp375–386

Metz, D. (2004a) 'Travel time constraints in transport policy', *Proceedings of the Institution of Civil Engineers: Transport*, vol 157, no 2, pp99–105

Metz, D. (2004b) 'Travel time – variable or constant?', *Journal of Transport Economics and Policy*, vol 38, no 3, pp333–344

Metz D. (2005) 'Journey quality as the focus for future transport policy', *Transport Policy*, vol 12, no 4, pp353–359

Metz, D. (2006a) 'Travel time and land use planning', *Town and Country Planning*, June 2006, pp182–183

Metz, D. (2006b) 'Time and motion: How limited travel time constrains mobility', *Traffic Engineering and Control*, vol 47, no 9, pp380–382

Metz, D. (2006c) 'Accidents overvalued in road scheme appraisal', *Proceedings of the Institution of Civil Engineers: Transport*, vol 159, no 4, pp159–163

Metz, D. (2007a) 'Eddington's conundrum and unresolved questions', *Traffic Engineering and Control*, vol 48, no 4, pp172–174

Metz, D. (2007b) 'The Newbury Bypass: What we can learn from before and after studies', *Traffic Engineering and Control*, vol 48, no 8, pp372–374

Metz, D. (2008) 'The myth of travel time saving', *Transport Reviews*, vol 28, no 3, pp321–336

Metz, D. and Underwood, M. (2005) *Older Richer Fitter: Identifying the Customer Needs of Britain's Ageing Population*, Age Concern Books, London

Miles, J. and Walker, A. (2006) 'The potential application of artificial intelligence to transport', *IEE Proceedings Intelligent Transport Systems*, vol 153, no 3, pp183–198

Mokhtarian, P. (ed) (2005) 'The positive utility of travel' (special issue), *Transportation Research Part A*, vol 39, nos 2–3

Mokhtarian, P. and Salomon, I. (2001) 'How derived is the demand for travel? Some conceptual and measurement considerations', *Transportation Research Part A*, vol 35, no 8, pp695–719

Mokhtarian, P. and Salomon, I. (2002) 'Emerging travel patterns: Do telecommunications make a difference?', in Mahmassani, H. (ed) *Perpetual Motion: Travel Behaviour Research Opportunities and Application Challenges*, Pergamon, Oxford

Monbiot, G. (2006) 'A new transport system', *Heat: How to Stop the Planet Burning*, Penguin, London, chapter 8

Mullainathan, S. and Thaler, R. (2000) 'Behavioral economics', working paper no.W7948, National Bureau for Economic Research, Cambridge, MA

Nash, C., Mackie, P., Shires, J. and Nellthorp, J. (2004) *The Economic Efficiency Case for Road User Charging*, Institute of Transport Studies, University of Leeds, and Department for Transport, London

Newman, P. and Kenworthy, J. (1989) *Cities and Automobile Dependence: A Sourcebook*, Gower Technical, Aldershot

Newman, P. and Kenworthy, J. (2007) 'Greening urban transportation', in Worldwatch Institute, *State of the World 2007: Our Urban Future*, Earthscan, London, pp66–89

Njegovan, N. (2006) 'Elasticities of demand for leisure air travel: A system modelling approach', *Journal of Air Transport Management*, vol 12, no 1, pp33–39

Offer, A. (2006) 'The American automobile frenzy of the 1950s' and 'Driving prudently: American and European', *The Challenge of Affluence*, Oxford University Press, Oxford, chapters 9 and 10

Olsthoorn, X. (2001) 'Carbon dioxide emissions from international aviation: 1950–2050', *Journal of Air Transport Management*, vol 7, no 2, pp87–93

Ott, R. (1995) 'Conurbation transport policy in Zurich, Switzerland', *Proceedings of the Institution of Civil Engineers: Transport*, vol 111, pp225–233

Pacala, S. and Socolow, R. (2004) 'Stabilization wedges: Solving the climate and carbon problem for the next half century', *Science*, vol 305, pp968–972

Page, P. (2005) 'Non-motorized transportation policy', in Button, K. and Hensher, D. (eds) *Handbook of Transport Strategy, Policy and Institutions*, Elsevier, Oxford

Palmer, K. (2006) 'Financing new electricity supply within carbon constraints', *FST Journal*, vol 19, no 2, p9

Peters, P. (2006) *Time, Innovation and Mobilities*, Routledge, London

Pinker, S. (1998) *How the Mind Works*, Allen Lane, London

Price, R., Thornton, S. and Nelson, S. (2007) 'The social cost of carbon and the shadow price of carbon: What they are and how to use them in economic appraisal in the UK', Department for Environment, Food and Rural Affairs, www.defra.gov.uk/environment/climatechange/research/carboncost/pdf/background.pdf

Pucher, J. and Dijkstra, L. (2003) 'Promoting safe walking and cycling to improve public health: Lessons from The Netherlands and Germany', *American Journal of Public Health*, vol 93, no 9, pp1509–1516

Pucher, J., Peng, Z., Mittal, N., Zhu, Y. and Korattyswaroopam, N. (2007) 'Urban transport trends and policies in China and India: Impacts of rapid economic growth', *Transport Reviews*, vol 27, no 4, pp379–410

Putnam, R. (2000) 'Mobility and sprawl', *Bowling Alone*, Simon and Schuster, New York, chapter 12

Quarmby, D. (1989) 'Developments in retail markets and their effect on freight distribution', *Journal of Transport Economics and Policy*, vol 23, no 1, pp75–87

Ragauskas, A., Williams, C., Davison, B., Britovsek, G., Cairney, J., Eckert, C., Frederick, W., Hallett, J., Leak, D., Liotta, C., Mielenz, J., Murphy, R., Templer, R. and Tschaplinski, T. (2007) 'The path forward for biofuels and biomaterials', *Science*, vol 311, pp484–489

Rajan, S. (2006) 'Climate change dilemma: Technology, social change or both?: An examination of long-term transport policy choices in the United States', *Energy Policy*, vol 34, no 6, pp664–679

Richards, M. (2006) *Congestion Charging in London: The Policy and the Politics*, Palgrave, Basingstoke

Riddington, G. (2006) 'Long range air traffic forecasts for the UK: A critique', *Journal of Transport Economics and Policy*, vol 40, no 2, pp297–314

Rogers, R. and Power, A. (2000) *Cities for a Small Country*, Faber and Faber, London

Rothengatter, L. (2003) 'Environmental concepts – physical and economic', in Hensher, D. and Button, K. (eds) *Handbook of Transport and the Environment*, Elsevier, Oxford, pp10–35

Sack, R. (1986) *Human Territoriality: Its Theory and History*, Cambridge University Press, Cambridge

Salomon, I. (2000) 'Can telecommunications help solve transportation problems?', in Hensher, D. and Button, K. (eds) *Handbook of Transport Modelling*, Elsevier, Oxford, pp449–462

Santos, G. and Bhakar, J. (2006) 'The impact of the London congestion charging scheme on the generalised cost of car commuters to the city of London from a value of travel time savings perspective', *Transport Policy*, vol 13, no 1, pp22–33

Saunders, J. (2005) 'The rise and fall of Edinburgh's congestion charging plans', *Proceedings of the Institute of Civil Engineers: Transport*, vol 158, no 4, pp193–201

Schafer, A. (1998) 'The global demand for motorized mobility', *Transportation Research Part A,* vol 32, no 6, pp455–477

Schafer, A. (2000) 'Regularities in travel demand: An international perspective', *Journal of Transportation and Statistics*, vol 3, no 3, pp1–31

Schafer, A. and Victor, D. (1999) 'Global passenger travel: Implications for carbon dioxide emissions', *Energy*, vol 24, no 8, pp657–679

Schafer, A. and Victor, D. (2000) 'The future mobility of the world population', *Transportation Research Part A,* vol 34, no 3, pp171–205

Schwartz, B. (2004) *The Paradox of Choice*, Harper Perennial, New York

Serbin, L., Poulin-Dubois, D., Colborne, K., Sen, M. and Eichstedt, J. (2001) 'Gender stereotyping in infancy: Visual preferences for and knowledge of gender-stereotyped toys in the second year', *International Journal of Behavioural Development*, vol 25, no 1, pp7–15

Shah, Y. (2004) *Crude: The Story of Oil*, Seven Stories Press, New York

Shaw, J. (2001) 'Winning territory', in May, J. and Thrift, N. (eds) *TimeSpace: Geographies of Temporality,* Routledge, London, pp120–132

Sheller, M. and Urry, J. (2006) 'The new mobilities paradigm', *Environment and Planning A*, vol 38, no 2, pp207–226

Singh, S. (2006) 'Future mobility in India: Implications for energy demand and $CO_2$ emissions', *Transport Policy*, vol 13, no 5, pp398–412

Skeer, J. and Wang, Y. (2007) 'China on the move: Oil price explosion?' *Energy Policy*, vol 35, no 1, pp678–691

Sloman, L. (2006) *Car Sick: Solutions for Our Car-addicted Culture*, Green Books, Totnes, Devon

Sperling, D. and Clausen, E. (2002) 'The developing world's motorization challenge', *Issues in Science and Technology*, Fall, US National Academy of Sciences, http://issues.org

Sperling, D., Lin, Z. and Hamilton, P. (2005) 'Rural vehicles in China: Appropriate policy for appropriate technology', *Transport Policy*, vol 12, no 2, pp105–119

Stern, N. (2006) 'The economics of climate change: The Stern Review', Cambridge University Press, Cambridge

Stone, L. and Lurquin, P. (2007) *Genes, Culture and Human Evolution: A Synthesis*, Blackwell Publishing, Oxford

Stopher, P. (2004) 'Reducing road congestion: A reality check', *Transport Policy*, vol 11, no 2, pp117–131

Strahan, D. (2007) *The Last Oil Shock*, John Murray, London

Tapio, P., Banister, D., Luukkanen, J., Vehmas, J. and Risto, W. (2007) 'Energy and transport in comparison: Immaterialisation, dematerialisation and decarbonisation in the EU15 between 1970 and 2000', *Energy Policy*, vol 35, no 1, pp433–451

Tol, R. (2007) 'The impact of a carbon tax on international tourism', *Transportation Research Part D*, vol 12, no 2, pp129–142

Tooby, J. and Cosmides, L. (2005) 'Conceptual foundations of evolutionary psychology', in Buss, D. (ed) *The Handbook of Evolutionary Psychology*, Wiley, Hoboken, NJ

Turner, J. (1999) 'A realizable renewable energy future', *Science*, vol 285, pp687–689

Tyler, N. (ed) (2002) *Accessibility and the Bus System*, Thomas Telford, London

Tyler, N. (2006) 'Capabilities and radicalism: Engineering accessibility in the 21st century', *Transportation Planning and Technology*, vol 29, no 5, pp331–358

van Tilburg, C. (2007) *Traffic and Congestion in the Roman Empire*, Routledge, London

Wachs, M. (2002) 'Fighting traffic congestion with information technology', *Issues in Science and Technology*, Fall, US National Academy of Sciences, http://issues. org

Watts, G., Nelson, P., Abbott, P., Staitt, R. and Treleven, C. (2006) 'Tyre/road noise – assessment of the existing and proposed noise limits', published project report 077, Transport Research Laboratory, Wokingham, Berkshire

Wollen, P. and Kerr, J. (eds) (2002) *Autopia: Cars and Culture*, Reaktion Books, London

Woodcock, J., Banister, D., Edwards, P., Prentice, A. and Roberts, I. (2007) 'Energy and transport', *The Lancet*, vol 370, pp1078–1088

Wootton, J. (1999) 'Replacing the private car', *Transport Reviews*, vol 19, no 2, pp157–175

Wootton, J. and Pick, G. (1967) 'A model for trips generated by households', *Journal of Transport Economics and Policy*, vol 1, no 1, pp137–153

Worldwatch Institute (2007) *Biofuels for Transport: Global Potential and Implications for Sustainable Energy and Agriculture*, Earthscan, London

Wright, C. and Curtis, B. (2005) 'Reshaping the motorcar', *Transport Policy*, vol 12, no 1, pp11–22

Wright, L. and Fulton, L. (2005) 'Climate change mitigation and transport in developing nations', *Transport Reviews*, vol 25, no 6, pp691–717

Zahavi, Y. and Talvitie, A. (1980) 'Regularities in travel time and money expenditures', *Transportation Research Record*, vol 750, pp13–19

Zhang, S., Jiang, K. and Liu, D. (2007) 'Passenger transport model split based on budgets and implication for energy consumption: Approach and application in China', *Energy Policy*, vol 35, no 9, pp4434–4443

Zhao, X. and Wu, Y. (2007) 'Determinants of China's energy imports: An empirical analysis', *Energy Policy*, vol 35, no 8, pp4235–4246

# Index